LAKELAND TOWNS

Kendal from Kendal Fell

LAKELAND TOWNS

Jim Watson

CICERONE PRESS
MILNTHORPE CUMBRIA ENGLAND

First published 1992

ISBN 1 85284 096 X

For Maureen

Without her tolerance and constant good humour this book would never have been finished

Royal Oak ~ Ambleside

Introduction

My association with Lakeland towns goes back almost 50 years. I was born in Penrith and spent my teenage years within walking distance of Keswick. I still consider both of them as home. They are special.

The other five towns first came into my life on a variety of bus trips from my home village of Threlkeld. Our football team travelled regularly to Kendal for a ritual drubbing. Nobody minded. We usually played on Blencathra fellside, so running out onto level grass at Netherfield Park was like an appearance at Wembley Stadium. There was even a tin sheeting shed for spectators.

Kendal was always first stop on our annual village trip to Morecambe. As we all poured off the coaches, the Outing Committee Treasurer presented each child with a crisp new ten-shilling note. They were immediately put to good use buying six-penny cornets from a bemused ice cream man in the car park. He ran out of change very quickly.

We played cricket at Ambleside. The little square below Loughrigg Fell is still a perfect place to be on a summer evening. My lack of cricketing ability banished me to bat at number eleven and field at long stop so I always had plenty of time to admire the scenery.

Then as now, Windermere was just a place you went through on your way to somewhere else. I went through with the church choir on my first visit to Bowness. Adult choristers sat on the Promenade cooing at the view while we boy sopranos, two of us strong, plundered the Bowness sweet shops.

Cockermouth bred hard men, Saturday night marauders at Keswick, big drinkers who fought over local female talent at the Pavilion dances. I never dared set foot in Cockermouth until I researched this book. I needn't have worried.

When I was 18, I moved away from the Lake District, never knowing then how much I'd miss it now, 30 years later. My return visits have been to tramp wind-blown fells, wander poetically beside tranquil lakes or brood about the meaning of life in desolate valleys. Towns crowded with people and shops were places to avoid.

Now here I was thrashing my car northwards up the M6 motorway to hang about on street corners taking photographs of buildings. With all that countryside temptingly close it seemed like it was going to be a tough assignment.

But there was no need for strong will power. Wandering around Lakeland towns turned out to be just as satisfying and interesting as wandering around the rural landscape. Recreating it all on paper became an absorbing task on long winter evenings. Scenes in the drawings are more or less as my camera saw them. Only TV aerials and ugly lampposts have been left out to protect the aesthetically squeamish. Traffic was a problem until I realised that without it the streets looked like ghost towns. I drew many cars.

Lakes and fells do get a look-in. You can't appreciate Keswick properly without seeing it from a hill, or go to Bowness and not look at Windermere. I've included walks and occasional drives for the same reasons.

This book can be used as a guide to the seven towns of Lakeland, but for me it is a record of memorable rediscovery during the summers of 1989 and '90. The sun shone endlessly. It was hot on the streets but there was nowhere else I would rather have been.

Jim Watson

RUGBY. 1992

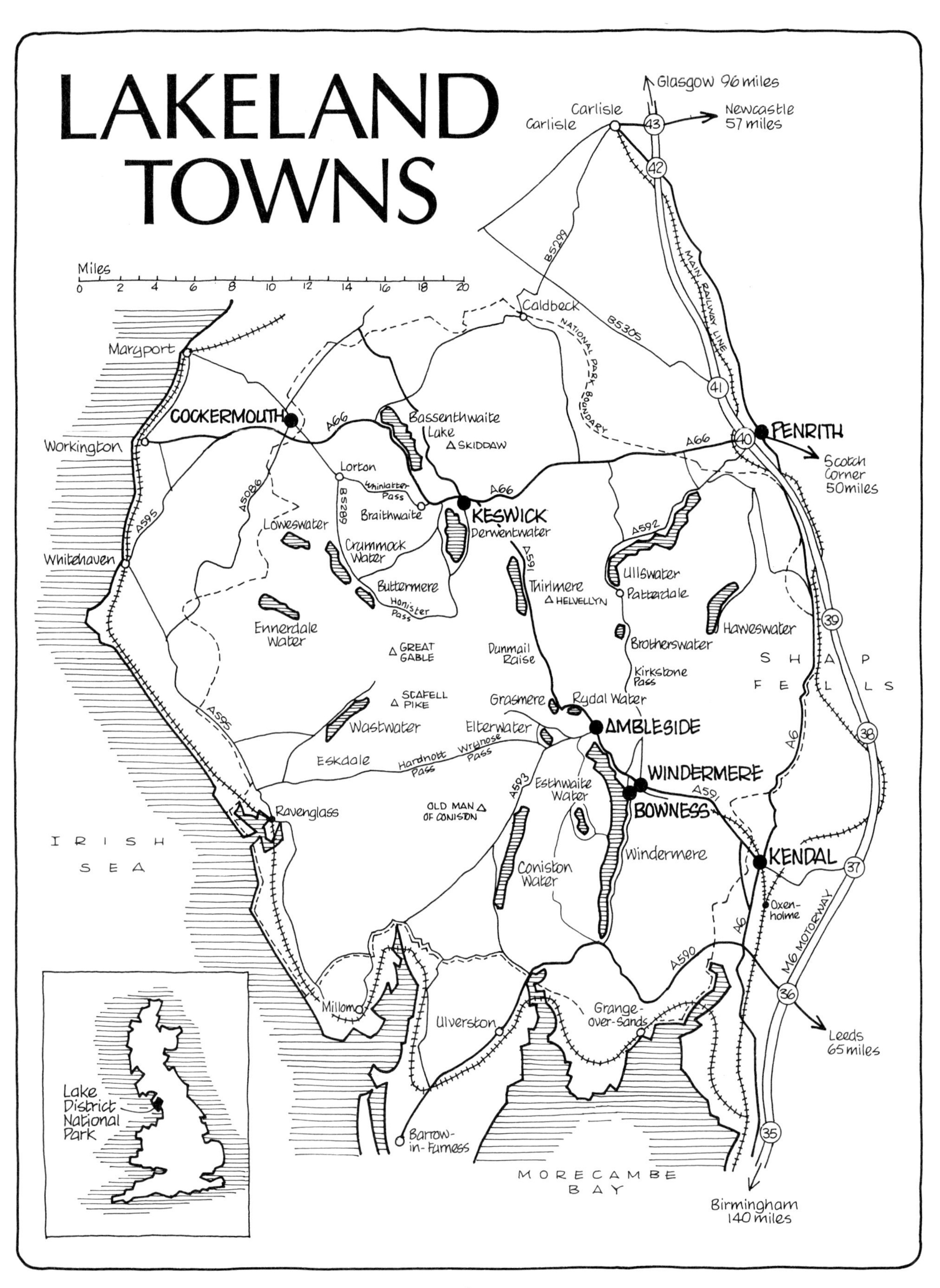
LAKELAND TOWNS
Glasgow 96 miles
Carlisle
Carlisle
Newcastle 57 miles
Miles
0 2 4 6 8 10 12 14 16 18 20
B5299
Caldbeck
B5305
NATIONAL PARK BOUNDARY
MAIN RAILWAY LINE
Maryport
COCKERMOUTH
A66
Bassenthwaite Lake
SKIDDAW
PENRITH
Scotch Corner 50miles
Workington
Lorton
Whinlatter Pass
B5289
Braithwaite
KESWICK
Derwentwater
A5086
A595
Loweswater
Crummock Water
A591
A592
Ullswater
Whitehaven
Buttermere
Honister Pass
Thirlmere
HELVELLYN
Patterdale
Ennerdale Water
Haweswater
Brotherswater
GREAT GABLE
Dunmail Raise
Kirkstone Pass
SHAP FELLS
SCAFELL PIKE
Grasmere
Rydal Water
AMBLESIDE
Wastwater
Elterwater
Eskdale
Hardknott Pass
Wrynose Pass
A6
WINDERMERE
A593
Esthwaite Water
BOWNESS
Ravenglass
OLD MAN OF CONISTON
IRISH SEA
Windermere
KENDAL
Coniston Water
Oxenholme
M6 MOTORWAY
A590
Millom
Ulverston
Grange-over-Sands
Leeds 65 miles
Lake District National Park
Barrow-in-Furness
MORECAMBE BAY
Birmingham 140 miles

Aynam Lodge ~ Kendal

Contents

Rothay Road and Church Street

Rydal Road and Wansfell

Ambleside

I drove into Rydal Road car park with the realisation that Ambleside is situated at just the right place on the A591. Whether coming north from Windermere or south from Keswick, by the time you get here scenery saturation has set in. You need to stop, walk around a bit and convince yourself you're still in the real world and not stuck in some kind of video paradise being projected onto your car windows. With four lakes and many famous fells and beauty spots, this 21 miles must be one of the most scenic stretches of road in the country. It gets hideously busy in summer.

Centrally situated, Ambleside is the best town base for exploring all the Lake District. The steep road to Kirkstone Pass and Ullswater climbs direct from Rydal Road, and the bounteous riches of Great Langdale and Coniston are within easy reach. Take a walk out of town in any direction and you will not be disappointed, though walking due south beyond Waterhead is not recommended if you want to avoid wet feet. Take a boat instead.

Walking out of the car park I was immediately engulfed in the tide of tourists sweeping along Rydal Road. Brown-legged walkers wearing sun-bleached shorts strode resolutely fellwards. Parents in designer shell suits wrenched kids scoffing ice cream from under the wheels of oncoming camper vans. We spilled from the pavements. Cars stopped to let us pass. Ambleside's narrow roads were not designed for modern traffic, mechanical or human. An ingenious one-way system relieves Market Place of north-bound vehicles, but chokes to a steaming standstill at holiday times. Everyone ambles at Ambleside.

Old Gale Farm

The town has generally escaped the worst horrors of modern development. There are few garish shop fronts and no unsightly housing estates. Gothic gable ends still soar from Victorian slate houses, faithfully following the fell skyline. Tourism is unmistakably the mainstay, but conducted with commendable restraint. There are no flashy gimmicks here. Ambleside is a tourist town with good manners.

How long it will all last unadulterated is anyone's guess. The modern buildings of a timeshare complex already blight the hillside below Old Gale Farm, and now the battered old bus station has closed, it looks ripe for development. I'm keeping my fingers crossed.

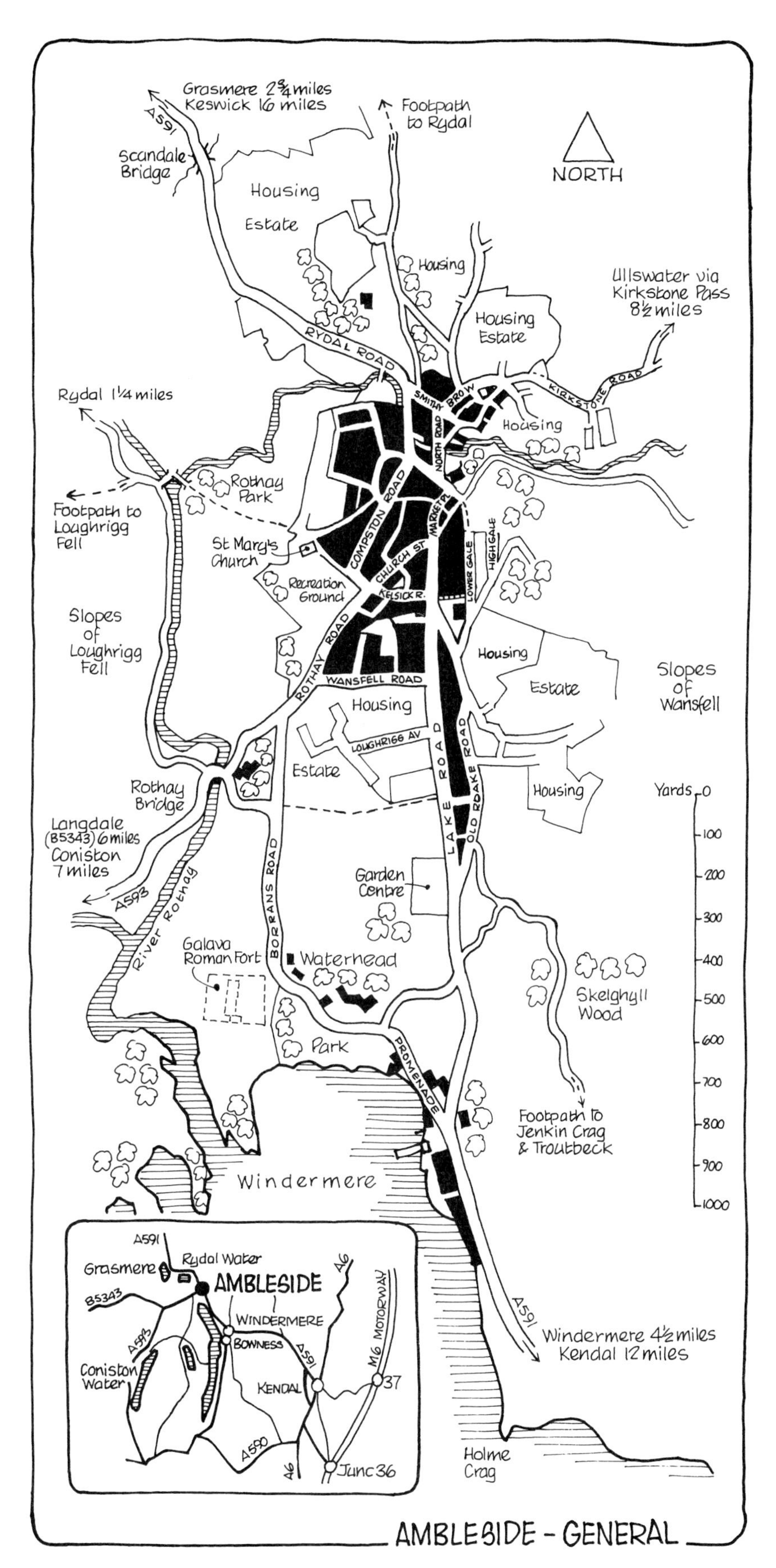

Market Place

Stock Beck
Smithy Brow
Rydal Road
Bridge House
Stock Beck
One way streets
Market Pl
Main through route
Compston Rd
St Mary's Church
Kelsick Road
Rothay Rd
Street Parking. Wansfell Road
Lake Road
CAR PARKS

The Rothay Valley was first settled in AD 79 by the Romans, who built a fort at Borrans Park beside the lake. A village later developed further north above Stock Beck. Even then Ambleside was a popular stopping place for travellers. By the end of the 17th century it had five ale-houses and a weekly market. The tourist flood gates opened when the railway came to Windermere and was planned to continue through Ambleside to Grasmere. With the prospect of big city money flowing into their pockets, the local ale-house owners set about extending their premises and building virtually a new town to accommodate the visitors. Modern Ambleside was up and running.

The untidily-placed buildings around Market Place have changed little in appearance over the last century. An old photograph shows Victorian trippers outside the Queen's Hotel setting off for Ullswater in horse-drawn carriages. It must have been a terrifying journey over Kirkstone Pass. I'd never trust the brakes on a horse.

Most of the intrepid ladies carried parasols to protect them from the sun. It didn't appear to bother the scantily-clad modern females I saw around Ambleside. Some of them even lounged outside the Salutation Hotel, smoking cigarettes and drinking beer. Victorian ladies couldn't do that.

Market Place - C1900

Church Street

Birkett's cakes are irresistible. I bought one of their large coffee-cream creations, then like a true tourist ate it while wandering down Church Street. The lady in the shop selling paintings gave me a funny look so I didn't go in. At another place, which had an extensive display of pop star mirrors, I noticed the blob of cream on my nose.

Suitably wiped clean, I went into the homely looking building that was once the town's police station and now serves as Ambleside's tourist information bureau. It was packed with sweating visitors but as usual the staff were coping magnificently. Unfortunately, none of their leaflets told me much about Ambleside.

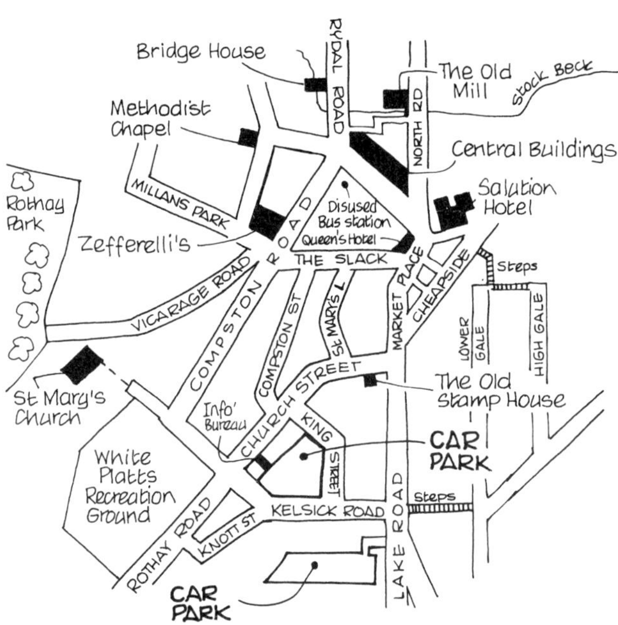

The Old Stamp House at the top of Church Street stands on the site of the office used by poet William Wordsworth when he was Collector of Stamps for Westmorland. At that time stamp duty had to be paid to the government on all legal documents. Wordsworth's job was to distribute official stamps to shops all over the county then collect the money when they were sold. He was elected to the post soon after his family had moved to their smart house at Rydal Mount, in 1813, so the £200 a year pay probably came in handy. It was the only proper job Wordsworth ever had.

The Old Stamp House

The spire of St Mary's Church caused great controversy when it was first built. Niggly little gables do give it the look of an ecclesiastical pigeon loft, but the massive 180-foot-tall structure has now become an integral part of the Ambleside landscape.

Inside the church, a lady acting as guard and guide was overjoyed to see me. She explained that church visiting is not popular during sunny weather and I was the first person she'd seen all afternoon. Male ego totally deflated, I was led to the west wall where my guide pointed out where the painting of the church's famous rushbearing ceremony had been obscenely vandalised with a blue biro. "Ignore this," she instructed, "we've been told by experts that it can be painted over." With a discrete cough I dutifully averted my eyes and she returned unabashed to shuffling the hymn books.

Rushbearing is an annual ceremony at Grasmere and Ambleside churches, commemorating the renewal of rushes in pre-Elizabethan days, which used to be laid on the bare earth floor every August then taken up the following spring. The mural, 26 feet long by 12 feet high, features 62 life-sized figures including the vicar and verger of the time. It was painted in 1944 by Gordon Ransom, a student at the Royal College of Art when it moved to Ambleside during the war.

St Mary's Church

The rest of the church, designed by Gilbert Scott, seems rather colourless in contrast. Large and airy, a symbol of Victorian self-assurance, it was consecrated in 1854 after four years of building literally on solid rock. Pneumatic drills had to be used to dig foundations for a new vestry in 1968. Wordsworth is said to have chosen the site before he died and he is commemorated by his own chapel furnished with two chairs from Rydal Mount.

War Memorial

The entrance to St Mary's extensive graveyard from Rothay Road has an attractive lych gate flanked by slabs of slate. There's a delightful view from here of the church backed by High Pike. A Gothic-style war memorial stands high on a rock beside the church door. Starkly silhouetted in the setting sun it looked like a scene from a Hammer horror film. I headed up Vicarage Road at a brisk pace, well before darkness fell.

When you're driving, the best part of Compston Road is when you manage to get out of it. When walking, it's Zefferelli's splendid arcade, a sympathetic modern development incorporating shops under a cinema and cafe, with a wholefood pizzeria upstairs. Red paintwork and blinds are a welcome splash of colour in the rather dull road. Ken Russell held the world premiere of his controversial film *Gothic* at Zeff's. The road wasn't so dull that night.

Compston Road

Methodist Chapel

A large Methodist chapel gazed sombrely at the passing holiday scene from between the buildings at the top of Compston Road. I turned up the hill and crossed the road for a browse in the excellent little bookshop in Central Buildings. This huge slate-built edifice of Victorian shops towers over the little Market Cross, which until the 19th century stood, complete with an ornamental headstone dated 1651, outside Cross House in Market Place.

Empty coke tins propelled by the breeze rolled aimlessly across the wide open spaces of the bleak 1950s bus station, now closed and neglected across the road.

Central Buildings

Though now fronted by a modern woollen goods store, the Salutation Hotel is one of Ambleside's oldest inns, dating from 1656. It was an important stop on the turnpike road, opened in 1761, where horses were changed for the journey to Keswick. A coach and six would regularly travel between Kendal and Carlisle, passing through Ambleside, in about six hours. That wouldn't be a bad time in a car these days, considering how crowded and slow-moving the A591 can be.

Salutation Hotel

From Stock Bridge

North Road took me into the oldest and most attractive part of town where there was once five water mills driven by Stock Beck. One of them, originally a bark crushing mill for making tannin for the leather trade, makes a wonderful picture set amongst rustic stone walls and cascading cottage gardens. Another, equally picturesque with a replica overshot waterwheel, used to be a corn mill.

Bridge House in the early 19th C. From a painting by William Green

Bridge House

Bridge House, which survived the construction of Rothay Road in 1833 and mega-stardom on countless chocolate boxes, calendars and postcards since, is now a rather cramped National Trust shop. A minor sport for visiting day-trippers is to see how many can cram inside. As I left, two coach loads of diminutive Japanese tourists were arriving, heavily armed with camcorders. The Bridge House cramming record was about to be shattered.

An interesting old alley goes down past the mill to Bridge House. English wags reckon the tiny building was built over Stock Beck by a Scotsman to escape land tax, but actually it was an apple store for nearby Ambleside Hall. The roof still has its original 17th-century 'wrestler' slates along the ridge.

William Green, a local artist who lived in Market Place where the post office now is, recorded the rural scene for posterity. He was a fine draughtsman and his studies of early 19th-century buildings around Ambleside are well worth seeking out.

The Old Mill

Ambleside's ancient market died out long ago, but a modern version is still held weekly in Kelsick Road car park. I went into the local library across the road to check a few things in its comprehensive collection of local books and to see if I could find the mysterious Armitt Collection of art treasures. A tiny notice pointed me upstairs to a single room packed with furniture, books and pictures left to the library by Mary Armitt (1851-1911). The kindly curator asked if there was anything in particular I would like to see, but how can you choose between Beatrix Potter's botanical watercolours, Ruskin books by the hundred, William Green's drawings, Roman remains, or priceless papers of the Lake Poets and other local notables?

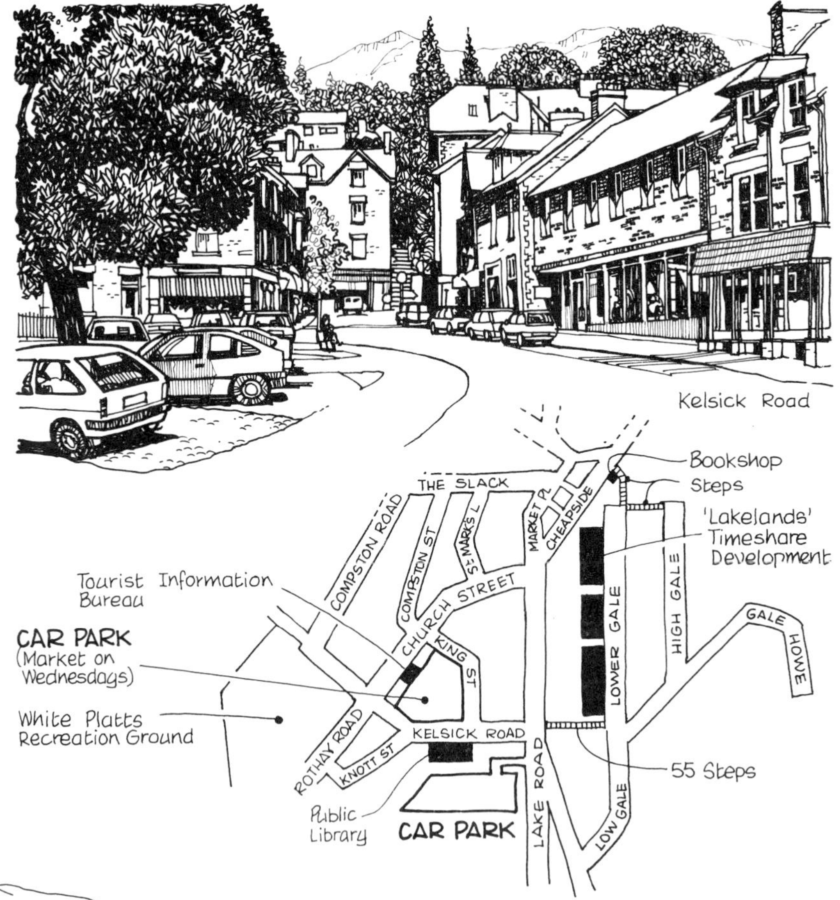

Kelsick Road

Lake Road and High Pike

The Armitt Trust has so much to show off but no space to show it. A plan to buy and convert Mill Cottage on Stock Beck to an exhibition and research centre had recently been abandoned when the money could not be raised. The price of a couple of the monstrous power boats that blast up and down Windermere would have covered it, and benefited infinitely more people too. It was easy to share the curator's disappointment, but there is some hope that the library will shortly move to Charlotte Mason College.

I left full of gloom and had a long browse through Wearing's excellent bookshop to lift my spirits. It was only partially successful. Nobody was buying my books. A walk down Lake Road for a look back to High Pike finally put me to rights. There's nothing so marvellously optimistic as a sunlit fell.

A tortuous climb up 55 stone steps from Lake Road brought me breathless to Lower Gale and The Lakelands, a timeshare holiday complex with its own indoor swimming pool, sauna, and bistro. Seen from St Mary's churchyard the modern buildings sit uneasily amongst Victorian slate. This kind of development causes heated argument all over the world and does pose serious ethical questions. The arrival of a closed, elitist and alien lifestyle in a poorer and long-established community is bound to cause friction. It did here. I stayed overnight at a Lower Gale guest house where the proprietors spoke bitterly about the way they considered their view had been 'hi-jacked' by the intruding buildings.

But even seen through a shimmering heat haze generated by The Lakelands' acres of roof, this view is a considerable commodity for any holiday venue. The glorious panorama sweeps from a glimpse of Windermere in the south, across Loughrigg to the great horseshoe of fells in the north crowned by Fairfield. Lit by the golden light of summer it was a heady sight. Sunshine danced lightly across the rooftops to Heron Pike, and so did I.

The Lakelands

Cheapside bookshop

With fells on three sides and a lake on the other, Ambleside is best situated of all the Lakeland towns. A yearning to live somewhere like this with fells coming down to my back door often aches at my heart. Unfortunately, the ache had now extended to my feet. Encased in unaccustomed boots and forced to walk on streets for longer than they thought reasonable on a hot summer day, they throbbed for release. I dragged them, and myself, back to reality down another long flight of stone steps to Cheapside.

The town and Fairfield Horseshoe from Lower Gale

The Ambleside area was a magnet for Victorian literary figures. Wordsworth and De Quincey lived at Rydal. Dr Arnold of Rugby School and his poet son, Matthew, had a holiday home in Rothay Park. Harriet Martineau, writer and close friend of Wordsworth, built The Knoll just beyond the car park on Rothay Road in 1846. She published a well-regarded guide book to the Lakes in 1855, which is still quoted from today. Apart from Wordsworth, none of them were native Lakelanders.

Charlotte Mason College

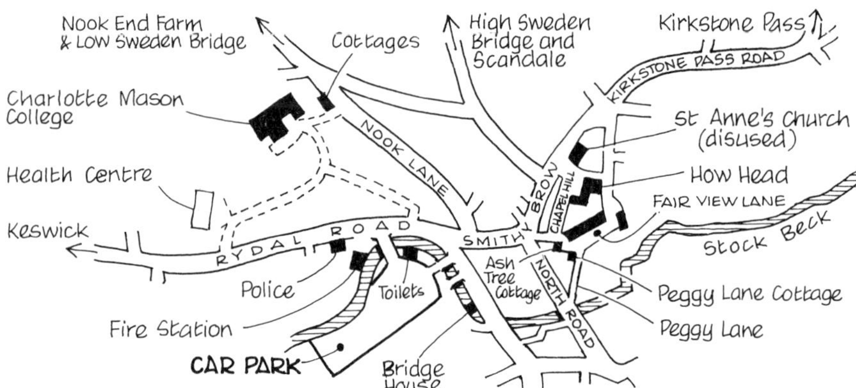

The sound of female and male laughter drifted through the open windows of the college. Miss Mason would not have approved.

Pathways edged by high slate walls led off Nook Lane to cottages dripping with pretty flowers. Larger houses stood soberly in their own grounds like country rectories, peaceful havens yet only 200 yards from teeming Rydal Road.

On the north side of Rothay Road, immaculate green lawns and exotic trees are a perfect setting for the white Colonial-style main building of the Charlotte Mason College. Miss Mason, a tiny but formidable figure, founded the college in 1864, for the education of 'earnest and well-bred young gentlewomen'. Men were strictly not admitted until more liberal times. A friend of equally high-minded Wordsworth and Rawnsley, Miss Mason taught here until her death in 1923 at the age of 81. She would have been appalled to see her name so prominently displayed across the wall outside. The grounds are a considerable temptation for the motorist looking for somewhere to park. Dire consequences may befall your vehicle if you succumb.

Cottages in Nook Lane

Smithy Brow climbs from Rothay Road to the 1,500-feet-high summit of Kirkstone Pass with scarcely a break in unrelenting steepness. Not for nothing is it called The Struggle. Years ago a gang of us recklessly made the descent on bikes. Our motley machines, assembled from rusting parts gleaned from rubbish tips, were not up to the job. Braking systems ranged from ancient levers held together with bits of binder twine, down to the soles of Woolworth's baseball boots fearlessly applied to back tyres. Dismounting from your bike was frowned on as 'soft', though falling off after running into a stone wall to stop was considered acceptable.

We all amazingly arrived in Rothay Road alive. However, first-degree burns to the feet of baseball boot wearers were widespread, and tattered and smouldering remnants of socks littered the roadside. Those with proper brakes had generated so much heat their inner tubes had melted to a black gunge unrestorable by any puncture repair kit. We all walked home, footsore but wiser.

Fair View Road

One of the delightful cottages off Smithy Brow has a huge slate chimney and walls of an unusual variety of stone. Its colours range from subtle reds and browns to almost black purples. The effect is remarkably beautiful, like a watercolour painted by a master.

Smithy Brow

Fair View Road has a terrace of pretty white cottages and a guest house at the end shaded by silver birch trees. A sign on its solidly-built porch bristles proudly with crowns awarded by the Cumbria Tourist Board. A well-kept garden with an old wheelbarrow overflowing with flowers, completed the rustic scene.

Fair View Road

Ash Tree Cottage is a carefully restored part of an ancient farmhouse, possibly once a store attached to the main building. The fashionable Victorian-style lamp posts don't look quite right, but they are infinitely preferable to the concrete monstrosities that I've left out of many drawings in this book.

Ash Tree Cottage

Peggy Hill

When you're stuck in a Compston Road traffic jam, it's difficult to imagine that only 200 yards away there's this peaceful backwater up Peggy Hill. The oldest part of Ambleside, much of it is now holiday homes. Generally speaking, it's the income from them that keeps the area so attractive. Serious money was parked around the narrow lanes in the gleaming shapes of top of the range GTIs and Volvos. Clearly this class of tourist doesn't struggle up Kirkstone Pass in a horse and cart. Sweaty from the heat of their extravagance, I climbed the hill at a leisurely pace to the small square at the top where the 16th century was waiting.

How Head is a superb example of a prosperous statesman's house, unaltered apart from being split into separate units. Vernacular architecture at its best, it was built during the 16th and 17th centuries by the Braithwaite family. They also owned Borrans Park where the Roman fort once stood. Ancient masonry from the fort is rumoured to have been incorporated into the How Head walls. Certainly the stones on the side facing the church look different from the slate used in the rest of the massive structure. Plastic dustbins stood outside, a modern intrusion into the otherwise idyllic scene.

St Anne's Church Hall

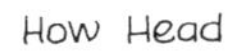
How Head

Walton Mount

The nearby Church of St Anne's was built in 1812 on the site of a 16th-century chapel. Of a plain uninspired design, the building was used as a church for only 42 years. When St Mary's was finished, St Anne's was de-consecrated and is now a church hall.

I settled down on the broad wall of the churchyard to eat my sandwiches and contemplate the distant view of Windermere. During my 30 years away Ambleside seems to have changed surprisingly little. It's still a manageable size, with only a third of the population of Windermere and Bowness, and you can easily wander round all of it in a day. There are some disturbing intrusions, such as the encroaching timeshare menace, but the bubble seems to have burst for this type of English holiday and anyway they do not seem to have been a runaway success in the Lakes.

Across the roof tops Loughrigg Fell beckoned. That's where I spent the afternoon, looking down on paradise. If I hadn't overshot by about 180 miles when I left home I could have been here for 30 years, but my going away was a preparation for coming back. Now my eyes are open I can see. And here at Ambleside things looked good.

Boat Landings

AMBLESIDE
Catholic Church of Mater Amabilis
CAR PARK
Pier for steamers from Bowness
Youth Hostel
Tourist Information
LAKE ROAD
COMPSTON ST
CHURCH ST
WANSFELL RD
Log Cabin
FOOTPATH
Garden Centre
CAR PARK
WATERHEAD
ROTHAY RD
BORRAN'S ROAD
Borran's Park
Windermere
St Mary's Church
R. Rothay
Langdale & Hawkshead
Galava Roman Fort

Windermere lake ends a mile short of Ambleside. This can come as a shock to visitors who leave the ferry from Bowness at Waterhead expecting to be in the town. An information bureau was opened on the lakeside to point them in the right direction. I joined the dazed walkers who had reached the town and were now returning down Lake Road.

At Wansfell Road end I was intrigued to see a party of Chinese nuns coming out of the Catholic Church of Mater Amabilis. I went into the church and was well rewarded by its startlingly beautiful interior.

An unusual wooden cabin was erected beside Lake Road in 1911 by the father of Grasmere artist, W.Heaton Cooper. He was also an artist and imported the cabin in pieces from Norway to use as a studio.

The new greenhouse at Hayes Garden Centre caused as much fuss as St Mary's church spire did when it was built. Ambleside wasn't ready for a miniature version of the old Crystal Palace. It looked great to me, much preferable to the boring square-shaped greenhouses.

Youth Hostel

Waterhead

Hayes Garden Centre

Catholic Church of Mater Amabilis

When you first arrive at a lake, there's always a quiet moment. The view across the water opens up and nothing else matters. Quiet moments at Waterhead are to be treasured. You may not get many.

Crowded around the bay are boats, hotels, cafes, tourist shops selling more tat than you'll find in the whole of Ambleside, and most important of all, a place selling food for the ducks. A large youth hostel has a magnificent position right on the lakeside. Youths dived straight from the sun-drenched grounds into the cool water of Windermere. How I envied them!

Borrans Park is a peaceful refuge where you can sit and admire the view down the lake. I had a look at the site of Galava Roman Fort, but to my inexpert eye it was only a few bumps in the grass. My return to town was by the scenic route, along Borrans Road and Rothay Road.

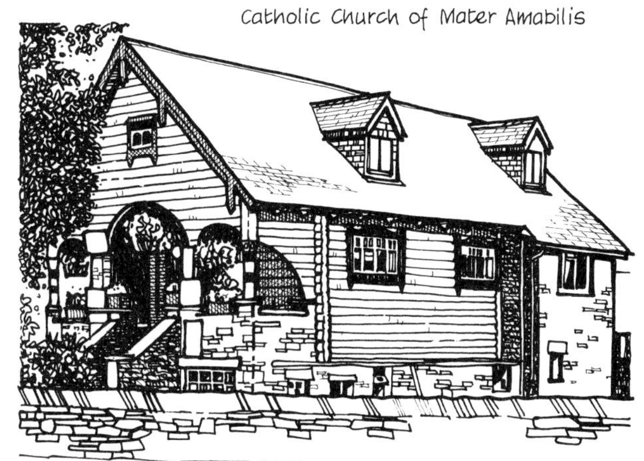
Norwegian Log Cabin

TOWN WALK

It's shops all the way between Rydal Road and Lake Road. In the narrows turn right into Kelsick Road for the library and Wednesday market. There are more shops up Church Street back to Market Place. Go behind the large buildings along Cheapside. Turn back to the Queen's Hotel and go past Sheila's Cottage down The Slack. Compston Road leads to the tourist information bureau in Church Street. Visit St Mary's church then go up Vicarage Road to Zefferelli's for refreshment and more shops. Cross Rydal Road into a cobbled alleyway lined by white buildings. There is plenty to photograph along North Street and up Peggy Lane to How Head. Return to the car park down Smithy Brow.

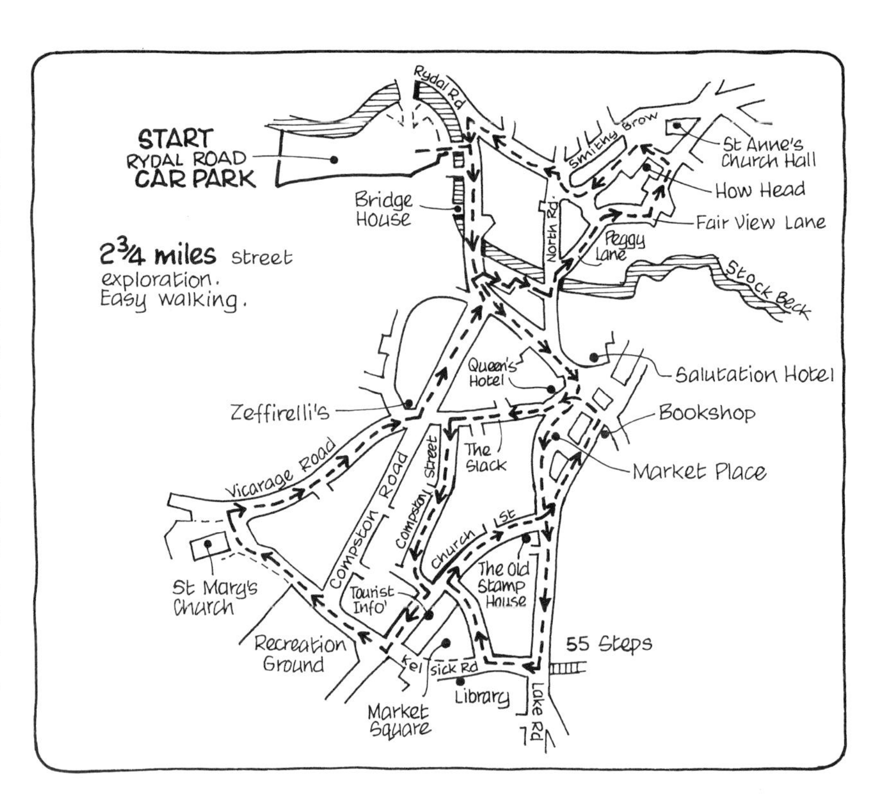

OUTSKIRTS WALK

Follow the obvious path from behind the Salutation Hotel to Stock Ghyll Falls. Return on the metalled road and take the lane along High Gale to Lake Road. Take refreshment at Waterhead. Visit Borrans Park then walk along the road to the Rothay Manor Hotel. Go left over bridge then turn right along narrow Rothay Park Road. Cross the next bridge on the right onto the footpath to Rydal Road. Walk through the college grounds to Nook Lane then double back to Smithy Brow. Go up to St Anne's Church. Return down Peggy Lane.

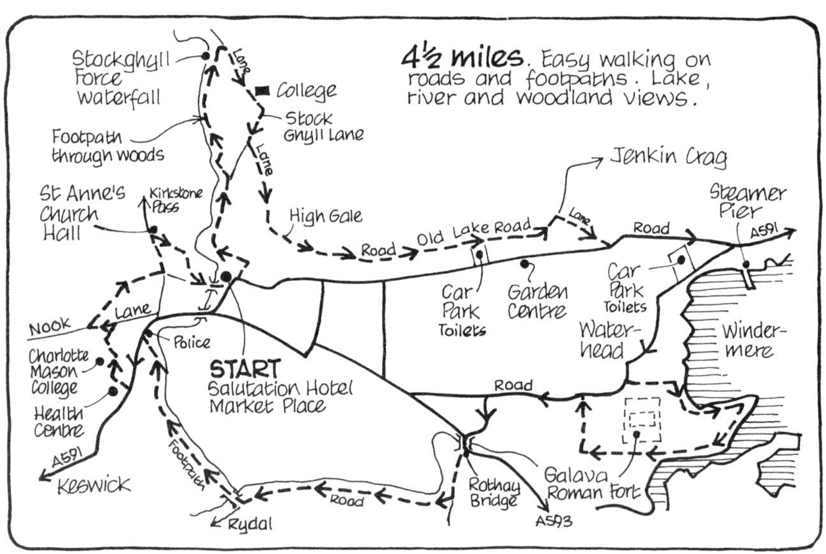

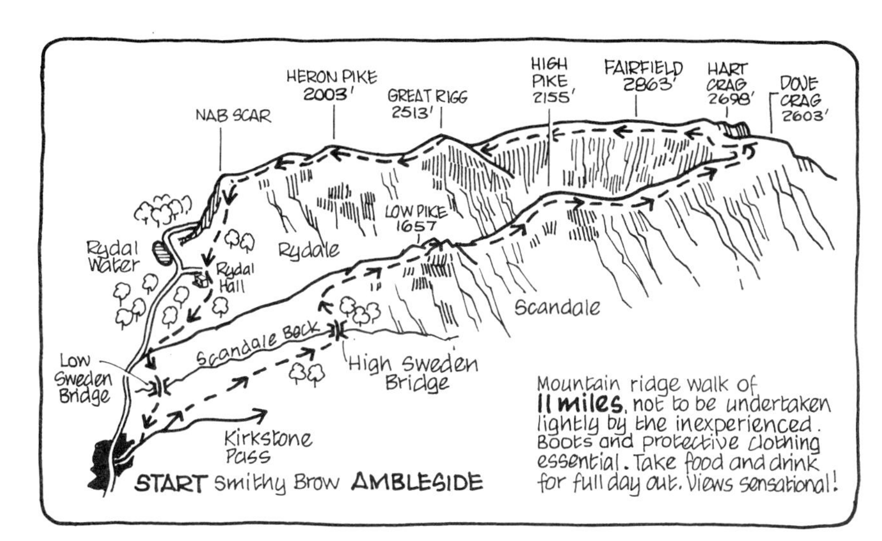

FAIRFIELD HORSESHOE

Sweden Bridge Lane takes you from Smithy Brow across the centuries-old High Sweden Bridge onto the slopes of Low Pike. A wall leads to the summit. All the horseshoe route can now be seen. If in mist, consider returning to town.

Take the obvious route to Fairfield summit for tremendous views into Deepdale. There is a gentle descent along a broad ridge to Nab Scar and a lovely low-level walk through Rydal Park back to Ambleside. A magnificent day out.

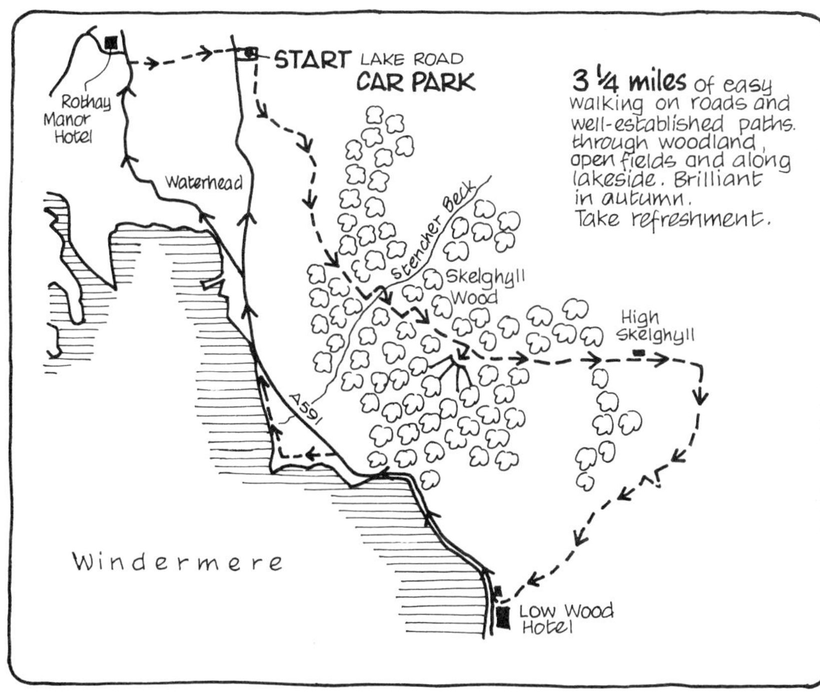

JENKIN CRAG WALK

The lane at the back of the car park climbs steeply into woods. Cross the bridge and continue climbing until a break in trees on the right reveals a wide platform of smooth rock. This is Jenkin Crag. Look at the view.

Return to the path, turn right and walk on through High Skelghyll Farm yard. Continue along the road and just before the next bridge, turn right. Follow the path through fields to Low Wood Hotel. Walk along the main road, with a short diversion along the lake shore, to Waterhead. Return to the car park along Lake Road or via the Rothay Manor Hotel and a footpath across fields.

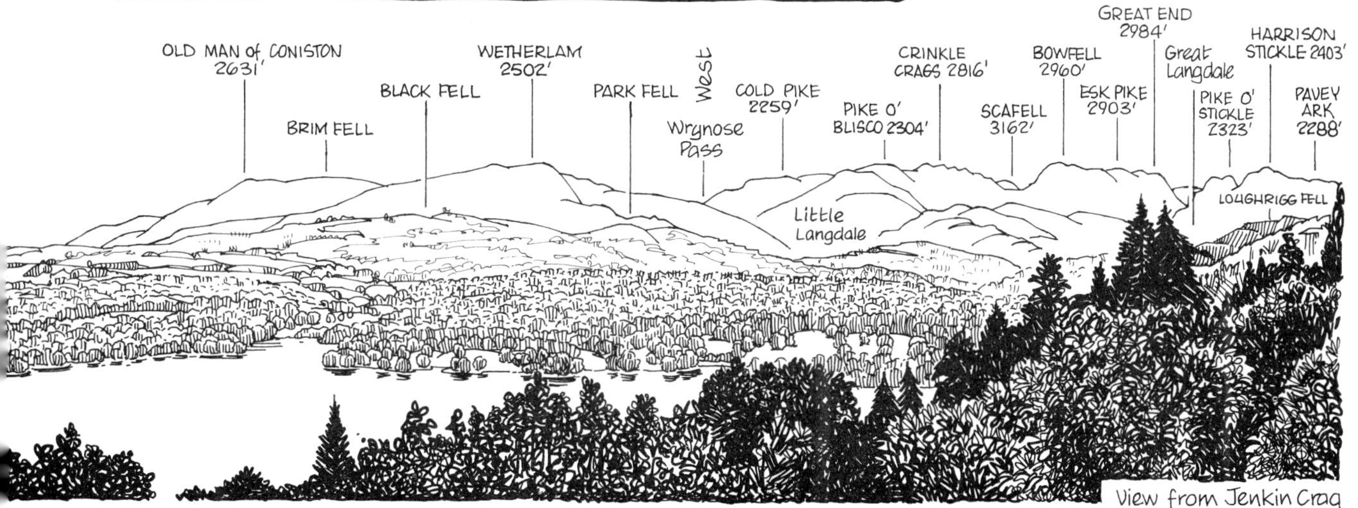

View from Jenkin Crag

LANGDALE DRIVE

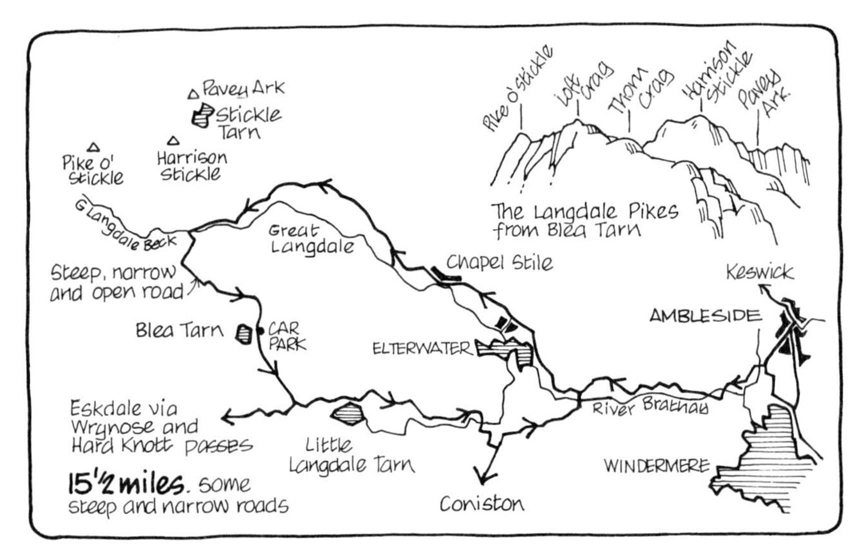

Langdale already attracts more cars than is good for it, but it's too good to miss. Go midweek, out of school holidays, and you'll miss the worst of the crowds. Stock-up on camera film and take a top coat. It blows a bit around Blea Tarn.

Follow the main road to the head of Great Langdale, then to Blea Tarn up a narrow road - steep but safe. Join the Wrynose Pass road through Little Langdale. Return to Ambleside on the Coniston road.

LOUGHRIGG FELL WALK

Though small in stature, Loughrigg is a delight to walk on. Go through Rothay Park, cross the bridge and go up the lane onto the fell. It is confusing but safe on top. Don't panic. Follow paths north. When Grasmere comes into view go down to Loughrigg Terrace. Take the wide track beside Rydal Water. Make a detour to see the impressive cave. Cross Rydal Beck and the A591 for refreshment at Badger's Bar.

Walk along the main road then cross Pelter Bridge for return to Ambleside through Rothay Park.

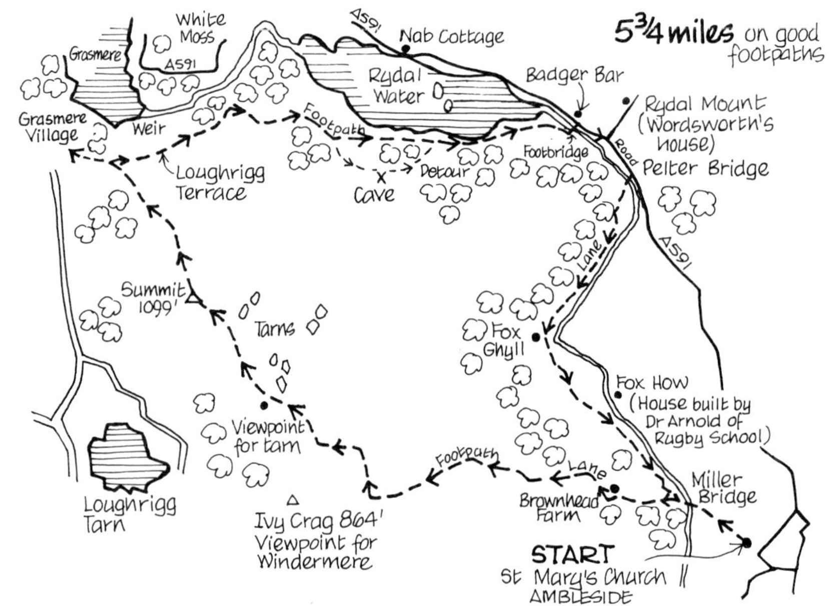

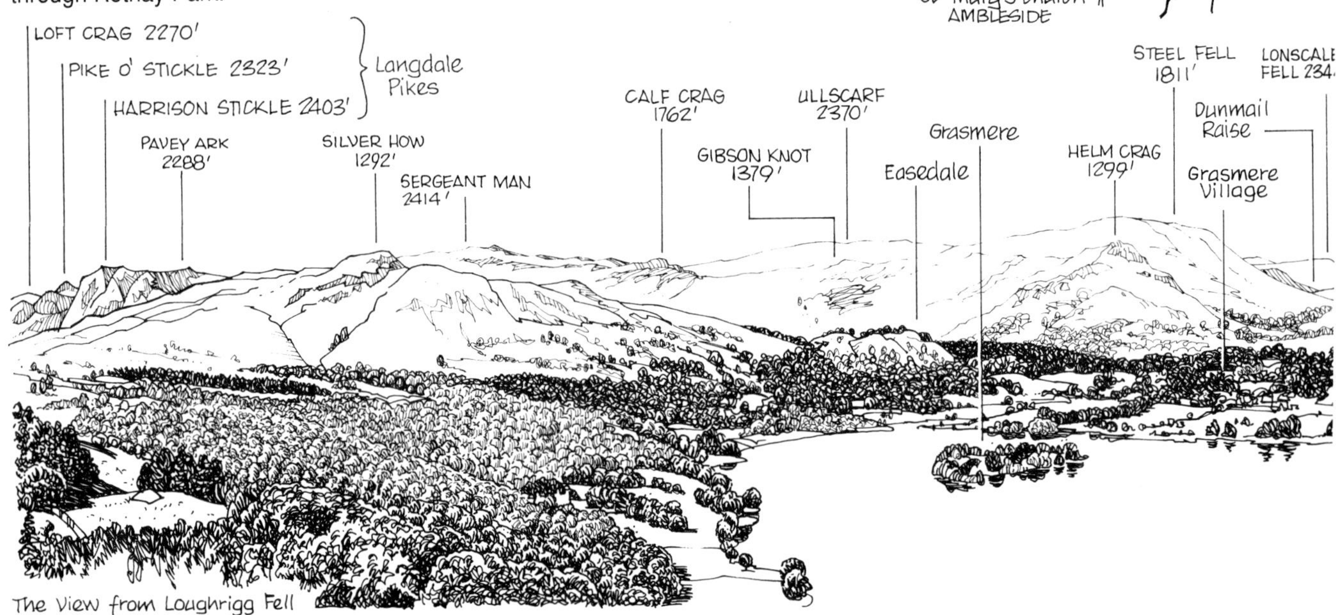

The View from Loughrigg Fell

KIRKSTONE PASS DRIVE

Lakeland in the raw - not to be missed. Drive up Smithy Brow. Stop at the inn on the summit for awesome crag views. Go down Patterdale to Glenridding.

Return up Kirkstone Pass, but at the summit keep on towards Windermere. Just before the Queen's Head Hotel take the village road on the right through Troutbeck. At Town End bear right along a minor road to the A591. Turn right for Ambleside.

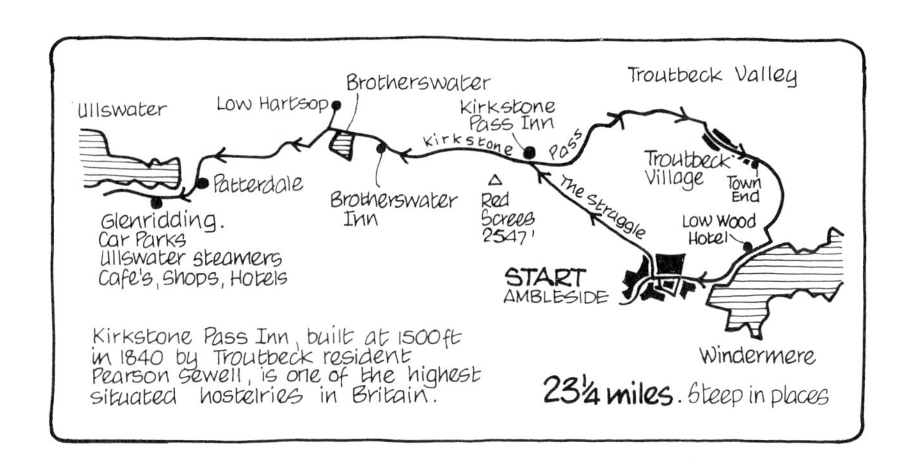

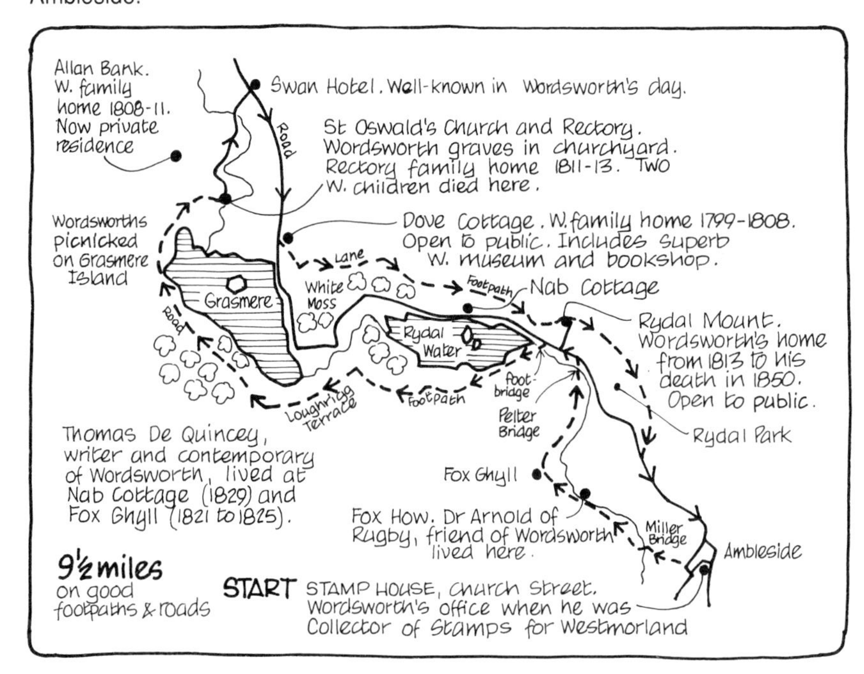

THE WORDSWORTH ROUND

Walk through Rothay Park onto Under Loughrigg Road to Rydal. Go left along the A591, then recross the river opposite Badger's Bar. Follow the path to Loughrigg Terrace. At the end go through the wood onto the old road into Grasmere village. Visit the church then go through the village to the Swan Hotel. Turn right along the A591. At Town End take a narrow road on the left to Dove Cottage and Museum. Continue uphill onto the fell. Go right along the footpath through many gates to Rydal Mount. Walk behind Rydal Hall to the footpath through Rydal Park back to Ambleside.

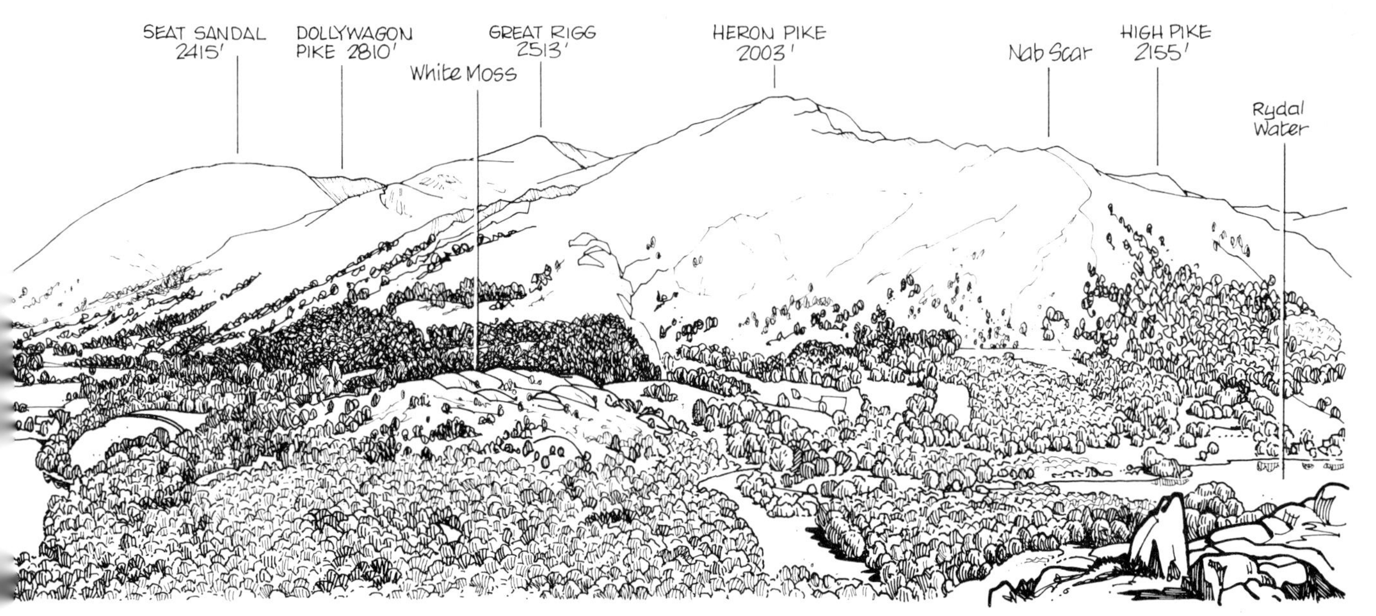

Crag Brow

Brantfell Road

Bowness

I left the A591 roundabout just north of Kendal and took the B5284 through Crook, my favourite road to Bowness. It follows a quiet undulating route across hummocky little valleys. Farmhouses peek shyly from behind trees and the road bends courteously to avoid them. Down a long hill I came to the park-like setting of Windermere and there, a great splash of white across the lakeside, was Bowness.

The A591 has been widened, straightened and diverted to avoid notorious bottlenecks like Staveley, so it is now possible to drive from the M6 motorway junction 36 to Windermere railway station in about 20 self-satisfied minutes, only to spend the next mile into Bowness stuck behind a forty-foot boat on a trailer trying to negotiate the narrow streets of Windermere. That's on a good day. Approach this area on a Bank Holiday and you could be stuck in a traffic jam tailing back to the M6. There has even been a serious suggestion to erect 'Lake District Full' notices at Forton Service Station. On a sunny August Sunday there can be 100,000 people heading north on the A591, and most of them are heading for Bowness.

The eastern shore of Windermere has long been a magnet for visitors. At the end of the 18th century it became a fashionable haunt of wealthy mill owners from Manchester and Liverpool. Who set about changing the place to suit their own ideas of Arcadia. Exotic woodland was planted. Flashy villas and fanciful temples sprang up along the lakeside. Many still stand, incongruous as ever.

In 1848 the railway came, opening up the area to floods of eager visitors and transforming the hamlet of Birthwaite at the railhead into the town of Windermere. Bowness, a mile away and a quiet shipping post for wool across Windermere from Hawkshead to Kendal, became a lively holiday resort overnight.

Windermere and Bowness have now grown to one town, largest in the National Park, with a population of 9,000. Impressionable coach trippers are brought here from all over the world for a glimpse of the English Lake District. They unfortunately see only a sham. The delights of Bowness are not those of Lakeland generally. Even the lake has become so taken over by frantic water pursuits, the magnificent mountains at its head are seen almost as an incidental backdrop.

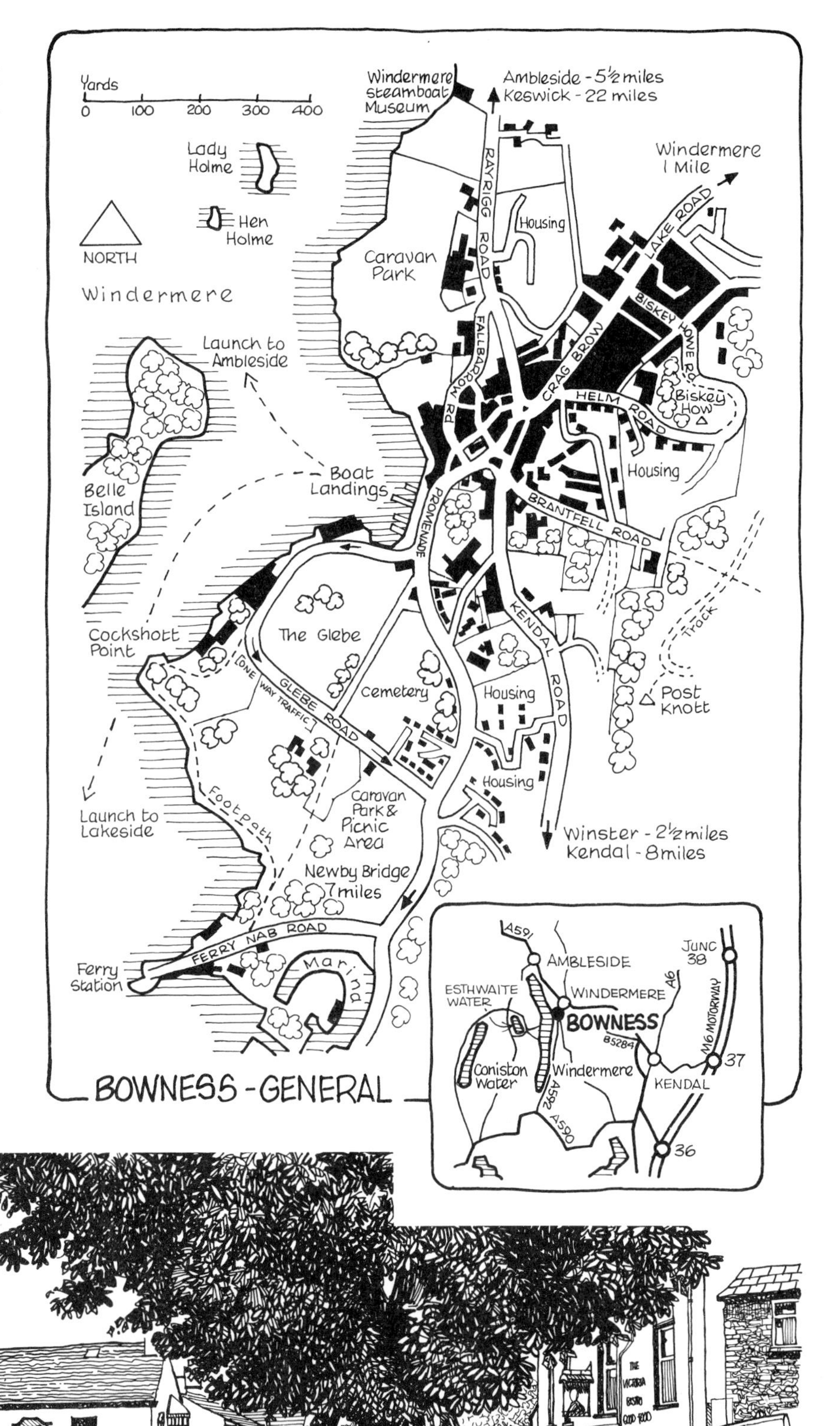

Queen's Square

St Martin's Square

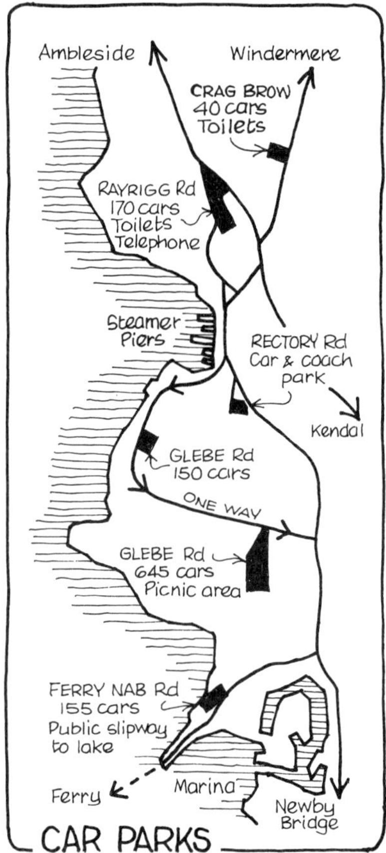

Parking in Bowness is a serious business; marriages and sanity have been known to crack under the strain. I grabbed a place in Glebe Road Car Park near the lake. Rayrigg Road is preferred if you want to be near the shops. But to go anywhere here you have to walk. Roadside parking is impossible.

I was once caught in a lightning police swoop on Glebe Road. Three van loads of shirt-sleeved officers booked scores of us for illegally parking - so much for safety in numbers. It was worth the cost of a fine for all the excitement. Only Jeremy Beadle was missing. I suppose we got off lightly.

The Mad Hatter Restaurant

Sepulcre Hill

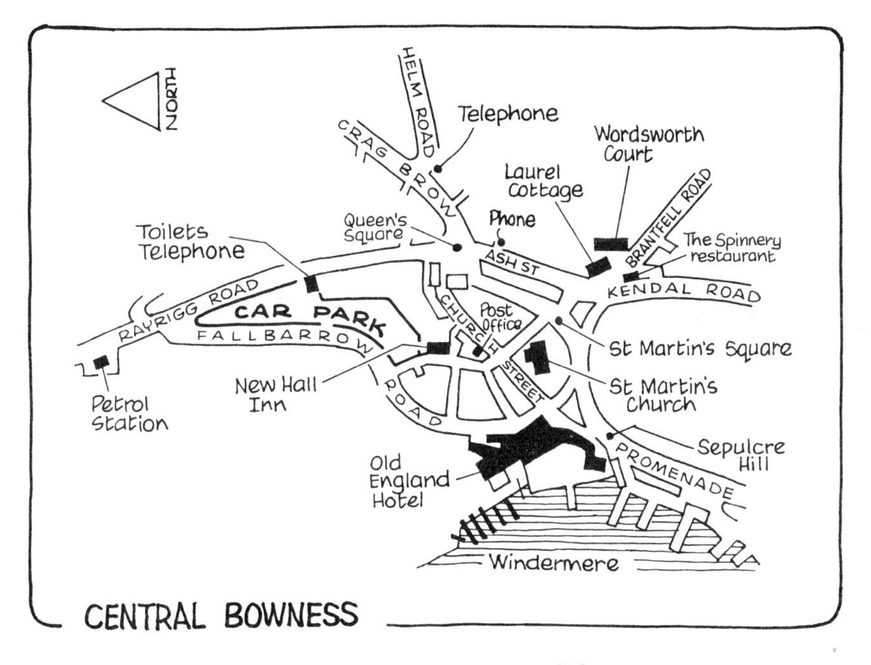

Despite heavy pollution at the busiest road junction in Bowness, a magnificent chestnut tree dominates Queen's Square. It's the survivor of two planted about 1900, and christened Martha and Mary in a quaint local custom still carried on today.

St Martin's Square once had an ash tree named Deborah. Notices pinned to it would be read to the illiterate for a small fee by villagers who gathered to gossip.

There was reputedly a cock-fighting pit hereabouts, but no trace remains. The only fighting I saw was people trying to get into the Ash Street souvenir shops and restaurants.

Whatever draws people to Bowness, it is not the architecture. The row of shops climbing up Crag Brow has a certain something, but whatever they've got it is not elegance. However, the odd mix of buildings gathered untidily around the two main squares do adequately reflect the town's energetic character. Sombre St Martin's churchyard overlooks the Royal Hotel's lively beer garden, while the Mad Hatter's Restaurant across the road is suitably housed in premises resembling the town hall of Toytown.

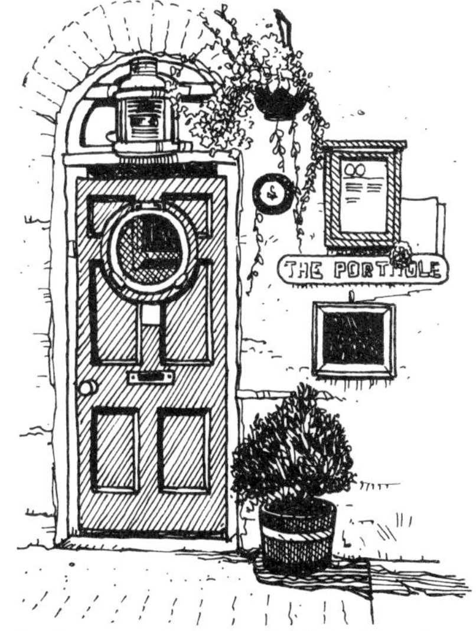

Restaurant doorway in Ash Street

A splendid half-timbered edifice richly decorated with barge boards and four brightly-painted carved heads makes unusual premises for a fish and chip shop. Unashamedly emblazoned across the front in large old English-style lettering is the unforgettable name of 'Vinegar Jones'.

You need never go hungry at Bowness these days. Eating houses to suit all tastes and pockets abound in this small area. Poorer times were chillingly recalled in 1912 when roadmen unearthed a mass grave beneath Sepulchre Hill.

Ash Street

The most historically interesting part of Bowness follows the route of the old village road, which began on the ancient packhorse trail from Kendal, then ran steeply down Brantfell Road, behind the church and along Fallbarrow Road.

I strolled around the narrow streets of Lowside and soon came across the New Hall Inn. Locally it's known as 'Hole in t'Wall', from the days when there was a smithy next door and sweaty blacksmiths were refreshed with ale passed through a hole in the dividing wall. The 17th-century tavern is reputedly the oldest in Bowness. A sign outside stretches the facts a bit by boasting it was 'frequented by Charles Dickens'. Another tells us that from 1852 to 1860 the landlord was Thomas Longmire, 'champion wrestler of England and holder of 174 titles'. That takes a bit of believing, too.

New Hall Inn (Hole int wall)

However, his wrestling prowess was in the Cumberland and Westmorland style of combat, only a local derivative, so perhaps the titles were more easily earned than it may first appear, though I wouldn't argue the point with the brawny Mr Longmire if he was still around.

Itinerant roughnecks used to hire packhorses at the Stag's Head Hotel. These days leather jackets and helmets are banned from its disco. Shutters and wrought iron window boxes give part of the hotel a Spanish look. A Chinese take-away on the corner completes the cosmopolitan character. Rambler-draped Rose Cottage offers bed and breakfast accommodation nearby. All buildings in central Bowness have to fulfil a commercial purpose. Houses for just living in are extremely rare.

Old Bowness

Rose Cottage

New shops

An old slate barn on the opposite corner has been converted into a row of modern shops. Unfortunately, the current architectural obsession with variations on a theme of Gothic towers has inflicted an appalling glass monstrosity on the otherwise excellent design. This tower is neither use nor ornament.

I studiously combed Lowside but was unable to find the 'Lakeland Experience', a much-advertised film show of Lake District sights embellished with suitably awe-inspiring music. The venture has probably closed; hardly surprising with the real thing so close by.

Recrossing St Martin's Square, I noticed a striking, Elizabethan-style building at the bottom of Brantfell Road was being converted from a bank into flats. Shock-horror! A commercially crazed place like Bowness with a redundant bank! Surely there must be some mistake?

Indeed. as I looked around the square flanked by parked sports cars and restaurants displaying the kind of prices that would buy a season ticket at Vinegar Jones, the down-market image of Bowness seemed inappropriate. Popularity with day trippers does not necessarily make a holiday resort cheap and nasty. Here you can step off the sometimes intolerably busy streets straight into a completely different world of prosperous gentility. The contrast is striking, much more noticeable than in the other Lakeland towns.

Kendal Road

Ancient buildings that have managed to escape the onslaught of modern traffic dot a clearing at the junction of Brantfell Road and Kendal Road. The Spinnery Restaurant looked so twee, I couldn't believe it's as old as it looks, but apparently it is - reputedly the oldest building in Bowness.

Laurel Cottage was the first local school, built in 1613. Now a bed and breakfast business, it's surprisingly spacious inside and full of creaky atmosphere. When I stayed overnight a pair of lively sisters from Liverpool was in charge. They served breakfast in great style with a non-stop barrage of one-liner jokes. I hear the girls have now moved on. What a pity!

In 1836 the original school was replaced by a new grammar school paid for by a local man, John Bolton of Storrs Hall, who make his fortune by trading in slaves. William Wordsworth, celebrity poet, laid the foundation stone. His address was full of common sense about education. "Too much attention is given to maths at the neglect of natural and civil history," he said, and "Parents are infinitely the most important tutors of children."

I wonder what Wordsworth thought about slave trading.

Laurel Cottage

Wordsworth Court

The Spinnery

Bolton died before his school was finished, but the grateful inhabitants of 'Applethwaite and Under Millbeck' provided a memorial stone. When the school was demolished in 1963 it was moved to another which had been built in 1867 to segregate boys from girls. That school closed in 1973 but still stands, converted to holiday flats and named Wordsworth Court.

The Royal Oak pub sign features a full-sailed galleon, a memento of the days when the inn was 'The Ship', and Bowness was more proud of its sailing life than it is now.

Green Farm Cottage

A snooker club in Fallbarrow Road marks the top of Sawpit Hill. Most parts of rural England used to have such a pit, where one woodman stood below the log and another above to heave the long saw. It sounds like hard work wherever you stood.

Down the grassy hill a charming country cottage dated 1751 nestles up against the huge trees that screen Fallbarrow Caravan Park. They are a text book example of how to site caravans with minimum damage to the landscape.

Beyond a garish petrol station in Rayrigg Road and hemmed in by parked cars, I discovered Green Farm Cottage, complete with traditional Lakeland chimney stack and marked ES1722.

Further along a rough lane on the right led me to a picturesque clutch of cottages. One dated 1719 has a mill-stone mounted on its porch. An outhouse with stone steps up the side had been converted to a couple of idyllic holiday hideaways, sparkling with colourful flowers. Another white-washed pair, sheltered by trees, had gardens overflowing with flowers and vegetables.

The short lane ends at a wide grassy track called Sheriff's Walk. Here I met a group of beautiful horses being exercised by long-haired girls with cut-glass accents. I thought it was Gloucestershire for a moment; all blissfully rural and just a ten-minute stroll out of teeming Bowness.

Cottages dated 1719

House dated 1751

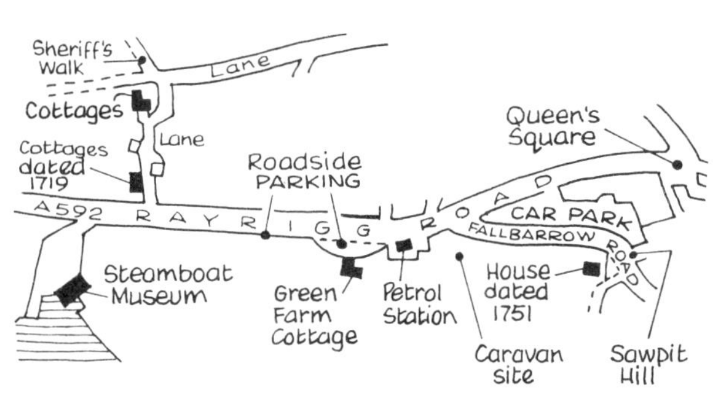

Cottages near Sheriff's Walk

Crag Brow, to the lake

Back on the heaving streets I tackled Crag Brow, which climbs steeply out of Queen's Square towards Windermere. A brass plaque set in the pavement made me stop suddenly. Less nosey visitors sucked irritatedly through their teeth as they crashed into my bent back. Initially I thought the plaque's message referred to the steepness of the hill, but later discovered that 'not dedicated to the public' means this is private land over which the public can walk although they have no right of way.

Before being trampled to death on the crowded pavement, I dived for sanctuary into the Lonsdale Gallery, a big and brassy gift emporium. Its hilariously rude merchandise made the rest of Crag Brow shops seem boring.

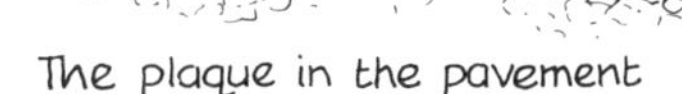

The plaque in the pavement

Crag Brow, to Windermere

However, there are bright spots among the dross. Designs Etcetera sells robust paintings of windswept Lakeland sheep and colourful scenes of racing cyclists toiling up mountain passes. Inside the shop, the artist was wielding a palette knife on his latest creation with all the ease of buttering bread.

That evening there was a ferocious storm, which made it a packed evening in the clean and comfortable Royalty Cinema where current big-feature releases are shown in summer. We saw 'Days of Thunder' - very appropriate!

The modern concrete lamp posts on Crag Brow stand uneasily against buildings designed for a more ornamental age. Some of the country's earliest lampposts once stood here. The Troutbeck, Windermere and Bowness area was the second in England to have electric street lighting - Preston was first. A hydro-electric plant at Troutbeck Bridge generated the local supply.

Just past the sheepskin centre in Helm Road, which has an amazing number of chimney stacks, I stopped to admire a view of Belle Isle and Claife Heights. Both are densely wooded. I tend to take trees in the landscape for granted, forgetting that most of them were planted by human hands years ago. The Browne family of Town End, Troutbeck, was responsible for much of the Scots pine and other coniferous tree plantations in the area. Another prominent family, the Curwens of Belle Isle, planted 30,000 larches on Claife Heights in 1774. They would be sorely missed today. Without its colourful afforestation the great hill across Windermere would resemble a stricken whale, harpooned at its summit by a cruel TV mast.

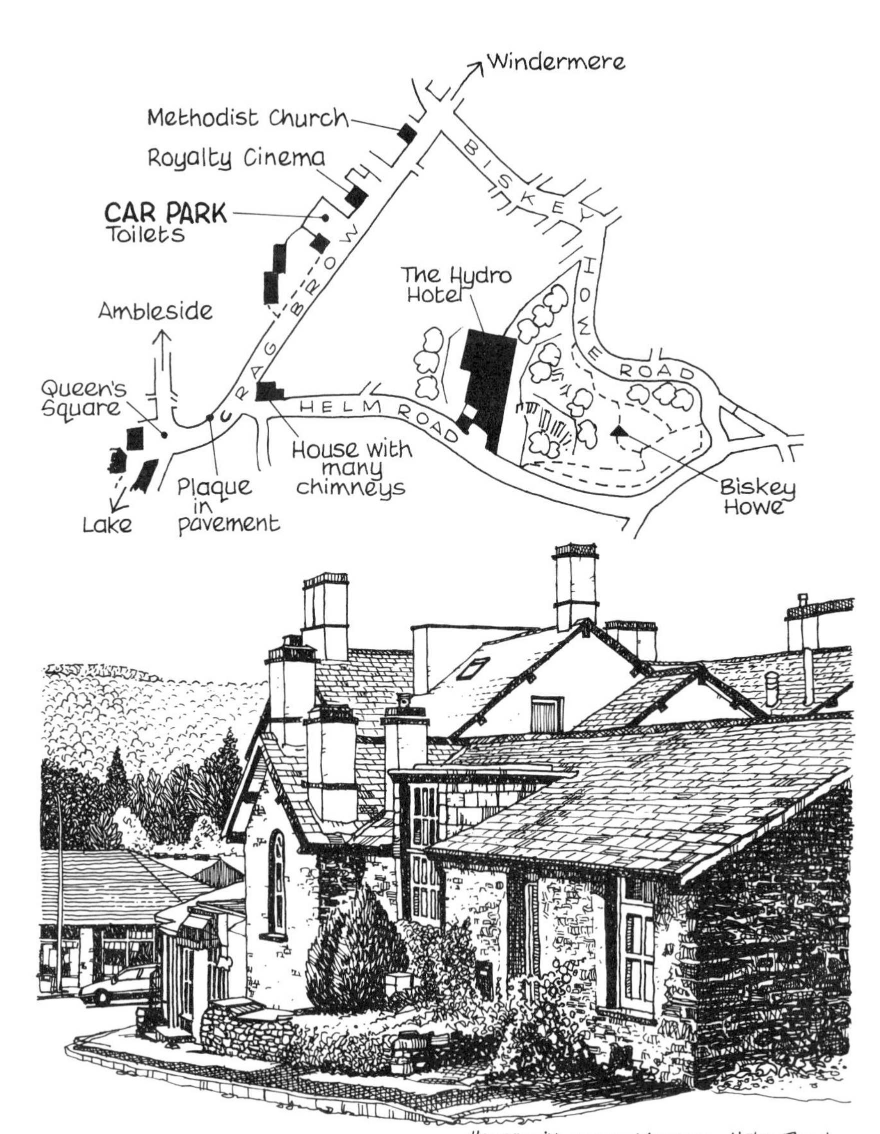

House with many chimneys - Helm Road

The Hydro Hotel

During 1881, the Windermere Hydropathic Hotel started to provide remedial baths in what was intended to be a private residence when building began in 1875. Before then, fashionable Victorians took the waters at the Old Bath House on Lake Road.

Now one of the town's premier hotels, the Hydro has 120 bedrooms, all with private baths. Taking the waters these days is still remedial, though considerably dearer than a century ago.

I found Helm Road beautifully shaded by trees. Vast rhododendron bushes exploded with blooms. All was peaceful, yet remarkably close to the busiest of Bowness streets.

BISKEY HOWE

This viewpoint was a wonderful surprise. No visitor to Bowness should miss Biskey Howe. It's easily accessible via Biskey Howe Road or Helm Road; just don't all go at once. Both roads are a steep walk, but there's parking at the top for about three cars. The Howe itself is level and suitable for wheelchairs. When I first saw the view it was sensationally decked out in autumn colours, but do try it any time. Bowness never looks better than from here.

The view over Bowness

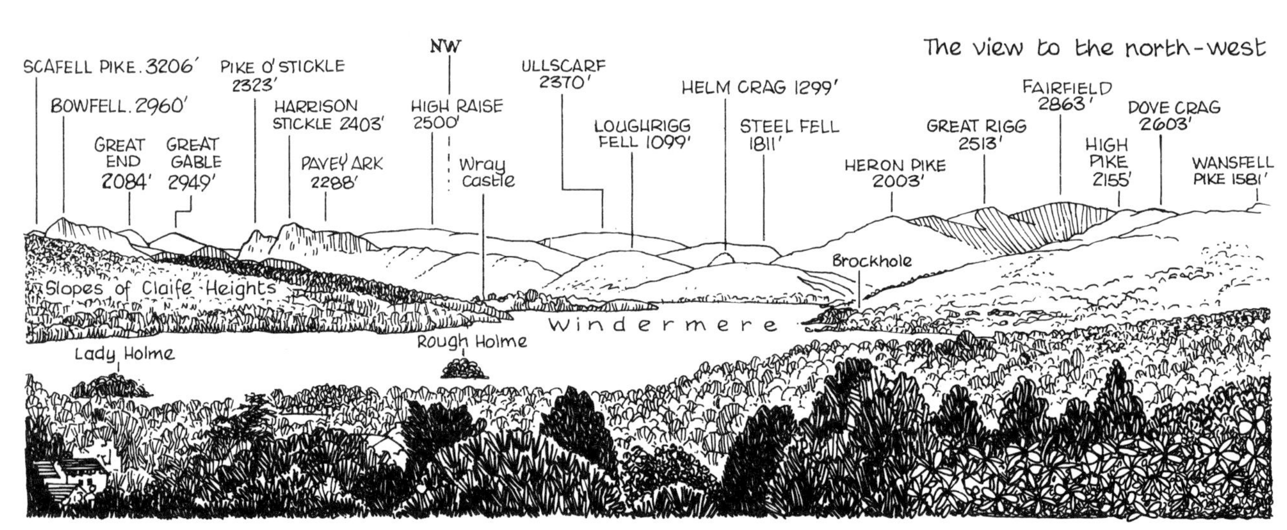

The view to the north-west

St MARTIN'S CHURCH

St Martin's Church stands in the busiest part of Bowness and looks understandably grumpy. However, inside the ancient slate walls I was pleasantly welcomed by sweeping stone arches and uplifting biblical texts painted across walls and roof beams.

The entire roof is unusually covered with lead, transported over Wrynose Pass by a local man without payment. His patronage is commemorated by a tiny piece of glass in one of the windows. Medieval glass dating back to 1260 was brought here from Cartmel Priory for safe keeping during the Dissolution and incorporated into the east window, St Martin's greatest treasure.

A church has stood here since at least 1203. The core of the present building was completed in 1436 replacing one destroyed by fire three years earlier. An 1870 restoration added the chancel and heightened the tower.

From St Martin's Square

Lychgate from St Martin's Square

Consecrated during the Great Plague of 1348, the churchyard has much of historical interest. Some of the yew trees are over 600 years old. Beneath the chancel lies the mass grave of 47 people drowned in 1637 when the Windermere ferry capsized as they were returning from a Hawkshead wedding. Burials ceased here in 1856.

The North side

The Belsfield Hotel

Down on the Promenade the seats were full. Pensioners queued to board lake cruisers that constantly manoeuvred blocking the bay view. Diesels throbbed unmercifully like disco basses. Oil slicks lapped dejectedly against the dreadful Aquarius building. Grubby swans littered the lake shore like abandoned bags of rubbish. Some ganged up with the ducks to mug tourists for egg sandwiches. It was a normal day.

I went back in the evening when the sun was setting spectacularly over Claife Heights. A gentle breeze skipped across the water, caressing the last yacht home and giving the reflected Aquarius lights a seductive twinkle. It was no time to be alone.

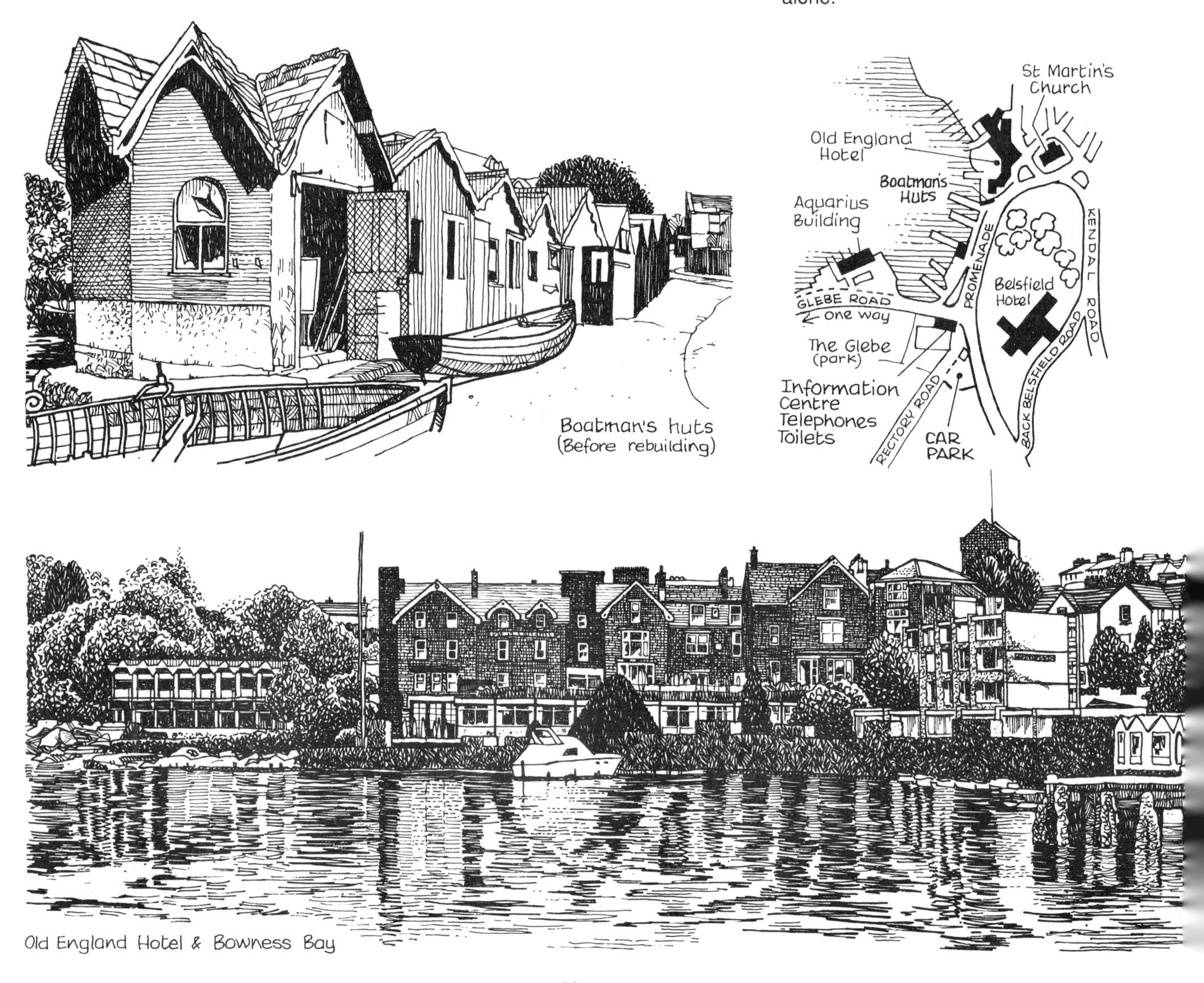

Boatman's huts (Before rebuilding)

Old England Hotel & Bowness Bay

And the Prom' does have much to enjoy. The graceful old steamers have long been converted to diesel propulsion, but are still far more beautiful than their modern glass-bubble counterparts.

I've always liked the old boatmen's huts, real hammer and nail jobs held together by countless layers of green paint. Their rustic charm was sadly replaced by breeze-block replicas in 1989.

The prominent Belsfield Hotel was built for the Countess de Sternberg in 1848. A wealthy industrialist, H.W. Schneider, bought the mansion in 1869 and built the pier for his private steam launch, the *Esperance*.

The Aquarius Building

Information Centre

The Glebe

'The Tern' at the pier

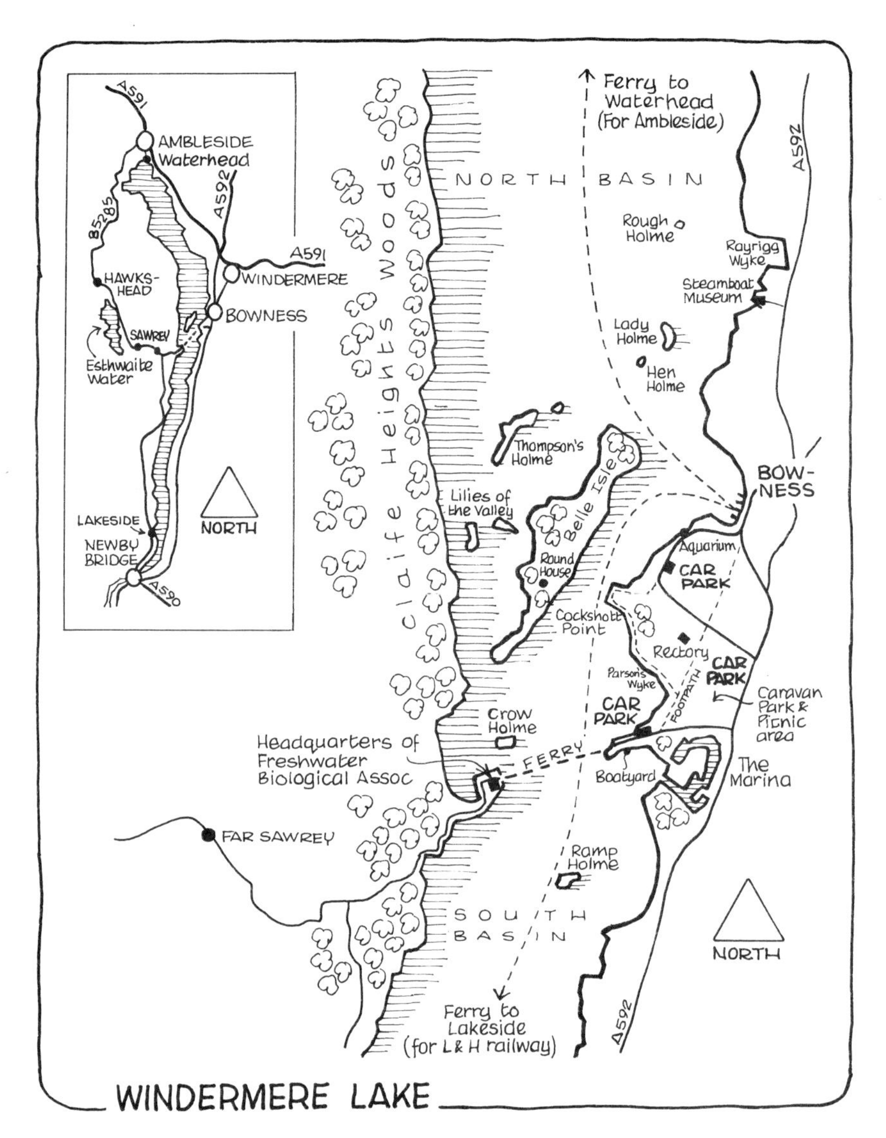

Windermere is England's largest lake: 10½ miles long, a mile wide and over 250 feet deep in places. A busy waterway since Roman times, it is now infested by all manner of pleasure craft. The surface area of deck out there often exceeds that of the water. Yachtsmen with masochistic problems queue for half a day to launch their boats, then queue for another half day to get ashore again.

The huge influx of people has brought problems for this most regal of lakes. Sewage pollution is killing off the famous Windermere char. The wash from large speed boats causes serious erosion on long stretches of shore line. Rowdy gangs land anywhere they fancy and cut down trees for boozy barbecue parties. One landowner became so incensed by their behaviour he mined his private beach with dynamite to keep them out. A party there would have gone with a bang.

As I write, a speed limit of 10mph across all of Windermere has been agreed in principle, which will effectively banish power boats and water skiers to other less populated stretches of water.

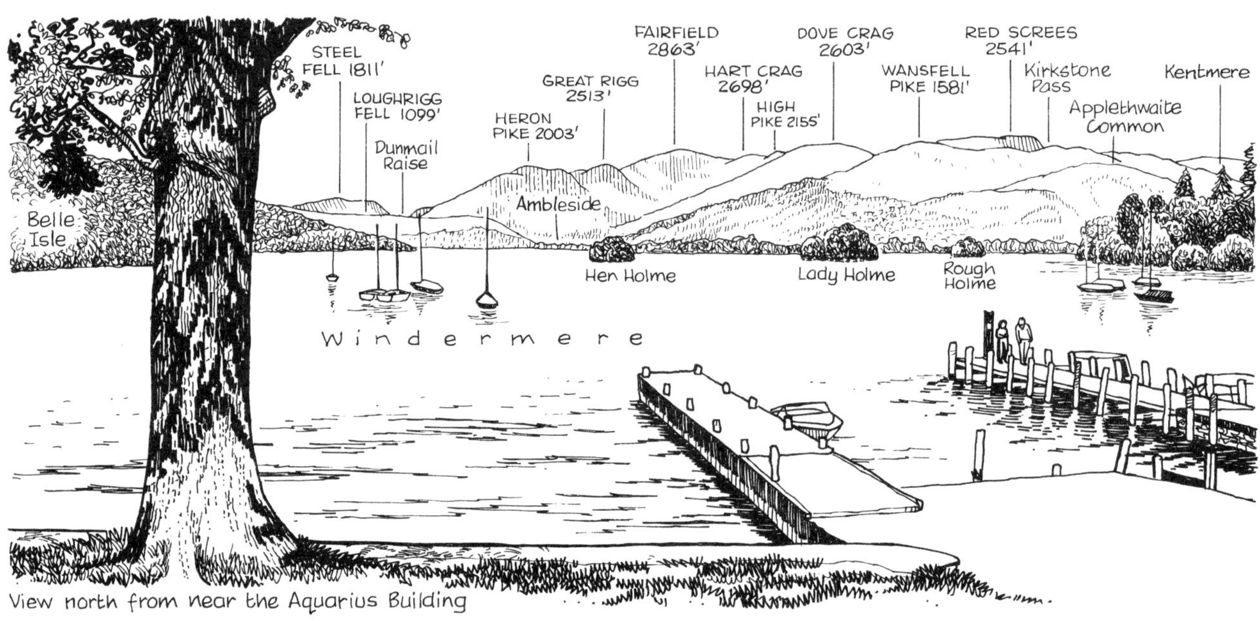

View north from near the Aquarius Building

Windermere steamer

Two launch companies operate from Bowness Bay. The Windermere Iron Steamboat Company runs a regular lake service, carrying up to 600 passengers to Waterhead and Lakeside on traditional 'steamers'. *Tern*, the oldest, was built in 1891.

The Bowness Bay Boating Company operates launches and water buses on a variety of trips, including round the islands and to the National Park Centre at Brockhole. Motor boats and rowing boats can also be hired.

The large steamers are terrific travelling grandstands, but the smaller boats give you a much better sense of scale

The circular house on Belle Isle

Situated just off Cockshott Point, the largest of Windermere's fourteen islands has 38 beautiful acres. In 1774, when the island was known as Longholme, the owner, a Mr English, asked architect John Plaw to design him a house. What he produced must have been quite a surprise. It would have modern planning board officers helpless with laughter. The island house is circular with a dome and a lantern, and a portico of four perfectly proportioned Ionic columns; first of the few round mansions in this country.

Perhaps Mr English got dizzy walking round his house, but seven years later it was sold for £14,000 to Isobel Curwen, who renamed the island after herself. After 200 years in Curwen hands the last of the family line sold Belle Isle in 1991 for a reported 'several million pounds'. We must hope that the fascinating 'pepper pot' house, with its curved furniture and fine paintings, will again be opened to the public.

If you like fishy curios, the rather ramshackle premises of the Windermere Aquarium is a storehouse of delights. See the char before it becomes extinct, or the fearsome local pike, which reminded me of a Glebe Road parking warden I once met.

The Aquarium

Rectory

Chapel in Glebe Road

I wandered dreamily across the large boulders placed to protect the Point from erosion. At Parsons Wyke placid cows paddled as if part of a Victorian painting. I returned to town across fields where the massive chimneys of the 600-year-old rectory pointed to the wide blue sky. It was a fitting end.

The town itself seemed to have changed little over the 35 years I've known it. More shops, more boats, more people, but Bowness still has style. You just have to search a bit to find it.

What had changed was my perception of the place. At the end of Rectory Road the morning's first day trippers were spilling from their coach. It was time for me to leave.

Parson's Wyke

My image of Bowness as only a day tripper's trinket faded as I explored the town. Cockshott Point one fresh October morning shattered it forever.

Mist rose sparsely from wooded hillsides just touched by the russets of autumn. Yachts bobbed at anchor, rigging jangling like the harness of racehorses anxious to be off. Strengthening sunshine found the whiteness of the day's first steamer from Lakeside, which shimmered silently by, sending ripples of greeting across the still lake to my feet. I was considerably moved. Bowness would never be the same again.

Ferry House from Cockshott Point

THE WINDERMERE FERRY

An early model

Steam-powered c.1905

There has been a ferry across Windermere for at least 500 years. The earliest craft were large rowing boats, often dangerously overloaded by people, coaches and animals. Passengers were expected to help with the rowing.

In 1870 the first steam ferry to run on cables strung under the lake surface was introduced. This was updated by another steam-powered model in 1915. Diesel-powered *Drake,* named after a Lancashire CC surveyor, was launched in 1954.

Every ten minutes the ferry crosses the 550 yards between Ferry Nab and Ferry House, headquarters of the Freshwater Biological Association, which monitors the condition of all Cumbrian lakes and river. Queues inevitably build up. Roadside markers tell motorists how long they will have to wait.

Modern ferry - 'Drake'

Ferry Nab boat-yard

Using the ferry cuts at least an hour off the road journey around Windermere, so having to queue for a while in lovely surroundings is no hardship. After I had drawn the illustrations for this page, the 36-year-old *Drake* was withdrawn from service and replace by *Mallard.* Was it something I said?

The new 1990 model, built at Borth on the Welsh coast, carries 15 vehicles and has increased passenger space. As the only static ferry across any of the lakes, it has become a minor tourist attraction in itself.

WINDERMERE STEAMBOAT MUSEUM

It was a gloriously sunny afternoon when I visited the Windermere Steamboat Museum. This place is well worth giving up valuable fine weather time for.

The collection was brainchild of George Pattinson, a local man whose family construction business built most of the old parts of Windermere and Bowness. His father, Captain T.C. Pattinson, pioneered flying boat development at Windermere during the 1914-18 war. He piloted the first glider to take off from water, and flew a Sunderland flying boat up Langdale valley from the wartime lakeside factory. Captain Pattinson was also a steamboat enthusiast, so young George grew up amongst the smell of steam and hot oil.

Miss Windermere IV (1958) & 'Bluebird'

S.S. Raven (1871) & T.S.S.Y Esperance (1869)

Built on the site of a former sand wharf, the museum was opened in 1977 by Prince Charles. He took a trip on SL *Branksome* and drank tea from its copper kettle that boils a gallon of water in ten seconds.

In the 'dry' part of the museum there are many famous and historical motorboats. *Miss Windermere IV* was built locally by Borwicks in 1958. Powered by a Jaguar XK1220cc engine and driven by Norman Buckley, the hydroplane achieved four world records between 1960 and 1971. The MV *Canfly* is fitted with the world's oldest Rolls Royce Hawk aero engine in working order.

A full-scale mock-up of the speed boat *Bluebird* was on display. It was constructed for the excellent TV film, *Across the Lake,* the story of Donald Campbell's last days before he was killed on Coniston Water. I can still remember the shriek of the original *Bluebird's* engine around Ullswater. The BBC eventually sold the TV prop elsewhere for a rumoured £30,000.

Some exhibits were lucky finds. An 1898 motor boat, probably the oldest in England, was rescued from a Windermere garden compost heap in 1955. Even more amazing was the 1780 sailing yacht, being used as a henhouse at Southport when identified.

There are novelty items too: the 1890 rowing boat Beatrix Potter kept at Moss Eccles Tarn; and the glider intrepid Captain Pattinson flew off Windermere.

In the covered floating dock next door fifteen exquisite steamboats are kept in full working order. All were locally built, mainly of teak with pine, oak and mahogany pieces. Funnels are white to a Windermere convention, fittings brass and copper. Glowing with mellow colour and framed by the natural wood of the building and walkways, they were a magnificent sight.

Steam launch *Dolly* is the world's oldest screw-propelled vessel. After sinking on Ullswater in 1895 she lay forgotten until Furness Sub-Aqua Club raised her in 1962. The engine still runs smoothly with its original piston rings. For ten years it ran with the boiler which had spent 67 years on the lake bottom.

Two iron-hulled craft are moored outside the main building. *Raven,* the oldest vessel on *Lloyd's Register of Yachts* with original machinery, delivered cargo around the lake until 1922.

Esperance was built for wealthy industrialist, H.W.Schneider of Belsfield. The high grade iron came from one of his own foundries. Arthur Ransome made her Captain Flint's houseboat in *Swallows and Amazons,* a role which *Esperance* played in the TV adaptation.

For anyone even remotely interested in local history, boats, or steam propulsion, this place is a must. I left reluctantly at closing time.

S.L. Osprey (1902)

S.L. Branksome (1896)

S.L. Dolly (1850)

S.L. Kittiwake (1898)

S.L. Lady Elizabeth (1895)

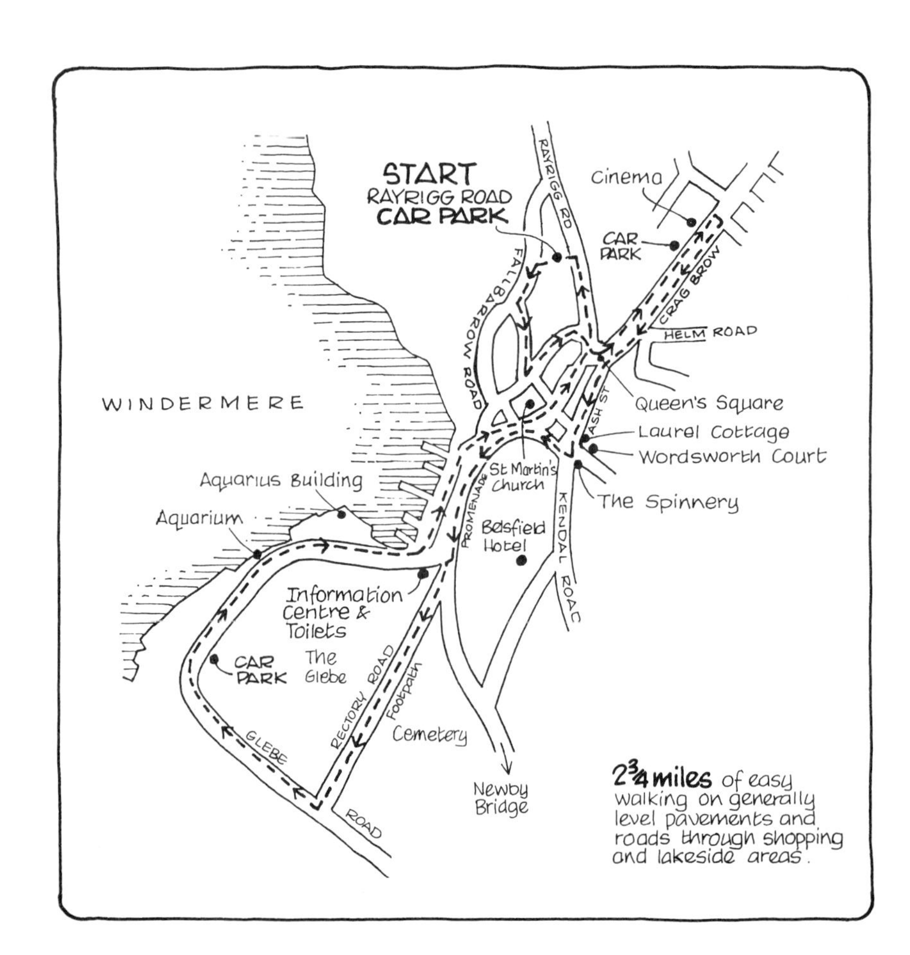

TOWN WALK

From busy St Martin's Square, walk along the Promenade into Glebe Road. Where the road turns sharply left, carry straight on through a gate to Cockshott Point. Follow the lake shore footpath to Ferry Nab and take the ferry across the lake.

On the quieter western lakeside head into the wood by following the shoreline to your right onto a peaceful road. Walk along this until you are level with Thompson's Holme, then take the path on your left into the wood. After climbing for a while you come back to lake level at a car park. Follow the road to Ferry House and recross the lake. Then take the path across the fields beyond Ferry Nab car park into Rectory Road to rejoin the town's holiday bustle.

LAKESIDE CONTRASTS

Explore Lowside, the oldest part of town, then take in the modern shops in Crag Brow and Ash Street. Go along the Promenade into Rectory Row where the aspect becomes more open. Glebe Road takes you past numerous boat yards to the inviting fell view up Windermere. Appetite suitably whetted, call in the Tourist Information Centre at the end of the Promenade.

You may fancy a trip on the lake now; well worth it if the weather is clear. Back in the town, have a look round St Martin's Church.

Return to the car park along Rayrigg Road. You pass 'Stan's Plaice', one of the best fish and chip shops I've come across. A visit here followed by refreshments at the New Hall Inn is an excellent way to round off the walk.

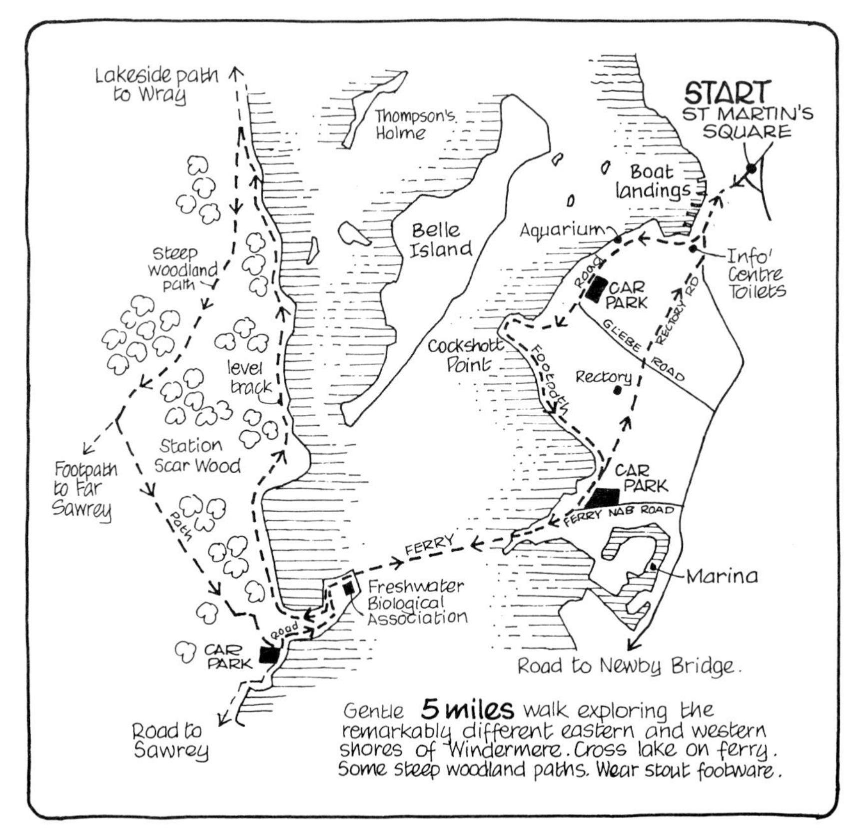

TOWN & COUNTRYSIDE WALK

The countryside around Bowness is unthreatening, no fearsome crags to clamber over and nowhere you can get lost. This restful route of about 4½ miles includes the two popular viewpoints of Biskey Howe and Post Knott. Stout footwear is recommended.

Begin by walking out of town along Rayrigg Road. Just before you reach the steamboat museum, turn right up a rough lane past some picturesque cottages (see page 35). A broad track on the right returns you to the town near the cinema. Cross Crag Brow for a steep but short climb up Biskey Howe Road to the first viewpoint (see page 38).

Return to the road. Go up the narrow lane opposite for a short distance then turn right onto a track which goes through a small wood to Post Knott, the second viewpoint. Get the sandwiches out, the delightful view across Windermere deserves a good long look.

When you can tear yourself away, head away from the lake onto the often muddy track past Brantfell Farm down to a quiet road. Turn right and walk to a junction where another right turn brings you onto the tree-lined B5284. A long hill, with fine views, leads down to the lakeside at Ferry Nab.

After a look at the multi-million pound marina and the famous Windermere ferry go through Ferry Nab car park onto the lakeside path to Cockshott Point where you can have a nose at the round house on Belle Isle.

Return to town along Glebe Road and the Promenade or, as I prefer, go behind the Belsfield Hotel into Kendal Road. Back streets can be very interesting.

Finally a stroll through the Lowside area of town brings you conveniently to the Hole in t'Wall for a well-deserved refreshment. Cheers.

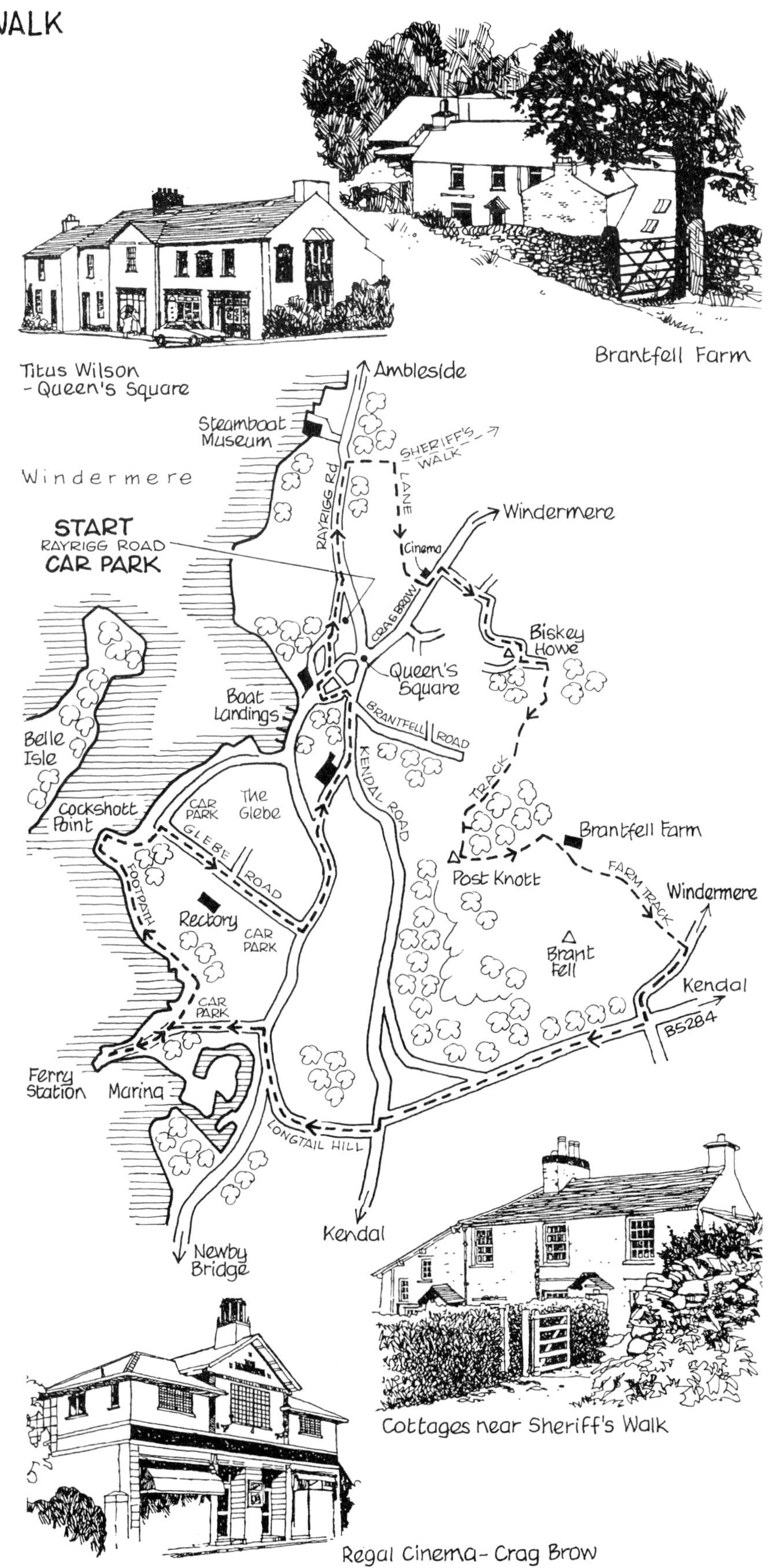

Titus Wilson - Queen's Square

Brantfell Farm

Cottages near Sheriff's Walk

Regal Cinema - Crag Brow

Market Place

Cockermouth

Skiddaw was rising sleepily from morning mist across Bassenthwaite Lake as the A66 swept me through the back door of Lakeland into a completely different landscape of scrubby trees and dusty low hills. Unmistakably limestone country.

The drab outlook brightened when the tempting mountainscape of Lorton Valley loomed into view on my left. Unfortunately, I was turning right, down what seemed the back road to Cockermouth.

Tourists don't flock here. Even the National Park boundary makes a sudden detour to avoid the place. I'd avoided it for years also, but was now heading for a face to face confrontation with the town I'd always written off as only a hard-bitten industrial wasteland.

Suddenly the futuristic buildings of the Lakeland Business Park reared up like pyramids. I thought I was on the wrong road, wrong planet even.

Then below me the town appeared, stretched out in the warm sunshine like a brown shaggy dog on a grey-green mat at the fireside. A minute later I was down the hill and comfortably parked in Main Street. Schoolchildren in neat uniforms queued quietly for buses. It was a promising start.

The Old Court House

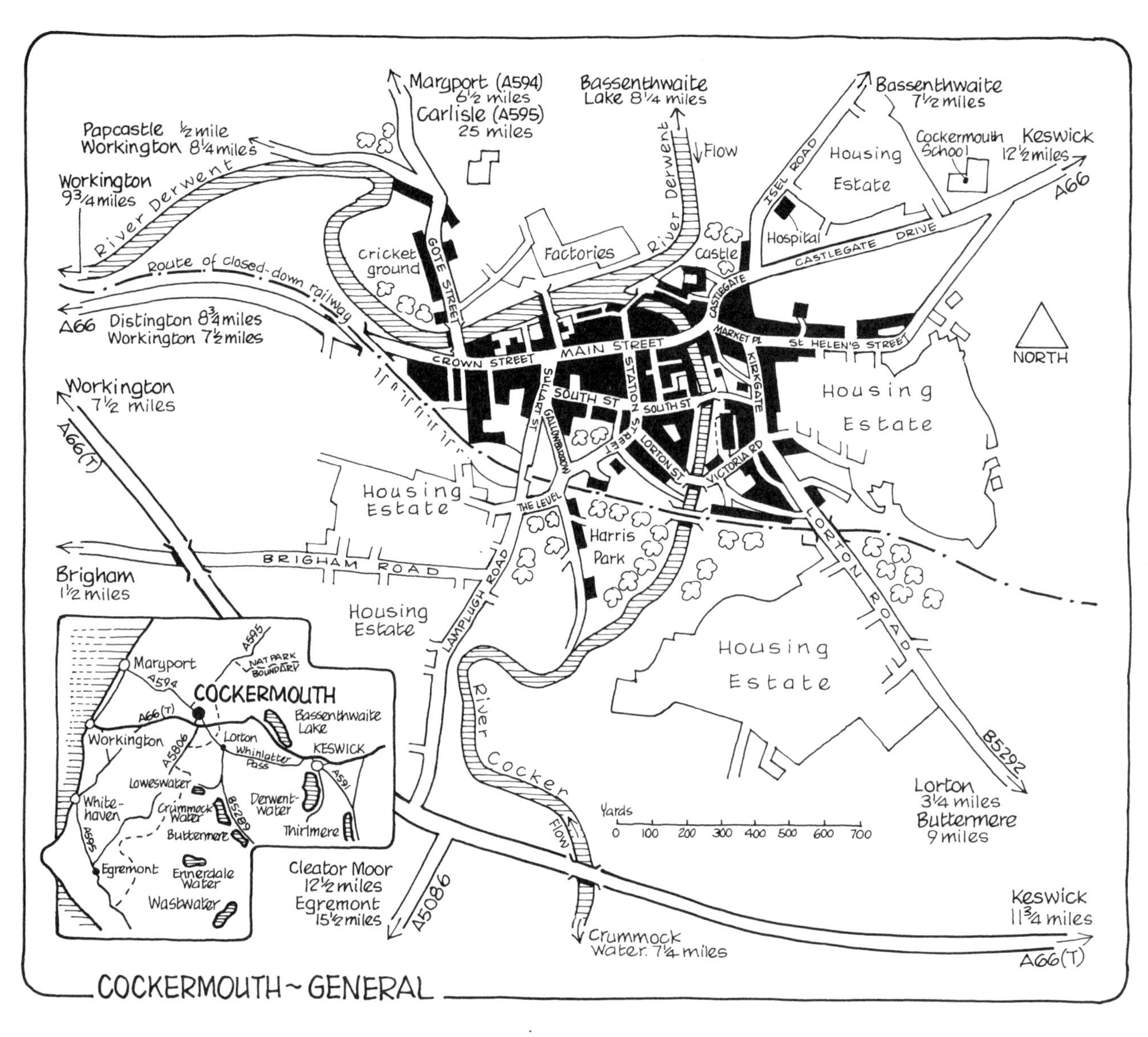

Lakeland Business Park

Main Street

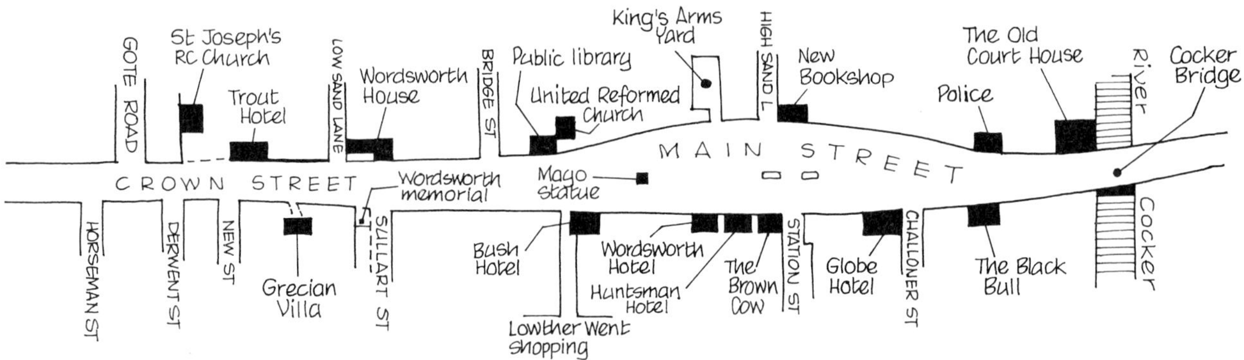

The Romans were first to make a lasting impression here. In the second century AD they built a fort, Derventio, at the junction of three important roads linking Maryport, Penrith and Carlisle, near what is now the village of Papcastle.

Another settlement gradually developed a mile away at the junction of the Derwent and Cocker rivers. Already strategically superior, this became the centre of power when a timber castle was built about 1140. Stone from the ruins of the Roman fort was used to rebuild the castle in 1220.

King Henry the Eighth was so impressed he awarded Cockermouth a market charter, only the second in Cumberland. The town rapidly grew in importance. By the 17th century it had become the county's main trading centre.

The Globe Hotel

Near Utd Ref Church

Medieval Cockermouth stretched between the two hills occupied by the castle and All Saint's Church. At the beginning of the 19th century the town had over forty industrial sites, many of them water-powered mills along the Derwent and Cocker. Corn, wood and cotton were the mainstays, tanning and hat making significant trades.

Since then Cockermouth industry has almost completely died out. Local people have to travel to find employment. Many work on the west Cumbria coast at the Sellafield nuclear plant, a place much feared, but not in this town. In winter, rumour has it, all the feet in Cockermouth are kept warm by BNFL protective socks.

Mayo Monument

WAKEFIELD RD
R. Derwent
CROWN ST
MAIN ST
CASTLEGATE
MARKET PL
SULLART STREET
STATION ST
SOUTH STREET
Foot bridge
R. Cocker
KIRKGATE
CAMPUGH RD
CAR PARKS

The Brown Cow

The Black Bull

Main Street developed in the 19th century from the town's market area where hiring fairs were held. The brawny lads I saw hanging about making eyes at the schoolgirls didn't have farm work on their minds.

The street, broad as some squares, is lined by lime trees severely pruned to the shape of out-sized toilet brushes. Buildings are brightly painted with none of the gloomy slate of Keswick or Ambleside.

The Mayo Monument, Lakeland's only statue, is a handsome white marble likeness of Richard Southwell Bourke, sixth Earl of Mayo and once MP for Cockermouth. In 1872 he achieved fame by becoming the only Viceroy of India to be assassinated. A convict in the Andaman Islands stabbed him.

His monument, erected in 1875, survived its own unprovoked attack in 1964, when it was hit by a rogue petrol tanker. The statue toppled over but was intact. The tanker was a write-off.

For my visit Cockermouth had arranged for a new sewer to be laid down the centre of the main street. Huge pipe laying machines filled one side of the road and temporary traffic lights were in operation. There were even traffic tail-backs, phenomena previously unseen in this town. The bus queues buzzed with comment, but a visitor from Ambleside would have considered it a quiet day.

All six Main Street pubs line up on the same side of the street, facing the serried ranks of the public library, United Reformed church, and police station on the other. Puritanism versus the Demon Drink. I noted the handsome good looks of the Bush Hotel, but more importantly, the Jennings logo across the front.

King's Arms Yard

Bush Hotel

Amongst all the gaily painted buildings the Gothic style of the United Reformed church stands out like a nun at a football match. However, behind the forbidding facade, which was added in 1856, there hides a friendly little church built five years earlier by Charles Eaglesfield of Maryport.

Further along Main Street I popped in the New Book Shop to consult a remarkable series of books compiled by a local man, Mr J.Bernard Bradbury, which contains everything you could possibly want to know about the history of Cockermouth and its buildings. Any town that can inspire that degree of devotion must have something special.

King's Arms Yard is a new development of small shops, pleasant enough with baskets of flowers and wrought iron work, but there were no people. They were all in Main Street, talking in tight groups. Maybe there was a hiring fair on.

United Reformed Church

Main Street - North side

I weaved my way back up Main Street between the trench-digging machines. The workmen were talking to someone in uniform. Alarms suddenly rang in my head. Sweating like one of the pipe layers, I reached my car. It was hot. No wonder, it had been parked on a yellow line for almost two hours. I drove off raggedly, passing the figure in uniform who smiled as he waved me through the lights. I never thought Cockermouth would have traffic wardens.

Trout Hotel

West of Wordsworth House, Main Street draws itself in like a waistline holding its breath, and becomes Crown Street. Even the Ionic columns and wrought iron railings of the long and low Trout Hotel seem to have been pushed into its front wall to make room for passing traffic.

I crossed the street to have a look behind a great wall of fir trees at the Grecian Villa, one of the town's most unusual buildings. Aging now, it was built in 1847 by Thomas Wilson, a hat manufacturer whose factory stood by Cocker Bridge. The rural district council used the villa as offices from 1930-50, then it became headquarters for the Cumbria Fire Service. In 1985 it moved to a new custom-built building on the site of the old railway station.

Cumbria Fire Service Headquarters

Grecian Villa

Low Gote Mill

The 'Hospice'

Across Derwent Bridge I drove into Wakefield Road Car Park, dutifully paid and displayed, then set off up Gote Street to see what I could find of Cockermouth's rich industrial past.

The two Low Gote Mills date back to the 17th century. Both have been used for grinding corn and textile work. Harris Linen Company occupied one from 1820 to 1847. It dried flax in a small chapel-like building, now a charming private house called The Hospice.

The main part of the mill has been converted to what looked to me-like holiday flats. The preserved water wheel gave the game away. Tourists are supposed to lap up stuff like this. I lapped up the view of open sunlit fields across the sparkling river instead. A large textile mill used to stand in the curve of the Derwent, but now no trace of it remains.

An impressive building of honey-coloured brick overlooks the river from a hillside of tall beech trees. It was once a pumping station for Maryport's water supply. According to Mr Bradbury's drawings it used to have a tall square and monumentally ugly chimney, which was demolished in 1974. What a pity, I'd like to have seen that. However, some beautiful brickwork patterns above the windows have survived.

High Gote Mill

The mills were once driven by a race, which was taken from the River Derwent at a weir upstream of the castle and rejoined it beyond Low Gote mills. The Derwent itself was diverted centuries ago to provide more protection for the castle.

Derwent Mill

On the other side of the busy Carlisle road, High Gote Mill was hanging about looking for something useful to do after a lifetime of grinding corn. I was surprised to find behind it the modern factory of James Walker which manufactures seals and gaskets.

A walled pathway led me to Derwent Mill. It looks just like a prosperous 19th-century mill should: solidly built with a proud chimney and an optimistic three floors for maximum production. Harris Linen made the well-known embroidery silks and thread here until the 1930s. After the war the building was taken over by Millars, the shoe company. It closed down in 1990, soon after my visit. I knew I should have bought something.

Despite being cast onto the scrap heap of unemployment Derwent Mill can still enjoy one of the best views of Cockermouth. When I was taking photographs across the river an old fellow walking along the grassy bank remarked, "Grand sight, isn't it?" I had to agree. The broad panorama spread between the castle and Derwent Bridge was the best I'd seen all morning.

House end in Gote Street

View across River Cocker to rear of Main St and Crown St

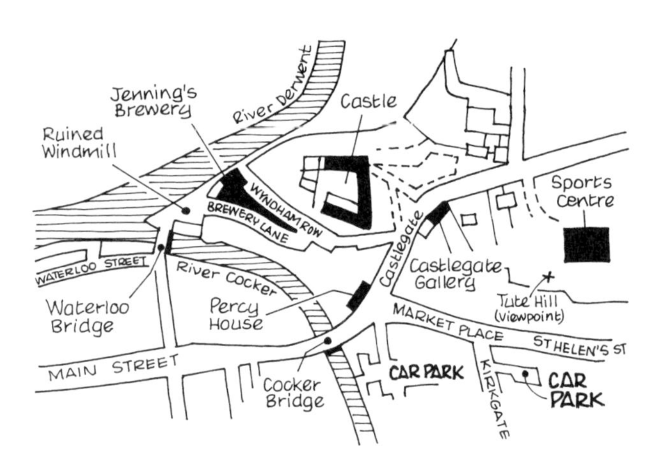

Jenning's Brewery & ruined windmill

Waterloo Street wasn't welcoming. An 1820 linen mill leaned alarmingly above a skinny Alsatian dog that sniffed hungrily at a bulging plastic rubbish bag. My foot splashed against an empty strong lager can in a puddle. So this was the mean streets of Cockermouth. Even the sun had gone behind a dark cloud.

Dry lipped, I hurried away, past the old tumbledown windmill that once ground down bark for a tannery, into the yard of Jenning's Brewery. This is hallowed ground. If I'd been wearing a hat it would only have been right to remove it.

Since the castle was built there's been a brewery here, using water from a well under the sandstone walls. At the end of the 19th century the premises were taken over by the family firm of Jennings, which had honed its brewing skills to perfection in the nearby village of Lorton. It has greatly modernised the plant but still uses traditional methods to keep its 77 pubs throughout Cumbria well topped up.

Slightly weak at the knees from prostrating myself beneath the towering maltings building, I decided not to visit the new visitor centre or the Museum of Brewing. Instead I returned to the Bush Hotel to sample the product at the workface. It never touched the sides.

Waterloo Street

Jenning's Brewery at junction of the Derwent and Cocker

Castlegate

For years the main road to Keswick climbed tortuously up steep and narrow Castlegate. The grime of heavy traffic still coats the elegant 17th and 18th-century houses. To counteract this deadening effect the ornate doorway of Strathearn House has been painted in vivid colours, but only succeeds in looking even more over the top amongst the rest of the plain, no-nonsense architecture. Castlegate House, dated 1739, stands back from the road at the top of the hill and looks very pretty in pink.

The oldest part of Cockermouth is preserved at the bottom of Castlegate. Percy House was built in 1598 by Henry Percy, ninth Earl of Northumberland. It was at one time the home of the earl's bailiff but was converted to three tiny shops a long time ago. You have to step down to enter them. An upstairs room still bears the Percy coat of arms in plasterwork and an ornate ceiling has the date of 1598 in its design.

A narrow alley between the shops leads to the Doll and Toy Museum, a large and fascinating collection of dolls from over 60 countries.

Percy House

St Helen's Street

After the grime of Castlegate the newly restored buildings in Market Place looked as bright and colourful as a paint catalogue. The Ship Inn is most attractive in Regency green with white window surrounds. An Elizabethan mansion, Old Hall, stood opposite until demolition in 1973. Mary Queen of Scots stayed here in 1568 when fleeing from the English.

St Helen's Street leads depressingly off Market Place, interesting architect urally but decaying badly.

Kirkgate

All Saint's Church

After a poor start Kirkgate opens gloriously to a small cobbled square lined by 18th-century Georgian houses shaded by chestnut trees. The great 150-foot-tall spire of All Souls' Church towers over all. Impressive Early English in style, the church replaced a 1711 building that burnt down in 1850. I found the door locked so had to rely on the Bradbury book on churches to take me round inside.

The largest east window, seen in my drawing, commemorates Wordsworth. A plaque honours Thomas Wilson of hat and Grecian Villa fame, remembered for his contributions to the church, not for his taste in houses. A Caen stone pulpit and the groined ceiling of the tower are also worth seeing.

The graveyard is full of interest. John Wordsworth, father of five including William and Dorothy, lies at the south-west corner. He died in 1783 at the tender age of 42. Other local worthies have their professions recorded on their headstones: a joiner, woollen weaver, draper, attorney, and a bookseller who died in 1856 aged 40.

Returning to Kirkgate I wandered past the Swan Inn, a lovely old 17th-century Jennings pub hung with baskets of flowers. The local brass band wet their whistles here but I resisted the temptation as was appropriate for a visit to the Society of Friends Meeting House at the top of the hill. The present 1884 building looks remarkably like a bank, which may not be quite what the Quakers intended.

Mackreth Row brought me to a fine view over the town hall and the best sight of the castle ruins that I'd managed all day. The castle is private and open only on special occasions. All very frustrating. I wanted to be in there having a good nose about. Again I rely on the indispensable Mr Bradbury for the facts.

Since the time of William the Conqueror, ownership of the castle has passed through the hands of several great northern families. The coats of arms of five of them hang about the 13th-century outer gatehouse. During the Civil War the castle was held for Parliament by the Percy family and was subject to a Royalist siege for two months in 1648. At the end of the Civil War the fortress fell into decay, but part was rebuilt in the 19th century by the Wyndham family who still live there today.

Deep inside the walls there is a couple of oubliette dungeons. Prisoners were lowered 18 feet into these windowless pits through a hole in the ceiling. Escape was impossible, unless you could fly. After a week in one of those you'd be flying very high indeed. There's also Mirk Kirk, a catchy name for another claustrophobic enclosure with a vaulted ceiling, which is thought to have served as the castle chapel at one time.

Society of Friends Meeting House

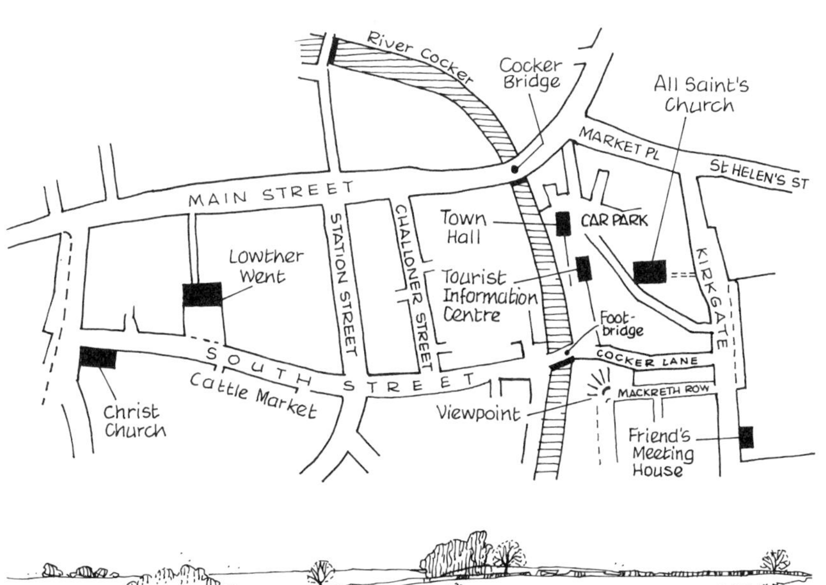

Castle ruins from Mackreth Row

Down some stone steps I came onto the bank of the River Cocker, once another of Cockermouth's busy industrial areas. The car park where I stood used to be a drying area for Sanderson's woollen mill. Across the river, a crumbling building with bricked-up arches was Cocker Bridge Textile Mill. On the opposite bank Thomas Wilson's factory stood, at one time turning out 4,000 hats a week.

Lined by high stone banks this part of the Cocker has the look of a benign canal, but the river can rise rapidly after heavy rain. The new Cocker Bridge was swept away in 1826 before construction was finished, and as recently as 1966 Market Place was hit by severe flooding.

From its source at the head of Buttermere, the Cocker flows a blissful course through Crummock Water then gently meanders down the Vale of Lorton. In town it's smaller than the River Derwent, which has a vast catchment area. Rain falling on Blencathra, Helvellyn, Skiddaw and the highest mountains at the head of Borrowdale eventually flows into the Derwent.

Town Hall

Tourist Information Bureau

I passed graciously through a stone archway that looks like the remnant of an ancient city wall, but was actually the unglamorous back entrance to an old factory yard. It now leads to the Tourist Information Bureau, a charming two-storey building, once the armoury of the local branch of the Cumberland and Westmorland fusiliers.

Cockermouth Town Hall is hidden shyly away nearby. It was originally a Wesleyan church, built in 1841. The Methodists moved to new Lorton Street premises in 1932 and a year later the building became offices for the Urban District Council. In the 1974 reorganisation Cockermouth Town Council was moved to premises ten miles away in Workington. The town hall became the department of Allerdale District Council responsible for all planning decisions affecting one quarter of the Lake District. If you don't like what is happening in Keswick this is the place to petition. Surprisingly there were no militant mobs outside.

Returning to the Cocker, I crossed into South Street over a hideous steel footbridge. It is no advert for the seat of good planning.

Cocker Bridge

Lowther Went

Lowther Went is a new supermarket development with some small shops. To someone like me, spoiled by the slick sophistication of a Sainsbury or Tesco, all Lakeland supermarkets seem garish and chaotic. This Walter Wilson's is a definite improvement.

Christ Church was a forlorn and bedraggled sight on the corner. A clock like Walter Wilson's on the tower would help. Inside things were more cheery, a typical 19th-century galleried church, built in 1863-65.

The atmosphere in Station Road was damp and clammy; there'd be more thunder before nightfall. I photographed the old cinema building, now a vet's practice, and wondered how youngsters amused themselves here. When I was young, Cockermouth lads used to invade dances at Keswick picking drunken fights, but all that harmless fun has gone now.

Suddenly I became aware I was being followed. Two rough-looking youths with shaved heads, tattoos, and earrings were keeping pace with my ever-increasing walking rate. This was it. I'd discovered the Cockermouth hard men. Or to be precise, they'd discovered me. Beneath some dark dripping trees I turned to face them. They stopped. The biggest bent towards me and lifted his hand. "Yer dropped this, mate." With shaking hand, I took my camera lens cover from him and muttered my thanks.

Christ Church

Along South Street the heavens opened. Rain in the Lake District knows no restraint until it hits the ground, and this rain was hitting the ground like a psychopathic pile driver. I dashed for cover through the nearest open door, which happened to be that of the cattle market auction ring. A sheep sale was in progress. Careful not to shake myself dry in case it was taken as a bid for 500 prime hogs, I examined the farmers gathered in the gloom away from the floodlit parade ring. They chatted conspiratorially like sheep rustlers, hands thrust deep in pockets to keep money safe from the auctioneer's probing eye. Flat caps, open mackintoshes and boots turned up at the ends seemed to be the agricultural fashion statements of 1990. My teeshirt, shorts and trainers looked positively eccentric.

Cumbrian sheep farmers all seem to have one leg bent more than the other. Developed over many generations, this is a useful attribute for walking across steep fellsides. On the flat it gives them the gait of drunken sailors.

With a monumental crash of thunder the rain stopped as quickly as it had begun. The impassive faces of the farmers never changed.

Station Road

Seen from Harris Park, All Souls' Church rises proudly from a forest of trees, just as it did after being burnt to the ground. Now the town itself is rising from the ashes of industrial decline to meet the challenge of tourism. Visitors who like to seek out their own pleasures rather than take whatever is on the tourist board platter will find plenty to enjoy here.

My visit had been a revelation. I wish I'd ventured here 30 years ago. But Cockermouth was different then, and so was I. We may not have hit it off.

The town from Harris Park

Fairfield schools and Christ Church

I took a final look at the town from Slate Fell (see page 67). Cockermouth looked small and vulnerable in the dusty green fields. Dark Scottish hills brooded above the bright slash of the Solway.

Behind me storm clouds still lingered over Buttermere where the sun was setting in a riot of red, yellow and purple. I turned away from the town and watched until the fells dissolved into the night. Cockermouth couldn't match that. No town could.

'Pepperpot' house

Wordsworth House

The finest house in Cockermouth, built in 1745 by Joshua Lucock, High Sheriff of Cumberland. William Wordsworth was born here on April 7 1770, the second eldest in a family of five. His father John was a solicitor who worked as land agent for Sir James Lowther, one of the richest landowners in the north of England. The house went with the job.

William's mother was Anne Cookson, the daughter of a Penrith draper. She died when he was eight so William and his sister Dorothy were packed off to relations in Penrith. Five years later John Wordsworth died and the family's links with Cockermouth were broken. William later wrote about his childhood in the town and visited it after his own son had become the vicar of nearby Brigham Church.

In 1937 the house was due to be demolished to make room for a bus station. There was a public outcry and an appeal saved the house for the National Trust to administer as a Wordsworth memorial.

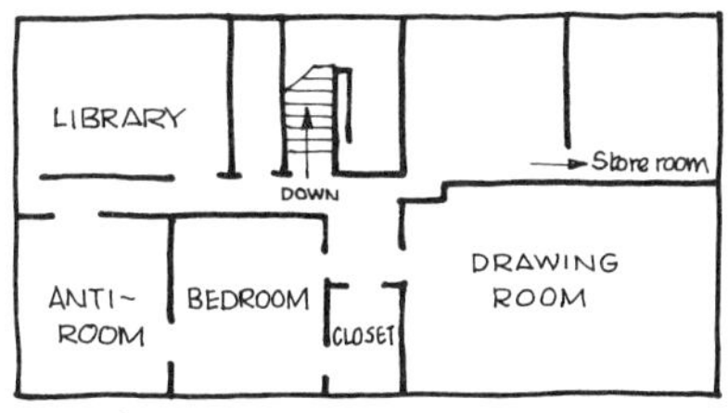

First floor

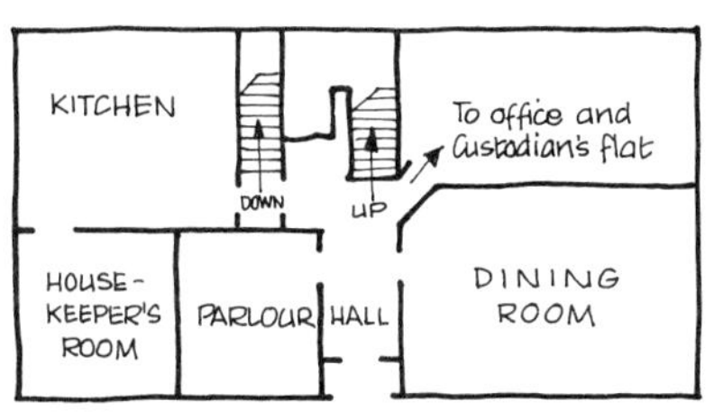

Ground floor

Wordsworth memorial

These days blinds drawn across the windows to protect the valuable furniture give Wordsworth House a rather cold and forbidding air despite its pretty pink paintwork.

The rooms are large and airy inside. Over the dining room fireplace hangs a landscape by Turner, who once stayed at Cockermouth Castle with his patron, Lord Egremont. The only significant items in the house that actually belonged to Wordsworth are a large painted bookcase, a mahogany bureau and a carriage clock.

The Trust has tried very hard, providing contemporary furnishings for the house, even laying out the garden as Wordsworth would have known it, but there's none of the romantic atmosphere of Dove Cottage here. Perhaps that tiny house more suits the popular image of Wordsworth as an impoverished, drop-out poet. If nothing else, his birthplace in Cockermouth reminds us that Wordsworth actually came from a comfortable, privileged background.

A bust of the poet, which gives him the appearance of a Greek god, was unveiled opposite the house in 1970, the bicentenary of his birth.

TOWN WALK

From Wakefield Road Car Park cross the footbridge and turn left into Main Street. Past the shops go left down High Sand Lane to the remnants of the town's industrial past. Through Jenning's brewery yard turn left down Castlegate to the revitalised buildings of Market Place. Kirkgate leads off right to Georgian houses and All Saints' Church. Go into Victoria Road, then turn back along a path for a surprising view across River Cocker, even better further on from the end of Cocker Lane. Walk through the stone archway to visit the Tourist Information Bureau and hidden-away town hall. Return to Main Street across Cocker Bridge and go up Station Street to cattle market. Return to Main Street through Lowther Went. Visit Wordsworth House and Grecian Villa before returning to the car park across Derwent Bridge.

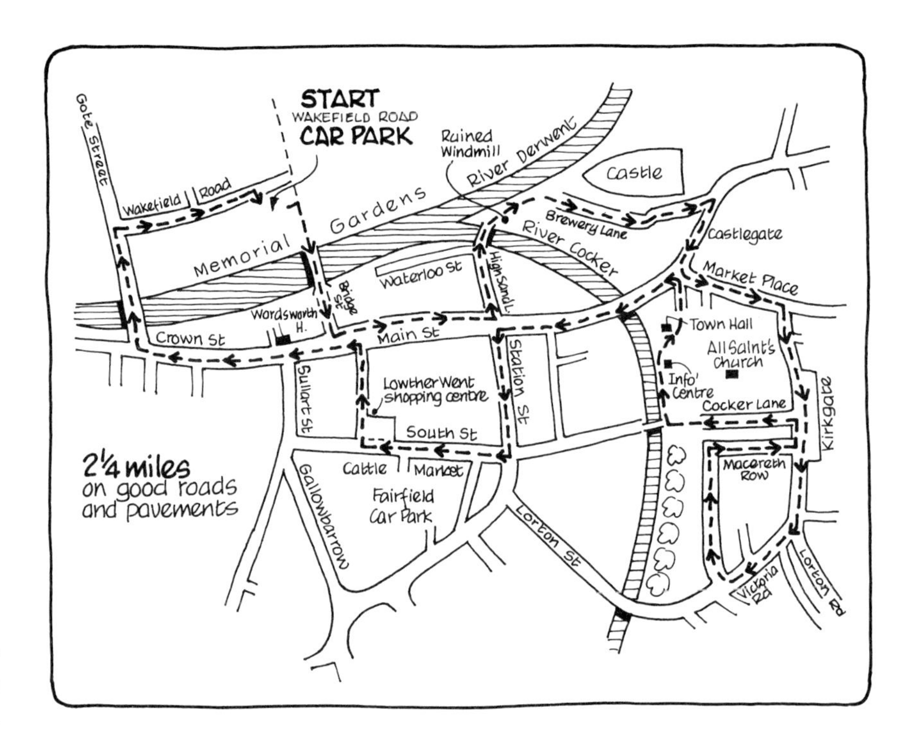

RIVER COCKER WALK

From Market Place walk to the top of Kirkgate. Continue along Lorton Road out of town. Beyond the A66 turn right down the minor road to Southwaite Bridge. Cross for a look at the old mill then return to the east bank. A stile leads to a riverside footpath back to town. Just beyond Double Mills Youth Centre go right over the footbridge into Harris Park. Follow paths under bridges to South Street. Cross the footbridge, turn left and go past the town hall to Market Place.

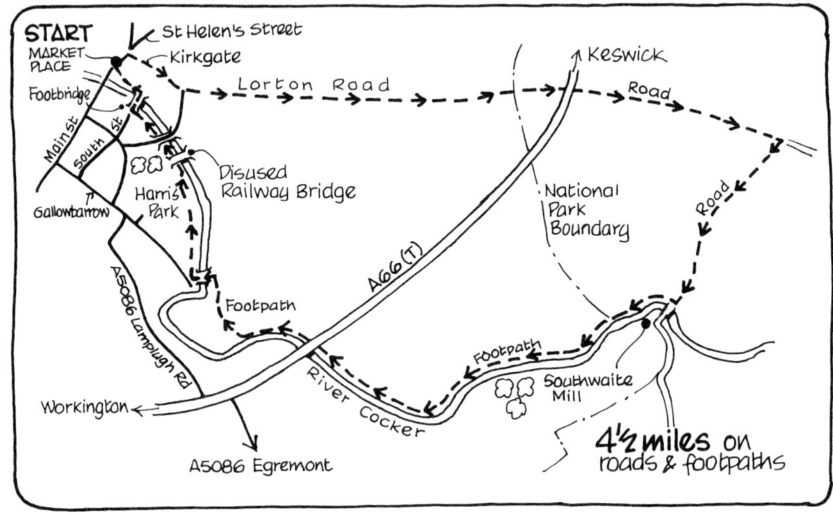

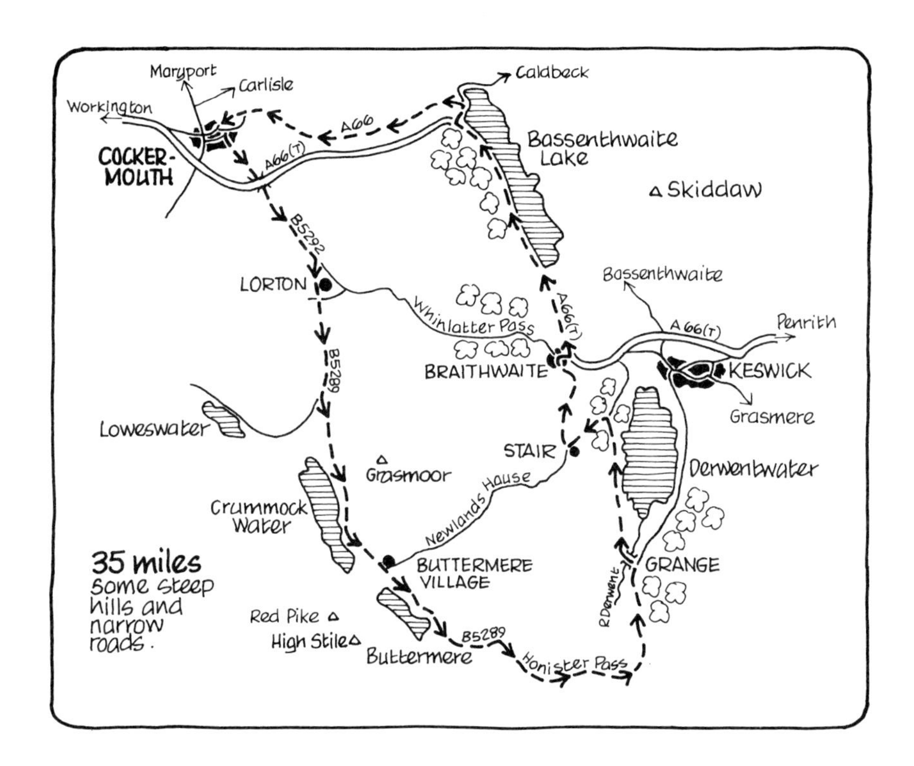

BEST OF NORTH LAKES DRIVE

Drive through Lorton onto the narrow road past Crummock Water to Buttermere village. It gets terribly busy. Past Buttermere lake drive up steep Honister Pass. Stop at the summit car park for views. Descend the pass into Borrowdale. Seatoller at the bottom has refreshments, information and toilets. Continue down the valley to Grange. Turn left over the bridge through the village. Go through woods to sensational views across Derwentwater. Beyond Catbells, take the road to Stair on the left just as more woods are entered. Through the village turn sharp right onto a narrow unfenced road below Barrow. At Braithwaite turn right onto the A66. Take the old road off to the right beyond Bassenthwaite Lake back to Cockermouth.

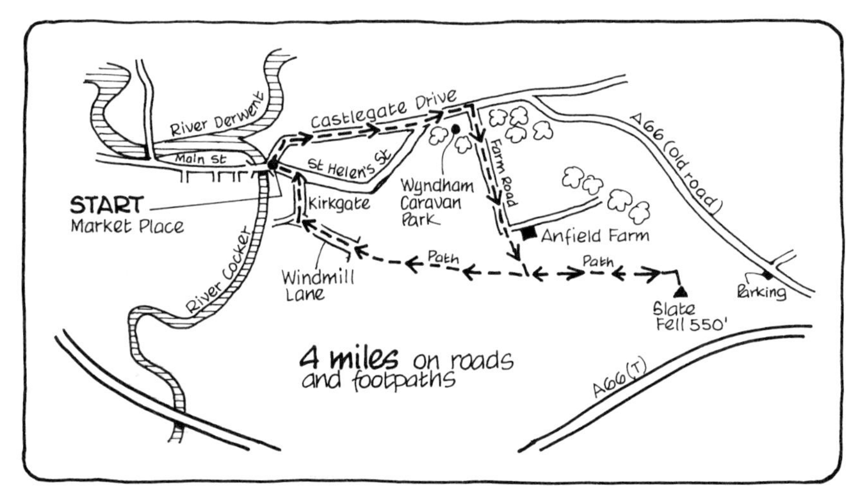

COUNTRY WALK

Walk up Castlegate and out of town to Wyndham Caravan Site on your right. Go down the farm road and cross a stile into a field. After another stile is crossed, turn left uphill to Slate Fell. An extensive view opens up. You may think why am I walking here when there's all that over there? Return downhill along the same path but continue straight on through a housing estate back to Kirkgate and the town.

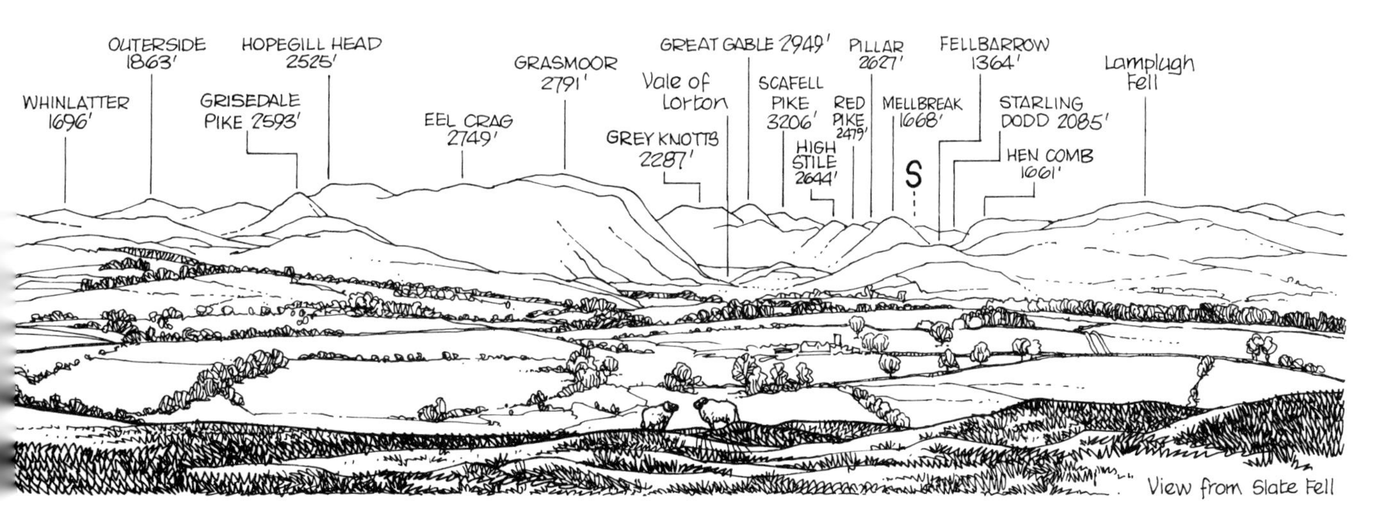

View from Slate Fell

Highgate

Kendal

We all streamed from the M6 at junction 36: cars, motorbikes and caravans all heading for the promised land. Lorries, banned from the sacred A591 tourist route through Lakeland, carried on to the Penrith turn-off. After five speedy miles down a dual carriageway I turned off for Kendal and parked in Kirkland Car Park five minutes later.

Coming south from Penrith the M6 sweeps majestically through open fell country giving fine views of the Howgills. The fearsome A6, once the main north-south highway over Shap Fells and frequently described on the wireless as 'impassable' after the lightest of snowfalls, is now the haunt of ageing lorry drivers reliving their greatest gear changes.

Kendal is where the Lake District meets the Yorkshire Dales. Often described as 'Southern Gateway to the Lakes', the handsome limestone town straddles a long valley that stretches north from Morecambe Bay to Grasmere. With a population of 23,000, it is largest of the Lakeland towns, and the best for shopping, cultural life and architecture. The fact that Kendal can also be enjoyed by a non-shopping barbarian like me makes it the place where miracles happen.

Branthwaite Brow

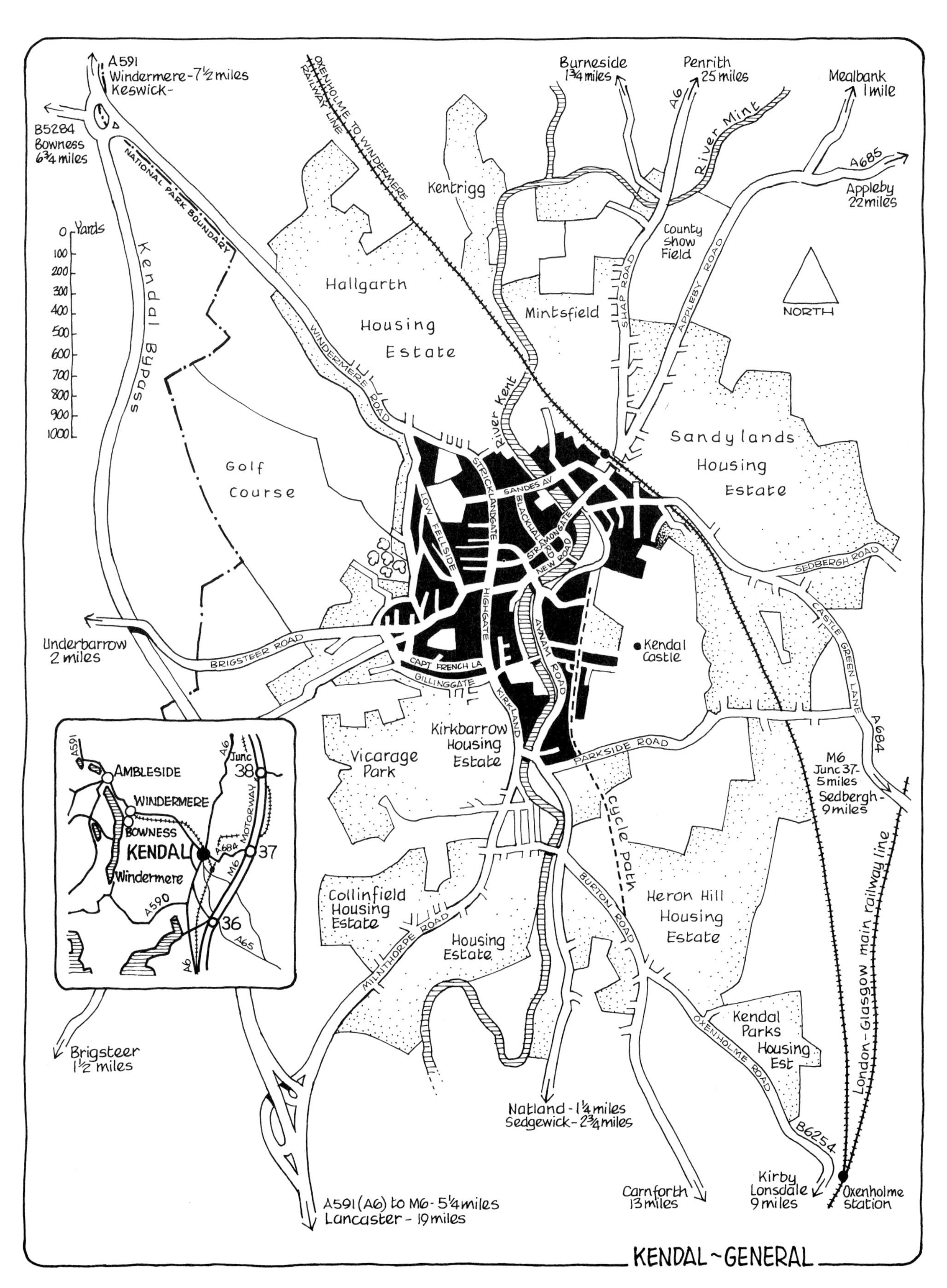
A591
Windermere - 7½ miles
Keswick -
B5284
Bowness
6¾ miles
OXENHOLME TO WINDERMERE RAILWAY LINE
NATIONAL PARK BOUNDARY
Burneside
1¾ miles
A6
Penrith
25 miles
Mealbank
1 mile
River Mint
A685
Appleby
22 miles
Kentrigg
County
Show
Field
Yards
0
100
200
300
400
500
600
700
800
900
1000
Kendal Bypass
Hallgarth
Housing
Estate
Mintsfield
SHAP ROAD
APPLEBY ROAD
NORTH
WINDERMERE ROAD
River Kent
Golf
Course
Sandylands
Housing
Estate
STRICKLANDGATE
SANDES AV
LOW FELLSIDE
BLACKHALL RD
STRAMONGATE
NEW ROAD
SEDBERGH ROAD
HIGHGATE
AYNAM ROAD
CASTLE GREEN LANE
Underbarrow
2 miles
BRIGSTEER ROAD
CAPT FRENCH LA
GILLINGGATE
Kendal
Castle
KIRKLAND
A684
Kirkbarrow
Housing
Estate
Vicarage
Park
PARKSIDE ROAD
M6
Junc 37 -
5 miles
Sedbergh -
9 miles
Cycle Path
A591
AMBLESIDE
A6
Junc
38
WINDERMERE
BOWNESS
MOTORWAY
KENDAL
A684
37
M6
Windermere
A590
36
A65
A6
Collinfield
Housing
Estate
MILNTHORPE ROAD
BURTON ROAD
Heron Hill
Housing
Estate
Housing
Estate
Kendal
Parks
Housing
Est
OXENHOLME ROAD
London - Glasgow main railway line
Brigsteer
1½ miles
Natland - 1¼ miles
Sedgewick - 2¾ miles
B6254
A591 (A6) to M6 - 5¼ miles
Lancaster - 19 miles
Carnforth
13 miles
Kirby
Lonsdale
9 miles
Oxenholme
station
KENDAL ~ GENERAL

Today's bustling town dates back to the 8th-century settlement of Kirkland, which sprang up at a popular crossing place on the River Kent. In 1189 Kirkland was awarded one of Westmorland's first market charters.

Between the 13th and 19th centuries a significant manufacturing centre developed. Over thirty water-powered mills along the River Kent turned out wood and paper products, but it was the wool trade that put Kendal on the map. A variety of fabrics collectively known as Kendal cottons was produced. Shakespeare refers to 'Kendal Green' in Henry IV (Part I).

Other industries and trades blossomed, but by the mid-19th century the bubble had burst and a slow decline was under way - ironically, soon after the railway arrived and the Lancaster to Kendal canal was opened. However, shoes, paper, carpets and snuff are still made here, and also Kendal Mint Cake, the hard bar of almost pure sugar now more essential on Everest than oxygen.

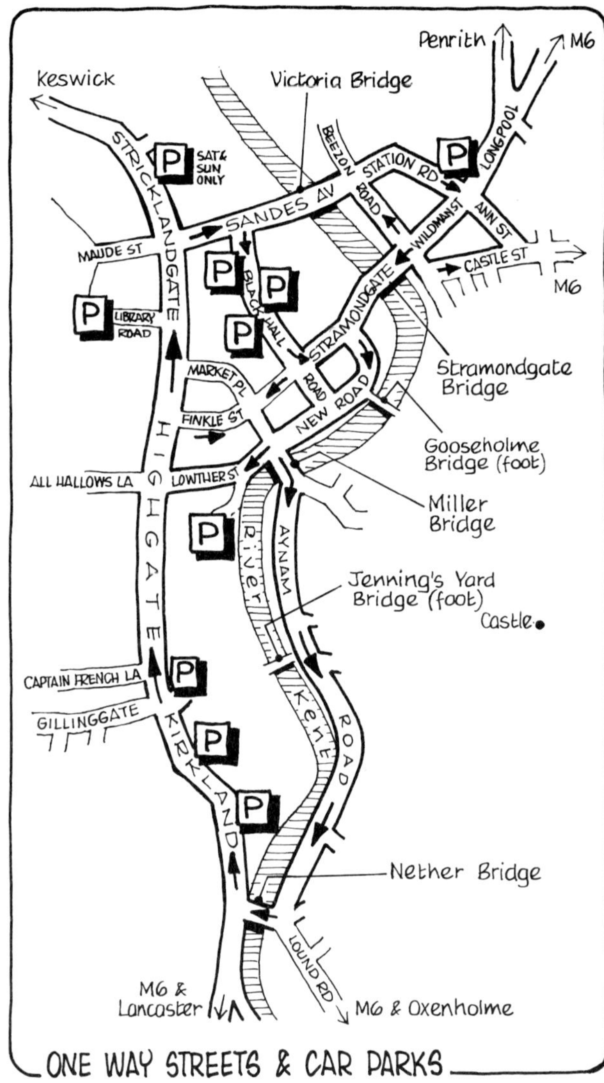

ONE WAY STREETS & CAR PARKS

All Hallows Lane

Kendal has many car parks, most of them cunningly hidden from strangers. Their line of defence is a mind-boggling one-way traffic system that takes you along both sides of the river. Spotting signs for car parks can be a frantic game for all the family to join in, usually ending in sulks for the rest of the visit.

It's safest to take one leisurely lap looking for signs then go for car park touch down on a second. Arriving from the south, I always parked at Kirkland then walked. Usually to find empty parking space right next to where I was going.

Kirkland

CAR PARK
CAR PARK
The Wheatsheaf
T'Crack
CAR PARK
Nether Bridge
Romney House
Jenning's Yard Footbridge
Park
Museum of Lakeland Life & Industry
Abbot Hall Art Gallery
Parish Church
Church Hall
Colonel's Walk (Riverside path)
GILLINGGATE
HIGHGATE
AYNAM ROAD
KIRKLAND
River Kent

I never tired of Kirkland. This oldest and most attractive part of town was built on church land with its own manorial court. It resisted being included in the Borough of Kendal until 1908, and still has a separate and distinctive character all of its own.

The ancient houses, packed round a double bend in the road, are now a lively mixture of shops. Local fell racing hero Pete Bland sells running tackle with free advice, bridal wear is sold in a quaint timber-framed building, and still-warm bread fills the window of a traditional family bakery. There are three pubs too!

WHEAT SHEAF
THE WHEATSHEA

The Wheatsheaf & T'Crack

Between Cobbler John's and the Wheatsheaf Hotel, I squeezed along t' Crack, an age-old cobbled path leading to the modern Kirkbarrow housing estate where Kirkland's original Saxon church once stood.

Beside the Wheatsheaf's old stables I had to stretch up on tiptoe to see a popular view of the church tower and castle between the stone chimney stacks. Ancient but uninteresting Kirkbarrow Hall was almost overlooked at the lane end where I was distracted by a familiar minty smell drifting from Wilson's mint cake factory in nearby Cross Lane.

T'Crack

Considered 'too elegant' to be scrapped during the 1939-45 war effort, the 1822 wrought iron gateway to the churchyard looks like something an irate angler has hurled hooks at in a moment of pique. The church itself is an inelegant pile, with a massive 80-feet-high tower and mismatched castellated walls spiked by pinnacles like rusty wood-screws. One fell off during a violent storm, breaking a woman's leg. Try proving that wasn't an act of God to the insurance company up the road!

Inside the building, I was most impressed by its great width, only a yard narrower than York Minster. In 1989 the suspension of a huge corona above the main altar began a commotion amongst church-goers that still simmers.

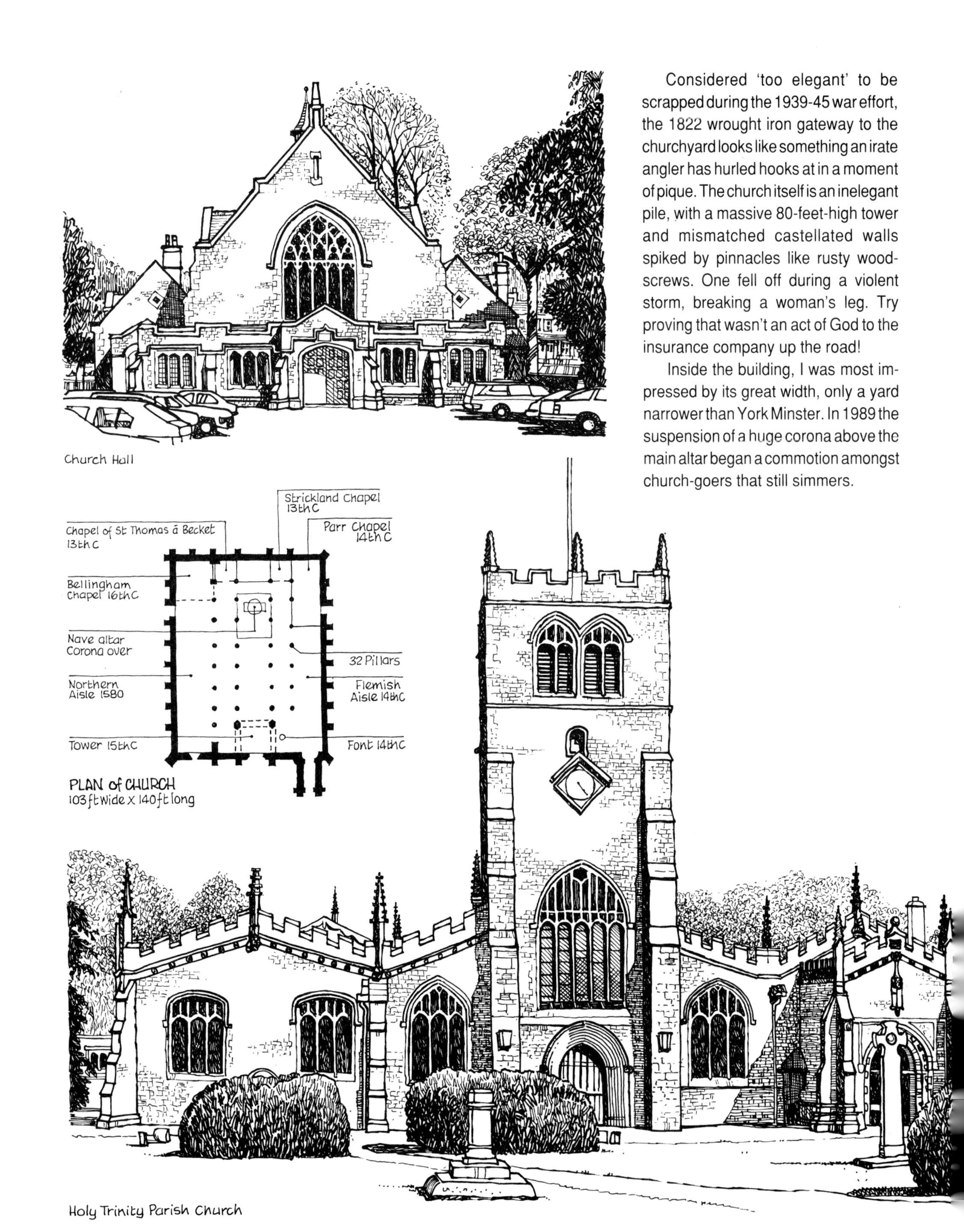

One of the four ancient chapels ranged across the east wall commemorates Katherine Parr, the strong-willed Kendal lass who survived marriage to King Henry the Eighth. The adjoining Strickland Chapel window has the church's only piece of ancient stained glass to escape 17th-century stone-throwing hooligans from the nearby grammar school.

In the Bellingham Chapel, gleaming brasses and Border Regiment flags and badges were a welcome splash of colour. A helmet and broadsword on display were allegedly left behind by Robin 'the Devil' Philipson, a Windermere Cavalier who rode into a service looking for a Roundhead enemy.

Holy Trinity has suffered other indignities. Two hundred years before psychedelia, painted cherubim and seraphim, green hissing serpents and flying dragons rampaged across the outside walls. Also during the 17th century, the communion plate was stolen and never recovered. The worst calamity of all occurred in 1210, when townswomen and children, gathered in the church for sanctuary, were all massacred by Scottish marauders. Sadness still haunts the place.

The Ring o' Bells

Non-attendance at church once merited a 12-pence fine, so children in the streets and fugitives skulking in Kirkland's dozen pubs were enthusiastically rounded up by churchwardens. Thirsty work, so Ring o' Bells was built in 1741 for the ecclesiastical press gangs to refresh themselves at parish expense. It's still a snug retreat and the country's only pub on consecrated ground.

Outside the church a man was feeding a jackdaw titbits. He told me that as a fledgling it had been injured in a fall from the church tower and was nursed back to health by a local builder. They became inseparable companions and even went to work together.

I mentioned building repairs going on above us. "Aye, that's him," said the bread man. As if on cue, the jackdaw left his crumbs, flew up the tower and disappeared. I wandered off into the town, unconvinced by the story teller's mischievous eye.

However, when I returned later the builder himself told me the same tale while preparing to go home. "Where is it then?" I demanded, confident that Exhibit A could not be produced. He grinned through his open truck window and whistled. With a flurry of black wings, the jackdaw flew in, settled beside a pack of Embassy on the dashboard, and gazed expectantly through the windscreen.

A cheery "Terra" and they were off home, one to his tea, the other to a comfy shed. Meanwhile, I was left pondering that old northern saying; 'There's nowt s'queer as folk' - except perhaps jackdaws.

Not knowing Kendal was a cultural hot spot, I was surprised to discover that Abbot Hall is one of northern England's finest art galleries. After years of neglect it was restored to 18th-century splendour and opened to the public in 1962, packed with period furniture, silver, glassware and porcelain. Paintings by local artist George Romney have pride of place, with a splashy Turner and a collection of 18th-century watercolours, including some Ruskins, worth a look. Displays of modern paintings are regular features.

Colonel George Wilson built Abbot Hall in 1759 on a riverside site once occupied by the local headquarters of the powerful abbots of St Mary's, York, who owned the area around the church. When the building fell into disrepair after the Second World War it was saved by a trust set up by concerned townsfolk. Abbot Hall is a pretty, limestone mansion in a wonderful setting.

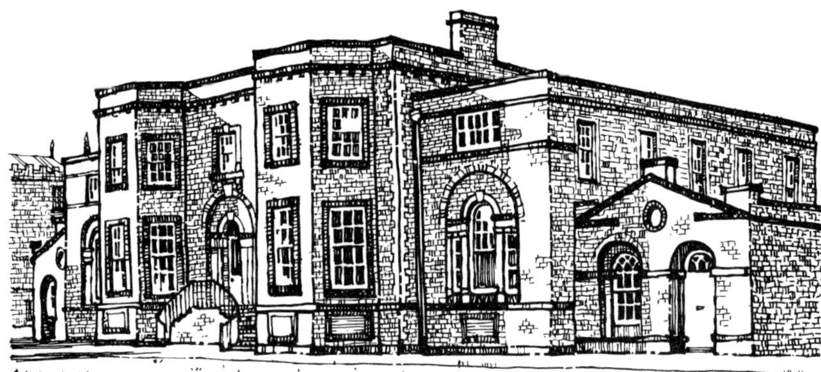

Abbot Hall

The valiant trust had another triumph in 1973 when its Museum of Lakeland Life and Industry, created in Abbot Hall's disused stables, won the first Museum of the Year award.

This is THE place for anyone even only remotely interested in Lake District history. There are few glass cases and you can touch, and even smell, everything. The displays are terrific, and creepily familiar for those of us brought up in the area, a bit like walking through your own 'Back to the Future' film.

The best bits include the recreation of a 1898 Kendal street, and a Lakeland mining shaft that vividly demonstrates the appalling working conditions. Arthur Ransome's considerable collection of pipes is on show. A display is planned on another world-famous local character, Postman Pat whose author John Cunliffe used to live in Kendal, renamed 'Pencaster' for the books.

The rather austere museum building is enriched by an elegant portico saved from the demolished Kendal gas works. A frieze carries the words 'Ex Fume Dare Lucem' (Out of smoke came light).

A separate farm barn has all the paraphernalia and implements of agricultural and veterinary life. It's worth the modest admission price for this bit alone.

Large trees hide the best views of Abbot Hall and the church from across the river. I have done a considerable amount of unauthorised pruning of these two drawings.

Museum of Lakeland Life & Industry

Parish Church ~ East elevation

Abbot Hall ~ West elevation

Nether Bridge

Romney House

Nether Bridge has been a busy eastern entrance to the town since before 1376, when it was only wide enough for one cart. Subsequent widening in 1772 and 1911 can be clearly seen under the arches.

I watched two boys fishing hopefully in the pitifully low river. Salmon are still caught but nothing like a century ago when poachers regularly took a hundredweight out in a night. A dead shark, 5 feet long, was found near the bridge in 1862.

From 1563 to 1910 the vicarage stood on glebe land now occupied by Kirkland Hall and the closed primary school. During the 18th century, the vicar let out his back field as an aromatic tanning yard, which can't have made him popular with the posh house guests at nearby Abbot Hall.

K Shoes, now the town's biggest employer, has occupied the factory across the bridge since 1843, taking over from a fancy waistcoat manufacturer. Just downstream, a footbridge has recently been replaced by Kendal's fifth road bridge - predictably named after painter Romney.

A plaque on Romney House Hotel reads, *Here lived for a time, and died, George Romney, Portrait Painter. Born at Dalton-in Furness 1734. Died 1802.*

Aged 22, Romney, (pronounced 'Rumney') married a Kendal girl, then immediately left her to pursue a wandering artistic career. He returned to Kendal stricken with senility, and died in the arms of his long-suffering wife three years later.

Romney was a better painter than a husband. Look at his work in Abbot Hall.

Park entrance

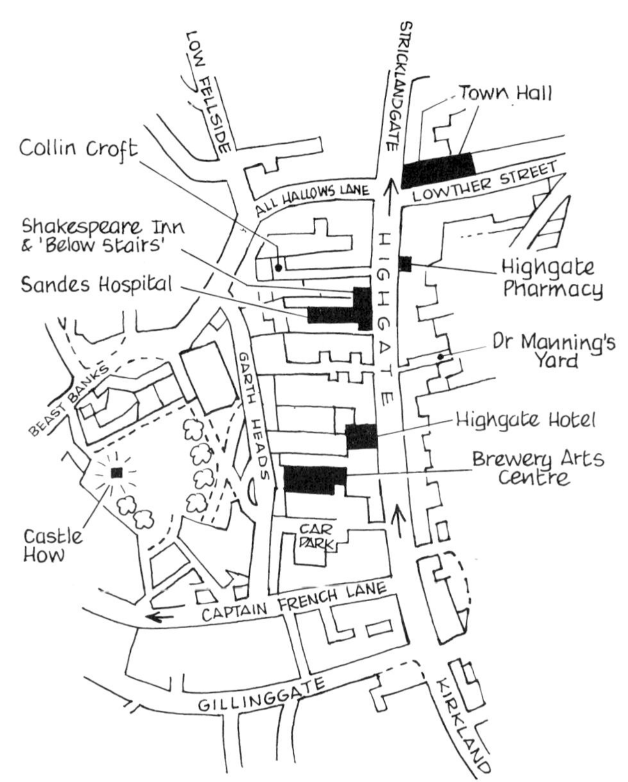

Highgate and Stricklandgate form the main thoroughfare of Kendal. They're almost a straight line, though I couldn't see along the whole length from street level as both sections go up and down hills.

Corner of Captain French Lane

Highgate Hotel

Datestone on Highgate Hotel

An odd-looking stone gateway into the park at the Kirkland end used to be the grand entrance to Abbot Hall. When the local corporation bought the hall in 1896 it turned the garden into a public recreation area. Blind Beck, the ancient border between independent Kirkland and the rest of Kendal, still flows by the children's play area.

On the corner of Captain French Lane stands one of Kendal's wonderful old chemist shops whose good looks haven't been spoiled by the garish advertising gimcracks that pharmacy companies inflict on outlets these days. They must do it to sell more headache pills.

Across the street, the inn sign of the Kendal Bowman commemorates the town's famous fighting men, appropriately clad in 'Kendal Green'. The ancient hostelry was once called the Bishop Blaize Inn after the 4th-century patron saint of woolcombers.

Two painted stones at the Highgate Hotel doorway inform passersby they are 135 miles from Edinburgh and 258 miles from London. In his invaluable *Kendal Town Trail* book, Arthur Nicholls says they inspired a woman to walk from Highgate, Kendal to Highgate, London, and write a book about her adventures.

Brewery Arts Centre

The Leyland Clock

Kendal's cultural life was considerably enriched in 1971 when the disused Vaux brewery was converted into the Brewery Arts Centre. The magnificent limestone complex always has something going on. You can watch theatre performances or films, enjoy jazz, rock or folk concerts, join workshops or just wander round art or photography exhibitions.

Brewing began here in 1853 when this was the back garden of Dallam Tower's town house (Dallam Tower itself is at Milnthorpe) and the family wanted a regular and handy supply of good ale. A thirsty lot, the Dallam Tower's folk. The house has a distinguished tippling history. Messrs Whilwall and Mark, who were residents in 1757, founded a prolific wine business with cellars reputed to hold 40,000 gallons.

Saved from destruction, local curios stand around the well-kept gardens. The Leyland clock, built like an early battleship, stood for years on the wildest part of the A6 over Shap Fells. Exposure to the worst of Lakeland weather has taken its toll, and the clock's timekeeping is now a bit of a joke. Any similarity to the rest of British Leyland is entirely coincidental.

Nearby stands the handsome drinking fountain rescued from the onslaught of traffic outside Windermere Railway Station (see page 159). Nice to see old friends enjoying peaceful retirement.

I sighed nostalgically at one of the much-lamented red telephone boxes. But warm feelings quickly evaporated when I almost dislocated my arm dragging open the door.

At the top of Highgate Bank I stopped to admire the fine view north up the street to the town hall. No two buildings look the same and the roof line is pleasingly erratic.

The tight frontages enclose a multitude of ancient yards and alleys, once the homes and workplaces of the poor and now Kendal's most distinctive feature. When industry mushroomed during the 18th century the town had well over a hundred yards. Those on the south side of Highgate used to reach down to the riverside where there were factories and even a windmill.

Many yards were miserable places where the sun rarely penetrated. Primitive sanitary conditions brought the cramped hovels frequent disease. By the 20th century most had become pitiful slums, unfit for human habitation and obvious candidates for demolition and replacement. Modern-day romantics consider the yard picturesque, oozing with communal spirit, but they never had to live in such squalor. The families who did must have been glad to see the back of them.

Dr. Manning's Yard

Gateway to Sandes Hospital

In 1971, Doctor Manning's Yard was generously 'improved' by South Lakeland District Council. I don't know what they looked like before the 'improvement', but when I saw the cottages they were sad, dirty and empty. Even 'yuppyfied' with ruched curtains and copper coach lamps they would at least have signs of some kind of life. This was once known as Braithwaite's Yard, site of a dry salters and dye stuffs business started by George Braithwaite in 1713. It must have been livelier then.

The prosperous factory owners lived on the north side of Highgate. One of them built Sandes Hospital, a yard full of charitable almshouses for the widows of wool industry workers. Graced by colourful cottage gardens, this is a much pleasanter place.

Outside on the street, two lanes of vehicles constantly stopped and started for traffic lights. The ancient entrance to Sandes Hospital, stained an unattractive grey colour, shook ominously. A panel, incorporating the arms of the Shearman Dyers Company and the date, 1659, hung on grimly over the gateway.

Sandes Hospital

The Shakespeare

Next door to Sandes Hospital stands The Shakespeare, a fine old coaching inn with a high arched gateway for the stagecoach trade to enter. Attractive Georgian buildings still line the back yard where a theatre was opened in 1829. Hence the 'Shakespeare' connection.

Underneath the inn, Below Stairs Antiques conducts business at a good two feet below street level. Patrons of The Shakespeare, going home 'tired and emotional', sometimes carelessly drop in on dark nights for an unexpected browse.

The town's first coal yard opened in Collin Croft where there was once an inn named The Malt Shovel. There's still a delightful little Georgian house in its own courtyard at the top end.

I was even more taken by the ancient passageway of stone steps that leads to Beast Banks. They were lovingly restored by Kendal Civic Society. The quaint archways, old beams and pretty doorways decked with flowers were good excuses for me to stop for frequent rests on the steep climb.

Collin Croft

Collin Croft

Below Stairs Antiques

The Highgate Pharmacy

Most people do a double-take when they first see Below Stairs Antiques, so here it is again in close up.

The olde worlde looks of The Highgate Pharmacy are spoiled by an electric sign hanging over the passageway. As all it does is repeat information already carried above the window, there seems little point inflicting this monstrosity on such a charming shop front. It's not in my drawing.

Until Gillinggate opened in 1888, the main road west was Captain French Lane, named after a churchwarden who lived in the narrow street after retiring from Cromwell's Roundheads in 1660. A small hospital, opened at the top of the hill in 1870 (closed 1991), overlooks two circular-shaped terraces of grass called Castle Howe. They are believed to be the site of a Norman motte and bailey type castle. Old maps show a bowling green on the lower 'bailey' part.

Crumbling stone steps lead steeply to the higher, 'motte' section, where a stark obelisk carrying the words 'Sacred to Liberty' was erected in 1788. It commemorates 'The Glorious Revolution' of a century earlier, when William of Orange landed in England and James II abdicated. After years of being ruthlessly plundered by murderous cross-border raiders, Kendal's dislike of Scottish kings is understandable.

Castle How

Captain French Lane

A Wainwright (1907~91)

Alfred Wainwright, the irascible fell walker, writer and artist, died in Kendal hospital, three days after his 84th birthday in 1991. He was the town's most famous inhabitant, more widely known than even Katherine Parr.

Born in Blackburn, Wainwright was seduced by the Lakeland scenery while on holiday. He moved to Kendal in 1942 to work at the town hall, becoming borough treasurer in 1948. Four years later he began to write and illustrate his seven classic guidebooks to the Lakeland fells, a task which dominated the next 14 years to the detriment of everything else, including his first marriage. Later he produced more handwritten books, including the definitive Pennine Way guide and a coast to coast route of his own invention.

Alfred Wainwright served Kendal well, both at the town hall, where he never missed a day through illness, and as treasurer of the Abbot Hall trust. In 1977 he published a fascinating book of his drawings of 19th-century Kendal.

Though shy and elusive, in old age he took to wandering our television screens where his quirky personality gradually emerged. Bestselling coffee-table books followed, but the much-admired penmanship was missing, dimmed forever by failing eyesight. Wainwright's masterpiece remains the seven superbly crafted Lakeland fell guides. We shall never see their like, or his, again.

Kendal's impressive town hall began life as 'Whitehall Assembly Rooms'. They were built in 1825 by Websters, a local company which is responsible for most of Kendal's dignified 19th-century buildings. Websters also did conversion work in 1858 when council business was moved from the moot hall in Market Place.

Further alterations in 1894, paid for by six-times mayor, Alderman Bindloss, included the erection of the present clock tower, which has been unkindly described as 'straight from a French architect's railway station pattern book'. But look what it replaced - a fantastic Alice in Wonderland creation of four massive gentleman's pocket watches! Every three hours carillon bells in the clock tower play a folk tune, a different one for every day of the week.

The Tourist Information Bureau on the ground floor sells posters about Kendal history, including one on Webster buildings.

Clock Tower, 1861-97

The Town Hall

Finkle Street

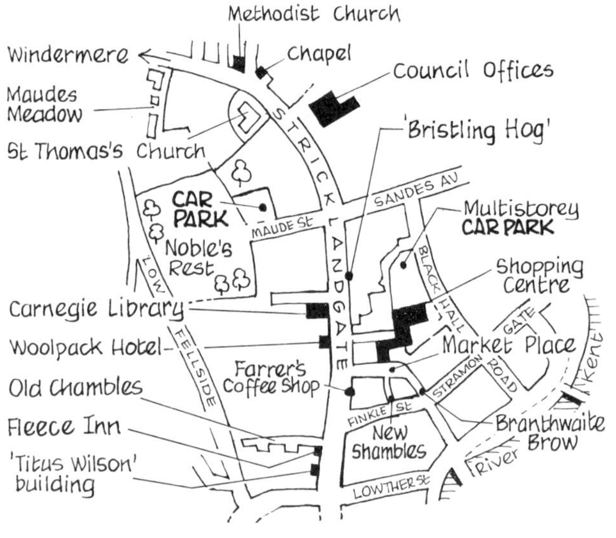

At the Finkle Street junction Highgate becomes Stricklandgate. Shops are more modern here, but there are still plenty of attractive Georgian and Victorian buildings to admire.

I like the New Shambles, a street of shops built in the 19th century to accommodate butchers when the Old Shambles closed. Also Farrer's delightful iron-fronted tea shop that remains much as it was in the 18th century.

Stricklandgate used to be a quiet backwater of inns and town houses, then Sandes Avenue was constructed in 1887 and almost overnight it became a main traffic route. There's been no let-up since. Now it's part of Kendal's Grand Prix circuit; crossing the road here can be as traumatic as crossing Sharp Edge on Blencathra.

The New Shambles

Farrer's Coffee shop

Market Place is lined by attractive buildings, but it really comes alive only on Wednesdays and Saturdays when there's a street market. The rest of the time it's yet another car park.

The corner next to the war memorial has a replica of the old moot hall, which burnt down in 1969 after standing on this site since 1591 and serving as town hall for a while when the castle was abandoned.

Market Place used to be closed off from Stricklandgate, first by medieval buildings, then by St George's Chapel. This was replaced in 1854 by a market hall, which was converted to a library when the present market hall opened in 1887. In 1909, when the Carnegie Library was built in Stricklandgate, the Market Place building was taken down and miraculously re-erected in Sandes Avenue (see page 97).

Market Place

Ancient iron-fronted buildings line Branthwaite Brow, a picturesque cobbled street that funnels Market Place onto Stramongate. I sat outside The George and Dragon at the top of the hill enjoying a sunny evening. It wasn't always so pleasant here. In the middle of the 19th century three of Kendal's ten slaughterhouses were situated in Market Place and the cobbles in front of me would have often been awash with blood and entrails flowing down to the Kent.

Branthwaite Brow

The Old Shambles

For a town made prosperous by wool, the amount of animal slaughter once performed on the streets seems a mite ungrateful. The Old Shambles, built in 1779, had 40 butchers' shops all swimming in blood and guts. In 1805, the butchers moved to the New Shambles, which was built on a steeper slope for better drainage. Their old shops are now cosy cottages, but a striking Georgian building across the yard end is little changed. It was once an inn, appropriately named 'The Butchers Arms', and later became a dye works for the woollen industry. The younger houses on Fellside awkwardly overlook the old yard like embarrassed teenagers towering above the 'wrinklies'.

Next door to the Old shambles stands the Fleece Inn, dated 1656, timber-framed, and the last remaining main street building with a projecting upper storey supported by pillars. There used to be a string of them along Highgate and Stricklandgate. It's said you could once walk under them for a mile when it was raining and never get wet. They'd be useful these days, Kendal can be very wet in wet weather.

Almost unbelievably, adjoining the inn is an amusement arcade. Talk about ancient and modern! However, the arcade front is tastefully done and the clash of cultures is not catastrophic. Kendal seems to have the happy knack of successfully combining old and new.

An awful exception could be the old Titus Wilson's shop, a splendid example of a typical Kendal town house dating back to Elizabethan times. I found it painted a most inappropriate shade of pillar-box red. However, after the expressions of shock I heard from passersby, I expect sanity has been restored by now, the woodwork repainted and the colour co-ordination expert returned to his proper job designing day-glo ski suits.

Built in 1791, The Woolpack Inn still has the high archway yard entrance where lumbering horse-drawn wagons piled high with bales of wool clattered in to unload. Nearby there was the printing works of the 170-year-old *Westmorland Gazette* that essayist Thomas de Quincey once edited.

The Fleece Inn

The Woolpack

'Titus Wilson's

I took a stroll through the new multi-million pound shopping precinct, opened in 1990. The old-established indoor market has been incorporated, but the old bus station in Blackhall Road disappeared beneath a monstrous concrete car park.

Many shops were still vacant but the escalators worked and the hanging baskets of plastic flowers were magnificent. It looked good, the proper place for modern shops to show off their glitz and glamour rather than out in the old streets upsetting people.

A large window in the precinct's upper floor had me sighing in appreciation. It overlooks an attractive new yard of shops. Their mellow brown colours that glowed warmly in the sunshine. The ancient chimney of Black Hall were a weighty grey contrast.

View from the shopping centre

The 'Bristling Hog'

Black Hall, now occupied by Halifax Building Society, was originally the rugged 16th-century mansion of Henry Wilson, first mayor of Kendal after the 1576 Charter. Two massive chimneys were added in 1820, and in 1838 the building became Hodgson's Black Hall Brush Factory with the distinctive 'Bristling hog' as company sign.

Next door there's a McDonald's restaurant. Another amazing juxtaposition of old and new! Now with the ultimate symbol of modern street cred, Kendal is right on for Century 21.

The Carnegie Library, one of the town's few sandstone buildings, glowers across the street at the flash newcomers. It has a look of old New York to me. Maybe the name helps.

The Carnegie Library

North Stricklandgate

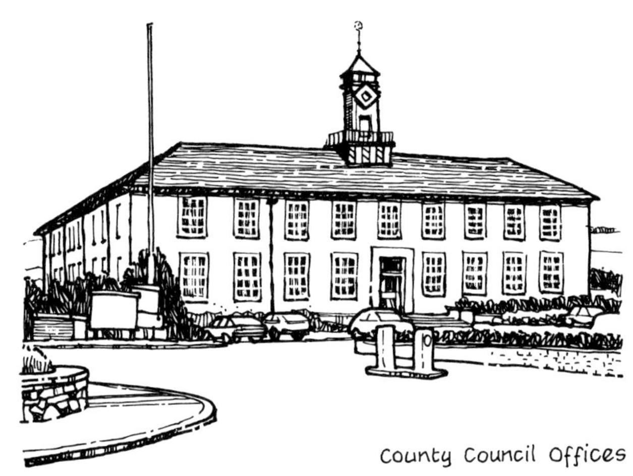
County Council Offices

Stricklandgate was originally a 'drift' road used for driving cattle to graze on common land outside the town. In the 19th century it became a fashionable street where borough dignitaries lived. John Macadam relaid the road in 1824, one of the first in the country to benefit from his ideas. He'd got the foundations and stone chippings sorted out, but it was not until after his death that the technique of using tar as a binding substance was mastered. These days, Stricklandgate's road surface is a very grand red colour.

Small shops, many of them old-established family businesses, cluster around the Sandes Avenue junction. A fish and chip shop has a cut-out wooden whale for a sign. How many chips do you get with a whale?

Maude's Meadow

19th Century House of Correction

Just beyond the county council offices, where Windermere Road begins its long climb out of town, there's an interesting collection of places to worship. The Parish church of St Thomas, built by Websters in 1837, stands across the road from a chunky limestone chapel and an impressive Wesleyan church. Just looking at it I could hear rousing hymns being belted out.

They are a continuance of the 16th-century sanctuaries that stood here so travellers could pray before entering or leaving the town. The Lake District must have been a frightening place then. Indeed, until demolition earlier this century, a fearsome eighty-cell 'house of correction' towered over the elegant Georgian terrace of Town View.

Methodist Church

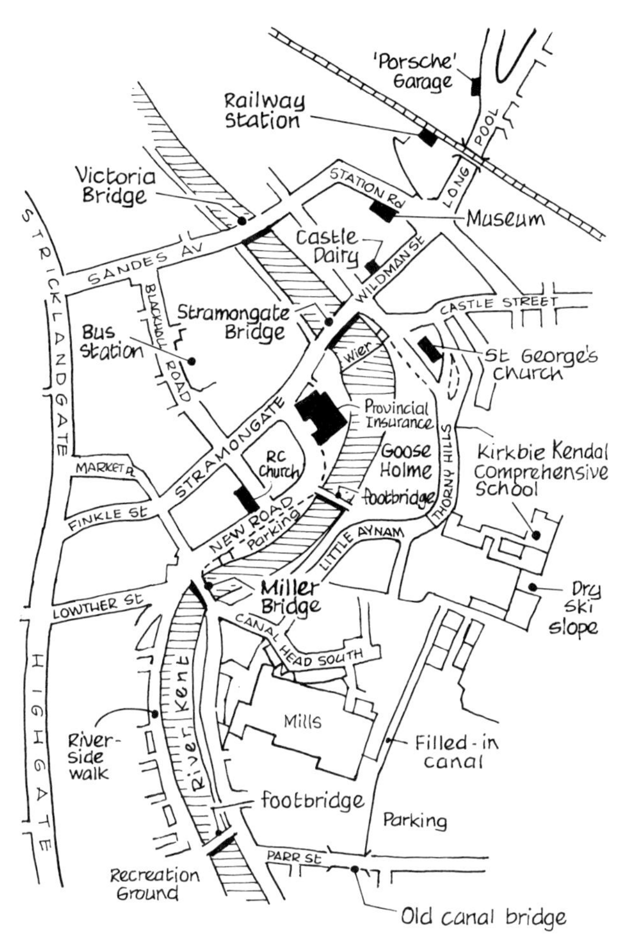

Stramongate

Stramongate has long been the main road north out of town to the A6 and Penrith. Unlike Kendal's other main thoroughfares, the street has its own market charter, a right, I found, still being exercised outside the Mercer's Arms.

A handsome Classical-style house built in 1827 on New Road corner used to be prone to flooding, so had a frequent turnover of disgruntled owners. Eventually it was bought by the Provincial Insurance Company for its headquarters. They were probably fed up with all the flood damage claims.

Unfortunately, the company outgrew the house and a hideous concrete office block, Kendal's first skyscraper, was added. The town should take advantage of the company's presence and insure itself against invasion by any similar alien eyesores.

Provincial Insurance Building

Miller Bridge - North elevation

The River Kent is one of the fastest flowing rivers in the country, dropping 1,000 feet in 25 miles. It once powered over 90 mills in the Kendal area. In 1848 a dam was built across the head of the Kentmere, the river's source, to ensure a regular flow.

New flats have been built on the site of the old yards that once filled the area between Main Street and the river. To me they looked just as cramped as the yards once were. Some residents had put out pots of flowers, but there were no gardens and the area for drying washing looked pitiful. I hope they're not the yards of the future.

Squealing tyres greeted my arrival at Miller Bridge where budding Mansells and Sennas were dedicatedly practising their skills on the fastest chicane of Kendal's one-way traffic circuit. The handsome stone bridge was erected in 1818, replacing a number of earlier models. One was destroyed by a flood. Now heavy traffic is the destroyer.

Miller Bridge - South elevation

Stramongate Bridge

In New Road cars parked beside the river twinkled in the sunshine. Across the road the twin-towered facade of Holy Trinity and Saint George's RC Church defiantly faces the castle ruins on the hill. Built between 1835-7, this is the only 'complete' church built by the famous Websters.

A footbridge leads to Gooseholme, now a pleasant grassy area beside the river, but until late this century the tenterground, where cloth or wool was stretched across hooked iron or wooden frames to dry. Long before then geese were pastured here by children. Gooseholme used to be an island, isolated by a mill race cut to provide power for Castle Mills. When they closed in 1955 the race was filled in.

Victoria Bridge was erected to commemorate the Queen's Jubilee in 1887. Seen from Stramongate Bridge the iron construction seems innocuous enough, but Wainwright was so disgusted that it wasn't built of stone like Kendal's other bridges he refused to draw it for one of his books.

Victoria Bridge

Holy-Trinity & St George's RC Church

Stramongate Bridge is the oldest of Kendal's five road bridges. Stone-built with four graceful arches, the structure we see today dates from 1794, but incorporated within it are two other bridges going back to the 14th century. A weir provided the first decent stretch of water I'd seen all morning. Seagulls weaved lazily and fish gently broke the surface.

It must have been different when the town ducking stool was in action here. Gossipy women were tied to a chair on a pole and ducked in the then highly polluted river as punishment. Their judges and juries were, of course, made up of equally gossipy men.

Castle Dairy

Railway Station

Museum of Archaeology and Natural History

The road narrows into the appropriately named Wildman Street where I was continually buffeted by passing traffic and exuberant teenagers hurling obscenities at each other after being let out of the nearby school for lunch. Half-eaten sandwiches lobbed towards the river were expertly caught by hungry seagulls before hitting the water.

Castle Dairy dates back to the 14th century, the present rambling structure virtually unchanged since a refurbishment in 1564. The dairy once served the castle. A popular legend that they were connected by an underground passage is high improbable. Period furniture and fittings are preserved inside. The house is open to the public, though at rather odd times that I was unable to manage. Castle Dairy is Kendal's oldest inhabited house. Anyone who lives in this noisy and depressing street deserves a medal.

I went past a closed-down cinema. A group of men stood drinking outside a pub. Skinny dogs tethered by bits of string looked on miserably. The sun blazed down without mercy on broken glass and rotting woodwork at the once proud railway station. Now closed, the old buildings are the haunt of vandals and graffiti artists. I wound my way between discarded drink cans and crisp packets to the platform. A new green slate shelter had been left half-built. The station was unmanned, unlovely and unworthy of a fine town like Kendal. A city-situated businessman with an expensive briefcase came onto the platform to ask me if the trains stopped here. Only if they have to.

A handsome stone building across the street, once a wool warehouse, houses an unusually comprehensive collection of bird and animal specimens, archaeological relics, Lakeland geology, and items relating to Kendal's social history. Social history was all around me, out on the streets.

Old Canal Bridge ~ Parr Street

The Lancaster to Kendal canal opened with great jubilation in 1819. Barges took out limestone and slate to build the new Lancashire towns then returned to Kendal loaded with coal.

When the railway came in 1847 the importance of the canal began to decline. The last load of coal was delivered in 1944. Final closure came in 1955 and the waterway that had served Kendal so well was filled in with town rubbish. Today it's a cycleway and car park.

Where the canal head used to be there are now allotments and tennis courts behind the factories. A dry ski slope sweeps down the steep side of Castle Hill to Kirkbie Kendal School. 'Kirkbie' is the old name for Kirkland.

Thorny Hills, an elegant terrace of Georgian houses, was built by Websters in 1823. Number four used to be George Webster's town house. The terrace is crumbling a bit, but still an impressive sight.

Thorny Hills

I went down to Longpool for a look at the Duke of Cumberland public house, named after the duke who forced Bonnie Prince Charlie back across the border in 1745.

A motor sale room across the road was a great surprise. It was packed with Porsche cars. One had a price tag of £36,000. I'd seen plenty of prosperous people around Kendal but I hadn't thought them that prosperous. It was good to see such optimism in this rather run-down part of town.

'Porsche' Garage ~ Longpool

Beast Banks was a sweaty climb up from the town centre on a hot summer afternoon. By the time I was at the top I was calling it Beastly Banks, and that was before I knew what used to go on here.

It looks just like a village green these days, split by a road and lined on both sides by houses with pretty gardens. Trees shade the grass.

This was an early settlement area, possibly connected to the 11th-century castle on the nearby Howe. Some of the houses stand on an old cemetery. The village green was once the Market Square where animals were baited before being slaughtered and butchered on the street. This odious practice, which still persists - even in Britain - is thought to improve the tastiness of the meat. Bull baiting was forbidden by law in 1791, probably because so many human beings were receiving injuries rather than any concern about cruelty to animals.

After the bustle of Highgate the green was too quiet. The hot afternoon had grown sultry and oppressive. I was tired and hungry, and the screams of tormented creatures seemed to still echo around the gloomy houses. A beautiful, long-haired girl lay in the grass chain-smoking cigarettes and reading a book. A Gothic novel perhaps? Or *Catcher in the Rye*? She studiously avoided my gaze, so I never asked.

Beast Banks

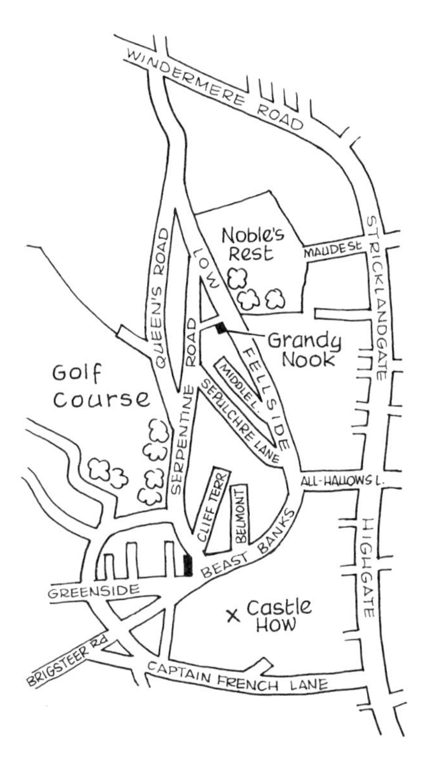

I turned to the three odd-looking houses that stand across the top of the green. The slope already made them tower above me, but in the oppressive atmosphere they appeared to take on monstrous proportions. Mount Pleasant was tightly shuttered. I caught a flash of a face at a window of the tall, silent house on the corner.

The girl in the grass still read, still smoked. I hurried past her for a look at Cliff Terrace, which spectacularly overlooks the town. Brightly coloured toys were scattered across the path outside, but there was no children, no noise.

My visit was turning into a Ken Russell film. I left Beast Banks and found urgent sustenance in the nearest hostelry.

Range Moor

Mount Pleasant

Cliff Terrace

The next day was clear and sunny. I felt fit and rested. It was just as well. Fellside had many steep steps to climb, and negotiating the maze of narrow lanes and modern look-alike houses took concentration. I still managed to get lost.

Steps....and more steps

However, Fellside is just like the fells - walk downhill and you're sure to come across something you recognise, only here it's safer.

It didn't used to be. Before the clearance acts of earlier this century, Fellside was one of the worst slums in Lakeland; a teeming warren of narrow ginnels and cobbled passages, cramped cottages built anywhere there was space on the steep hillside. Stone steps led in all directions. Living conditions were appalling.

Families were large. Ten or more children was common. They slept four or five to a bed, 'topped and tailed' like sardines to fit in. Sanitary arrangements were primitive. Passageways were open sewers. When St Thomas's Church was built nearby in 1837, part of the site was found to be compacted sewage, twelve feet deep.

Disease was commonplace, though surprisingly some Fellsiders lived to over 80 years old. The plague devastated Kendal on at least three occasions. In 1598, 2,000 people died - one third of the population. They are said to be buried in a mass grave near Scout Scar.

Today's Fellside is very different. Houses are modern and spacious, though the old, chaotic layout and many of the ancient cobbled lanes have been preserved. It's a wonderful area to wander, not knowing what's round the next corner.

Grandy Nook was originally Sandes Hall, the home of Thomas Sandes, mayor of Kendal in 1647-8 and founder of Sandes Hospital in Highgate. The delightful collection of cottages, painted in wedding cake colours, was restored in 1864 and is little changed since.

Grandy Nook

KENDAL CASTLE

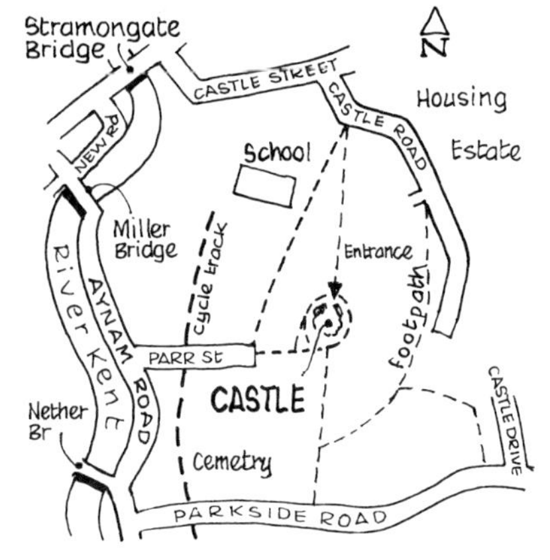

From Little Aynam

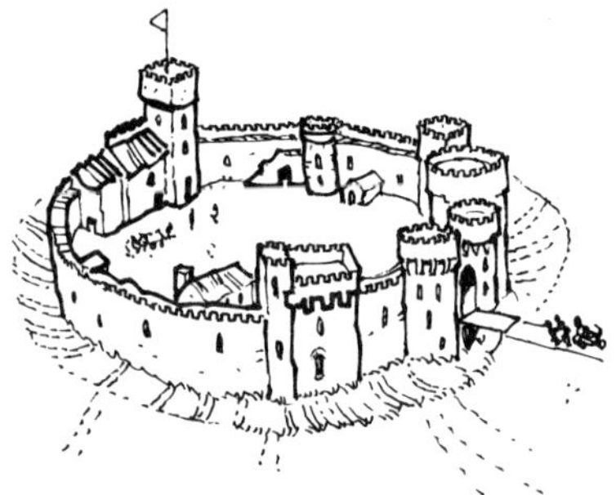

Possible layout ~1500

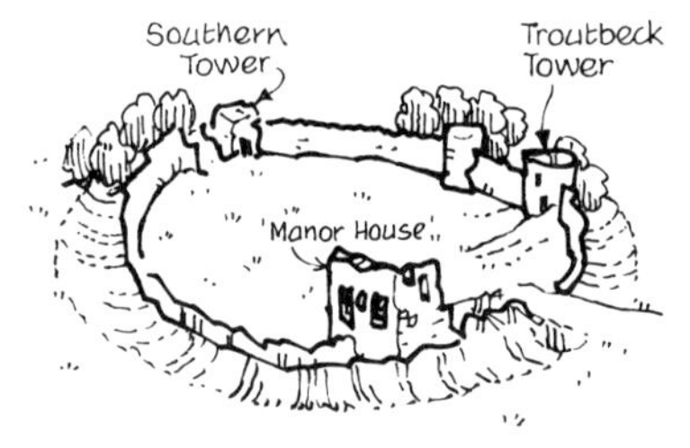

Present-day remains

From Parr Street it was a hard slog up the grassy hillside to the castle. I was glad not to be wearing heavy armour and have to storm the walls at the top. There's no evidence that anyone ever did. Kendal Castle was more a fortified manor house than a garrison.

It was built about 1220 for Gilbert Fitzrenfried, one of the powerful barons who forced King John to sign Magna Carta. From 1390 to 1571 the castle was in the hands of the Parr family. They lived there until the 1520s, but by then the place was in a bad state of repair. The last of the Parr line sold the barony back to the crown and the castle fell into ruin.

In 1813, when the ruins had reached the state we see today, the foundations were strengthened and trees were planted on the bare slopes. Kendal Corporation bought the site in 1897 and opened it to the public to celebrate Queen Victoria's Diamond Jubilee.

The situation, on a glacial mound, is just where you'd expect a castle to be. There are extensive views in all directions and the entrance from Castle Street follows a natural ridge. The walls, of local limestone with some sandstone, are thought to have been partially rebuilt in the 19th-century restoration. Some are 14 feet thick and would have once had battlements across their tops. They enclose a large circular area of uneven grass where a football pitch would easily fit. Cows chewed ruminatively as they watched me pick my way around their droppings. There's none of the park setting of Penrith Castle here. I wish I'd worn boots.

The Troutbeck Tower stands at almost its original height. A cow poked its head out of a doorway at the bottom. The castle once had seven towers. Parts of four remain. There's enough of the manor house walls standing to indicate the massive construction, but it can't have been a very comfortable place to live. The views, however, are fantastic.

'Manor House' remains

Troutbeck Tower

Katharine Parr 1513~48

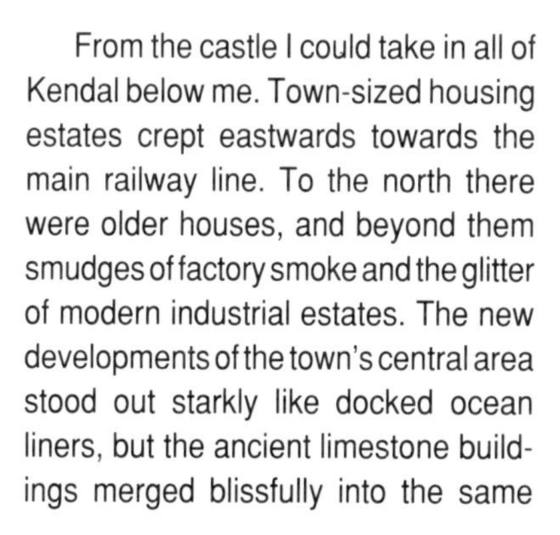

From the castle I could take in all of Kendal below me. Town-sized housing estates crept eastwards towards the main railway line. To the north there were older houses, and beyond them smudges of factory smoke and the glitter of modern industrial estates. The new developments of the town's central area stood out starkly like docked ocean liners, but the ancient limestone buildings merged blissfully into the same hillside their walls were cut from. In the distance, the rolling Lakeland fells reminded me that Kendal is still 'Gateway to the Lakes'.

It was difficult to leave. I still feel the 'Old Grey Town' has more to show me. On my way back to the M6, I drove round Kendal's one-way traffic system twice. Not because I couldn't find the right turn-off, but just for another look.

Kendal Castle was the childhood home of Katherine Parr, a tough Lakeland lass who had already seen off two geriatric husbands when she became the sixth wife of King Henry the Eighth in 1543. He too was in failing health and died four years later. Katherine quickly married Thomas Seymour, and within the year had given birth to her first child, a girl named Mary. Unfortunately puerperal fever set in. The baby lived but Katherine died, aged 36. She was buried inside Sudely Church. Her handwritten *Book of Devotions* is preserved in Kendal town hall.

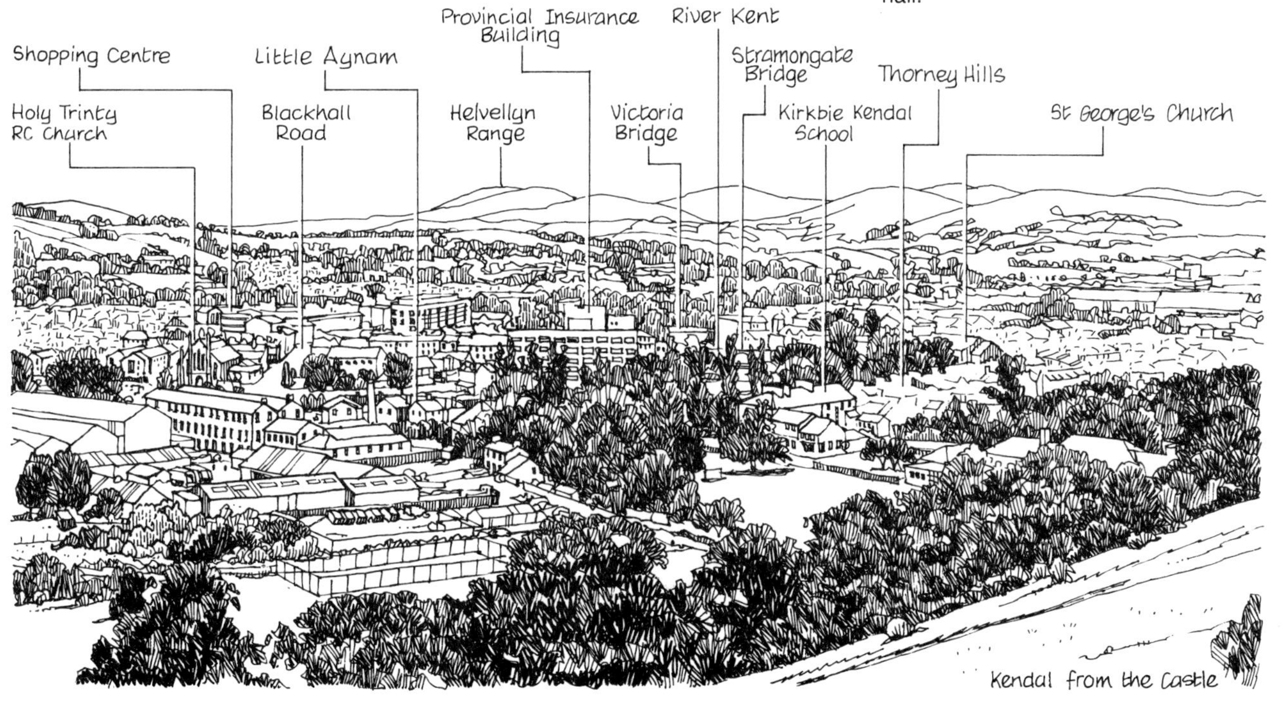

Kendal from the Castle

ODDITIES

Brewery Arts Centre car park

Near Stramongate Bridge

'Westmorland' Windows

Though Kendal floods are legendary, they were difficult to imagine when I stood on Waterside walkway. The highest mark on the flood level plaque was at my chin height, and the River Kent was dribbling by a good ten feet below my feet. In 1898, during the worst outbreak of flooding, water reached halfway up Lowther Street. Earlier, in the 18th century, graves in the churchyard were torn up by the torrent and Nether Bridge was swept away.

Lowther Street is narrow with high-walled buildings on both sides. Now that it's part of the Kendal one-way system, standing there looking skywards is a considerable health hazard. Nevertheless, I courageously flattened myself against the wall for a look up at the effigy of a Turk mounted above the offices of Gawith Hoggarth & Co, makers of the celebrated Kendal brown snuff.

The 'Snuff Turk' ~ Lowther Street

Kendal is full of surprises. I kept coming across 'Westmorland' windows. Some reach incredible heights. The tallest I saw was in a house near Stramongate Bridge, about 30 feet high I'd guess, with 99 panes of glass. Washing them would be bad enough, but imagine painting the frame! It would drive me crazy. And what about the curtains inside. What do they weigh? How do you get them in a washing machine? The mind boggles. Kendal's smallest window is in Castle Dairy. It looks about A5 size. I could cope with that.

Kent Tavern is oddly built out of the steep slope of Kent Street. The floor level at one end is about 8 feet higher above the street than it is at the other.

Kent Tavern ~ Kent Street

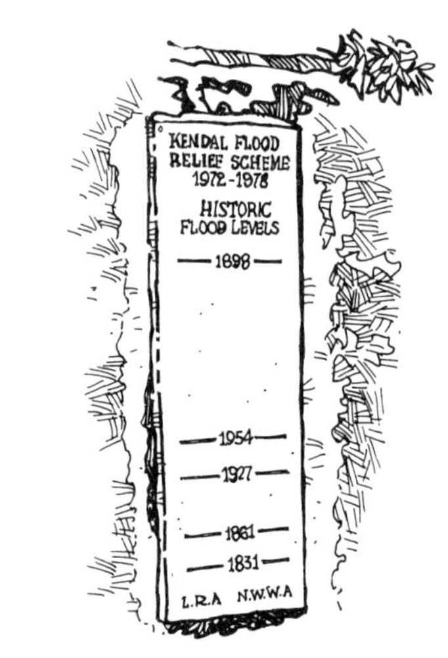

Flood Level Panel ~ Waterside

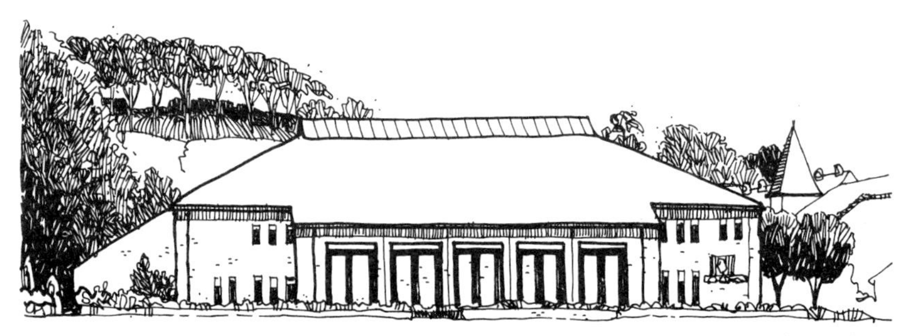
T.A. Centre

The striking mausoleum-like appearance of the riverside TA Centre caused great controversy when it was first built. In these days of draconian defence cuts it was a surprise to find new Territorial Army centres were being built at all.

Kendal was a pioneer of recycling long before it became fashionable. Even more unusual, the item recycled was a building. It was the old public library in Market Place, taken down in 1909 when the new Carnegie Library was opened in Stricklandgate and re-erected with its walls opened out in Sandes Avenue. The building now makes impressive premises for a shoe shop.

St George's Church on Gooseholme has not been so lucky as the public library. When its 100-foot-high towers became unsafe in 1927 they were dismantled and never replaced. The remaining lower sections look as if they're waiting for some kind altar lady to arrange a few daffodils in them. St George's is another Webster church, built in 1840 on a raised site to escape flooding. Rather bleak inside, the limestone building has a quiet dignity when seen from the outside.

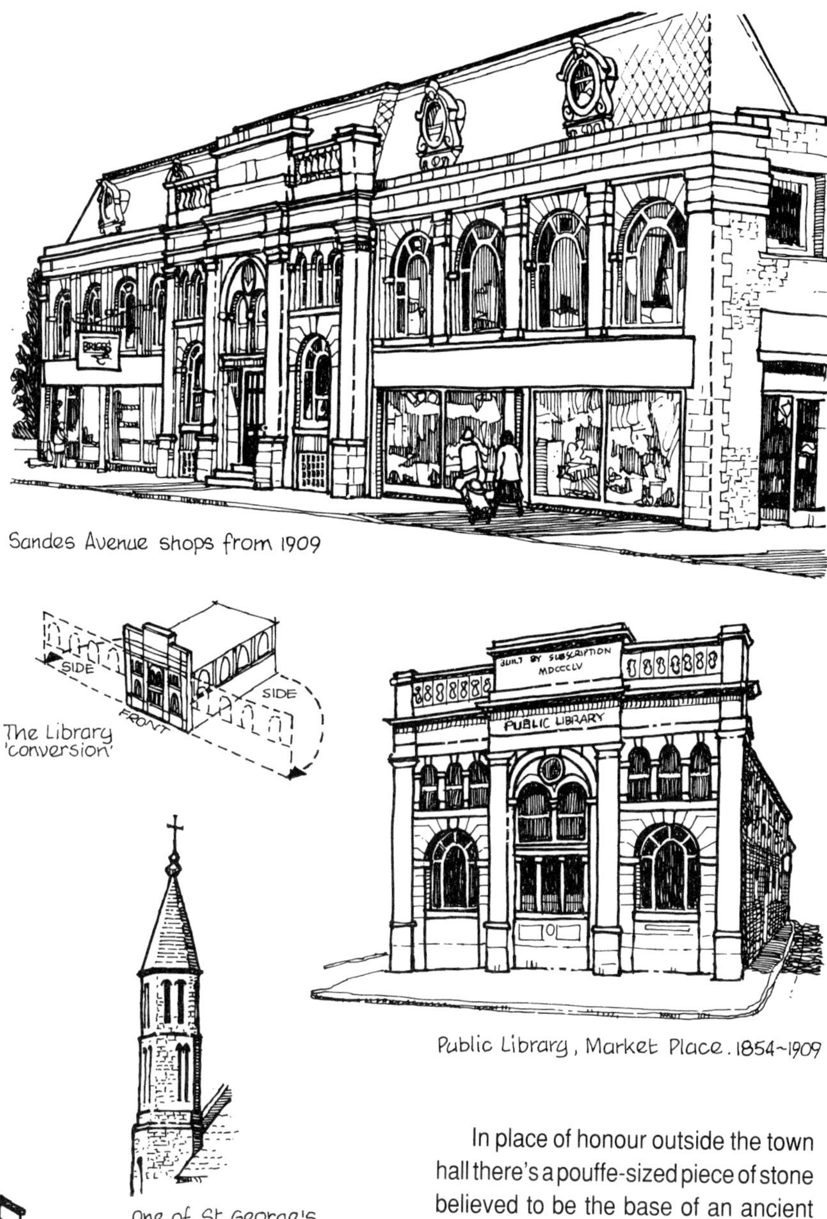

Sandes Avenue shops from 1909

The Library 'conversion'

Public Library, Market Place. 1854~1909

One of St George's dismantled towers

In place of honour outside the town hall there's a pouffe-sized piece of stone believed to be the base of an ancient market cross that once stood in Stricklandgate. Known as the Ca' (Call) Stone, royal proclamations are traditionally made from it.

Kendal was built on the wool trade. The town's motto is 'Wool is my bread'. Teazels and wool hooks appear in its coat of arms. There are still steps down to platforms at the side of the river where wool was washed. So it was a great surprise that, unlike the rest of Lakeland, the town is not overrun by stores selling woollen goods.

Indeed, this is the place where miracles happen.

St George's Church

TOWN WALK ~ SOUTH END

Walk up Kirkland and HIghgate for the ancient buildings and shops. Don't miss the Brewery Arts Centre. Go through restored Collin Croft and up Beast Banks. At the village green go through the alleyway opposite Serpentine Road onto Castle Howe. Climb the stone steps to the obelisk for a fine view of the town.

Return to the lower area of grass, then follow the footpath down behind a row of houses to Captain French Lane. Go down to the bottom, then turn right along Highgate. At the stone gateway across the road go into the park and walk down to the river. Follow the river bank footpath past the parish church to Nether Bridge. Turn right along Kirkland back to the car park. For optional extras, try a look round the church followed by refreshment at the Ring o' Bells.

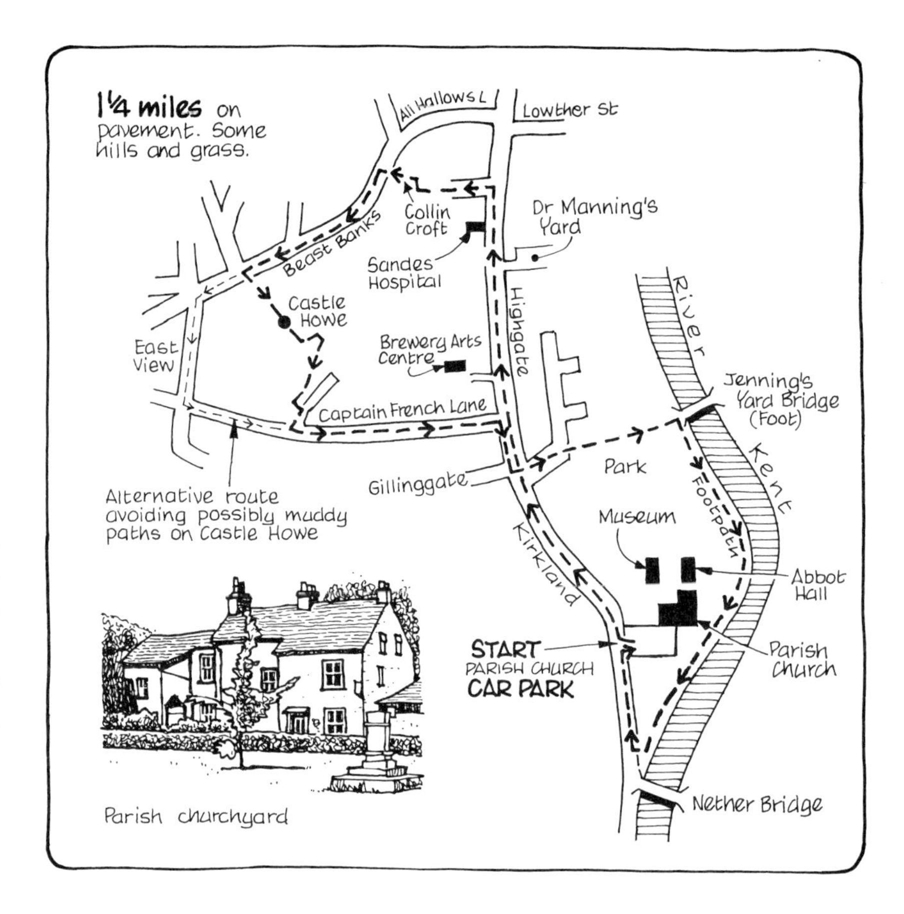

1¾ miles on pavement

Stricklandgate
Victoria Bridge
Station Road
River
Museum
Sandes Avenue
Kent
Beezon Road
Castle Dairy
Maude St
Noble's Rest
Brackhall Road
Castle Street
Stramongate Bridge
St George's Church
CAR PARK
Library St
PARKING
WC
Library
Woolpack Hotel
Shopping Centre
Stramongate
New Rd
Branthwaite Brow
Goose Holme
Market Place
New Shambles
Thorney Hills
Old Shambles
Finkle Street
Kent St
Footbridge
Fleece Inn
Town Hall
WC
Holy Trinity & St George's RC Church
Old Hallows Lane
Lowther St
START
TOWN HALL
Aynam St
Miller Bridge

TOWN WALK ~ NORTH END

From the town hall walk along the main shopping area of Stricklandgate. Follow the traffic flow at the lights into Sandes Avenue. Gasp at the shoe shop building, then cross Victoria Bridge. Call in at the museum if you like stuffed animals.

Give three cheers for the new station building, then continue along Wildman Street past Castle Dairy. Take in Stramongate Bridge, St George's Church and the Georgian terrace of Thorney Hills. Cross the footbridge over the river to New Road and Holy Trinity Church. Blackhall Road leads to Stramongate and picturesque Branthwaite Brow. Visit the new shopping centre. Go along Market Place, then left back into Stricklandgate. Turn left into Finkle Street. Return to Market Place up New Shambles. Branthwaite Brow, Kent Street and Lowther Street take you back to the town hall.

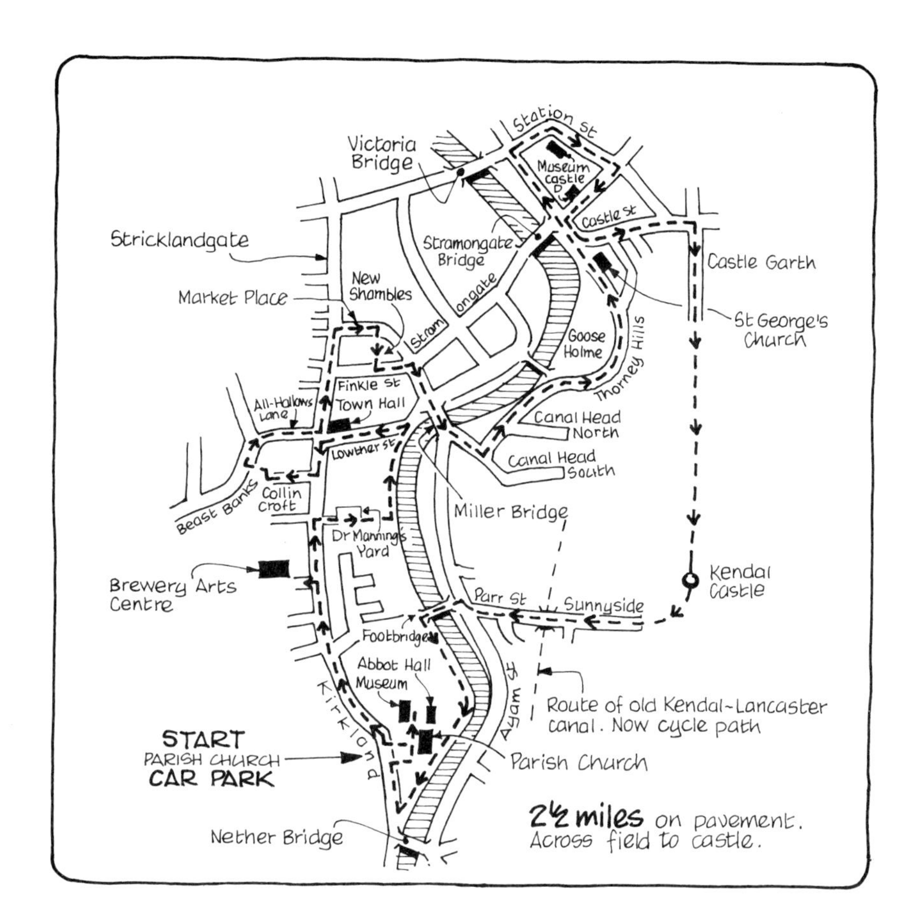

A HISTORY WALK

Go along Kirkland to the Brewery Arts Centre. Continue up Highgate, then turn right down Dr Manning's Yard to the river. Go left up Lowther Street. Cross Stricklandgate for Collin Croft up to Beast Banks. Walk down Allhallows Lane. Turn left up Stricklandgate to Market Place. Take in the New Shambles and Stramongate. Go down Kent Street. Cross Miller Bridge to the old canal head buildings. Go left along Thorney Hills. Pass St George's Church and Stramongate Bridge into Station Street. Go round the block for the museum and Castle Dairy. Walk up Castle Street, then Castle Garth. Go across the field to the castle. Walk down Parr Street, cross the footbridge and return to Kirkland along Colonel's Walk. Allow plenty of time for a tour of the parish church, and Abbot Hall museum and art gallery.

TOWN OUTSKIRTS

From Kirkland squeeze through t' Crack beside the Wheatsheaf and walk along the cobbled path into the housing estate. Go right into Gillinggate. Turn left up the hill, then right for Bankfield Road into Beast Banks. Cross the village green to Mount Street. Serpentine Road and Queen's Road take you across top of Fellside to Windermere Road. Walk down it to Sandes Avenue, then cross Victoria Bridge into Station Road.

Go round the block where Wildman Street leads to Stramongate Bridge. Head past St George's Church and along the Georgian terrace of Thorney Hills. Look out for a lane off to the left which takes you to the old canal, now a cycleway. Follow it under Sunnyside to Parkside Road. Turn right for Lound Road. Nether Bridge returns you back over the river to Kirkland.

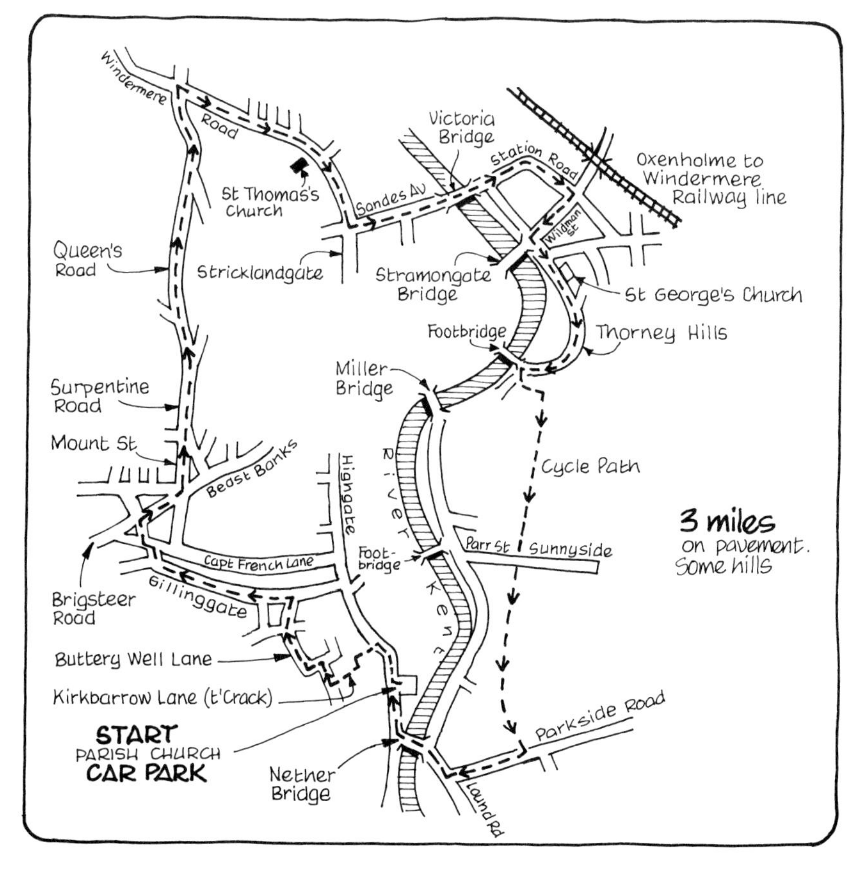

EASTERN COUNTRYSIDE

Go down Lowther Street from the town hall, then right along Waterside. Cross the footbridge to Parr Street. At the old canal bridge go down onto the cycleway. Walk along it under Parkside Road and past the new leisure centre to Burton Road. Just before the housing estate turn down Kendal Parks Road. Take the footpath at the end under two railway tracks. Follow the second track north to the A684 road. Walk along it back towards Kendal. Go under the railway branch line and pass a housing estate. Turn right up Castle Drive to the castle.

Leave the castle mound along a flat part of field into Castle Street. At St George's Church turn left across Gooseholme. Cross the river by the footbridge, then go along New Street to Kent Street. Finkle Street and Highgate return you to the town hall.

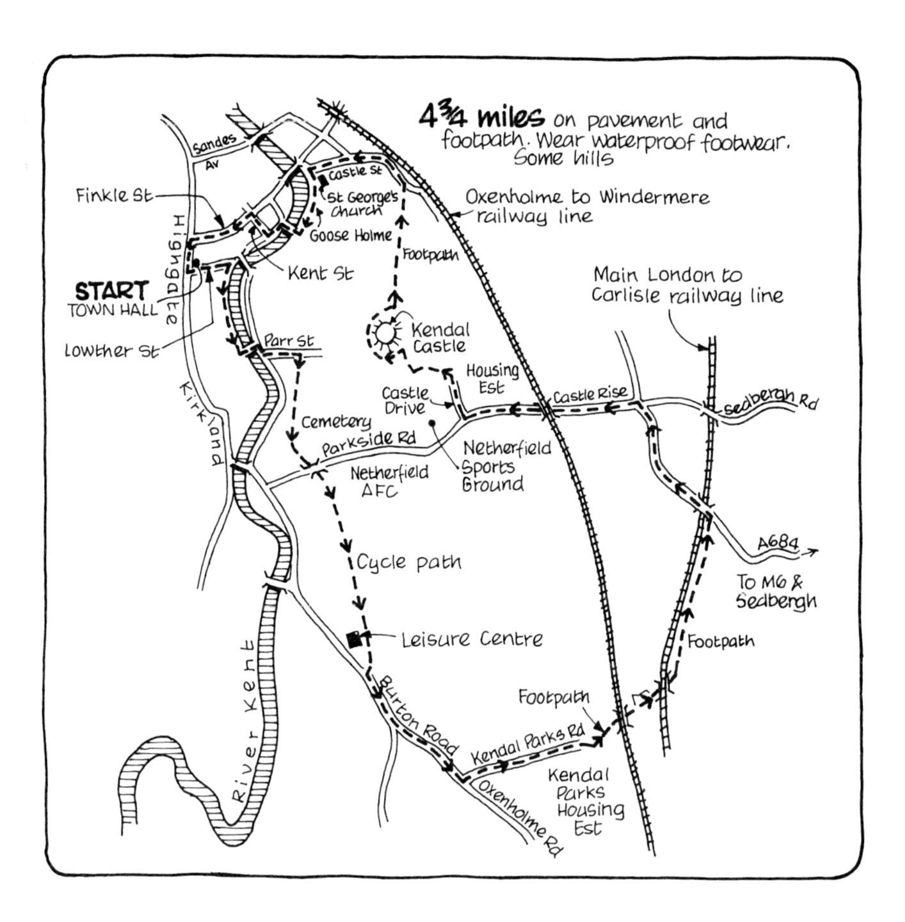

WESTERN COUNTRYSIDE

From the town hall walk up steep Allhallows Lane and Beast Banks. At the village green turn right along Serpentine Road. After 200 yards go through the marked entrance into Serpentine Woods. There's a maze of paths, but keep right and forward to a stile and gateway. These lead to a grassy hillside where there's a great view over town (see book title pages).

Continue across the hillside down to a well-established footpath which passes below Kettlewell Crag. Follow the footpath until it joins another leading back to town. Walk along this to Queen's Road. Cross it and go down Low Fellside. Don't miss Grandy Nook. In Allhallows Lane turn left to the town hall.

RIVER & COUNTRYSIDE

Go down Lowther Street. Turn right along Waterside. Pass Nether Bridge and the new Romney Bridge. Go onto the housing estate road to avoid the industrial area. At the next junction bear left to rejoin the river. Turn right through Scroggs Wood to the main road. Go left, then take the track on the right marked Helsington Barrows. After 100 yards, bear left under the Kendal by-pass.

Immediately turn left, then go through a series of three gates to Brigsteer Road. Go left along it for half a mile. At a signpost marked Helsington Barrows turn right. Follow the path up to Scout Scar. Magnificent views. Eat sandwiches.

Continue to the north end. Descend to Underbarrow Road and walk over the hill back towards Kendal. Take the track on the left through the wood onto Cunswick Scar. Cross the stile on your right and follow the path across five more stiles to Helsfell Nab. Continue past Kettlewell Crag. Climb towards the golf course and go through Serpentine Woods to Beast Banks. Stagger downhill to the town hall.

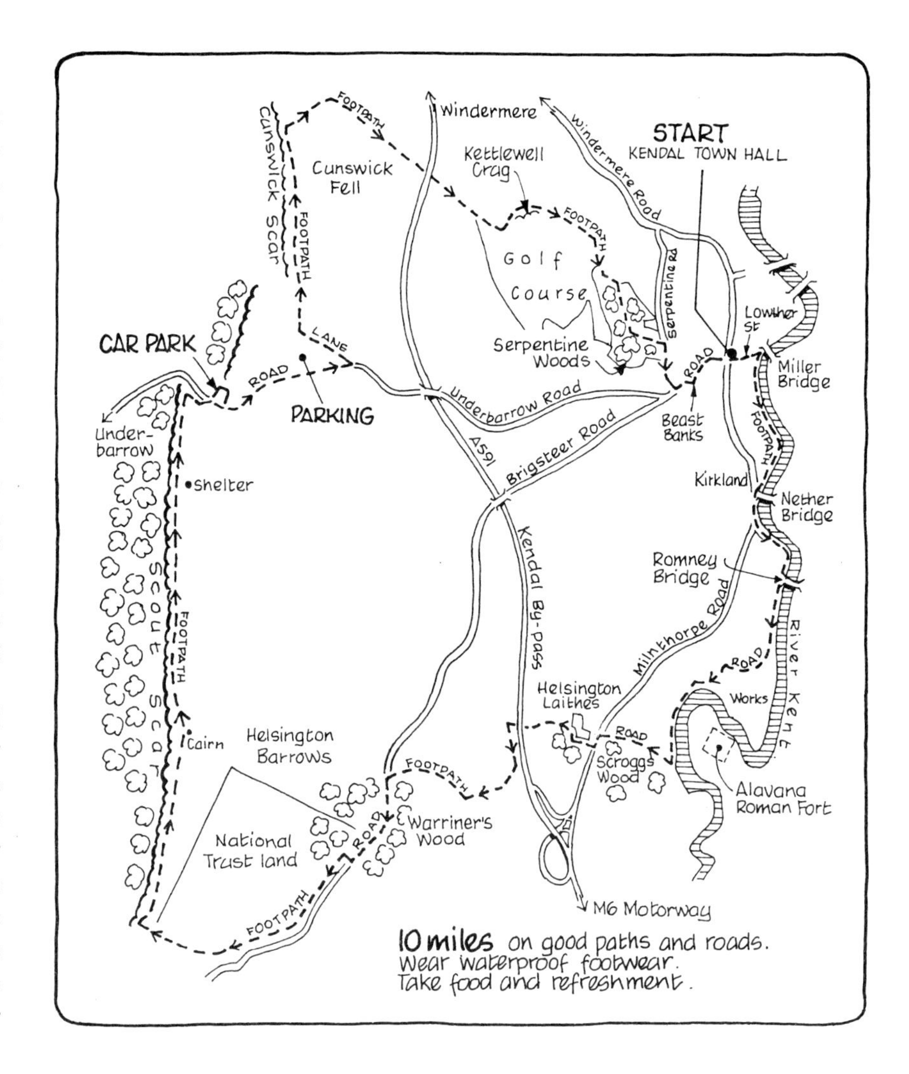

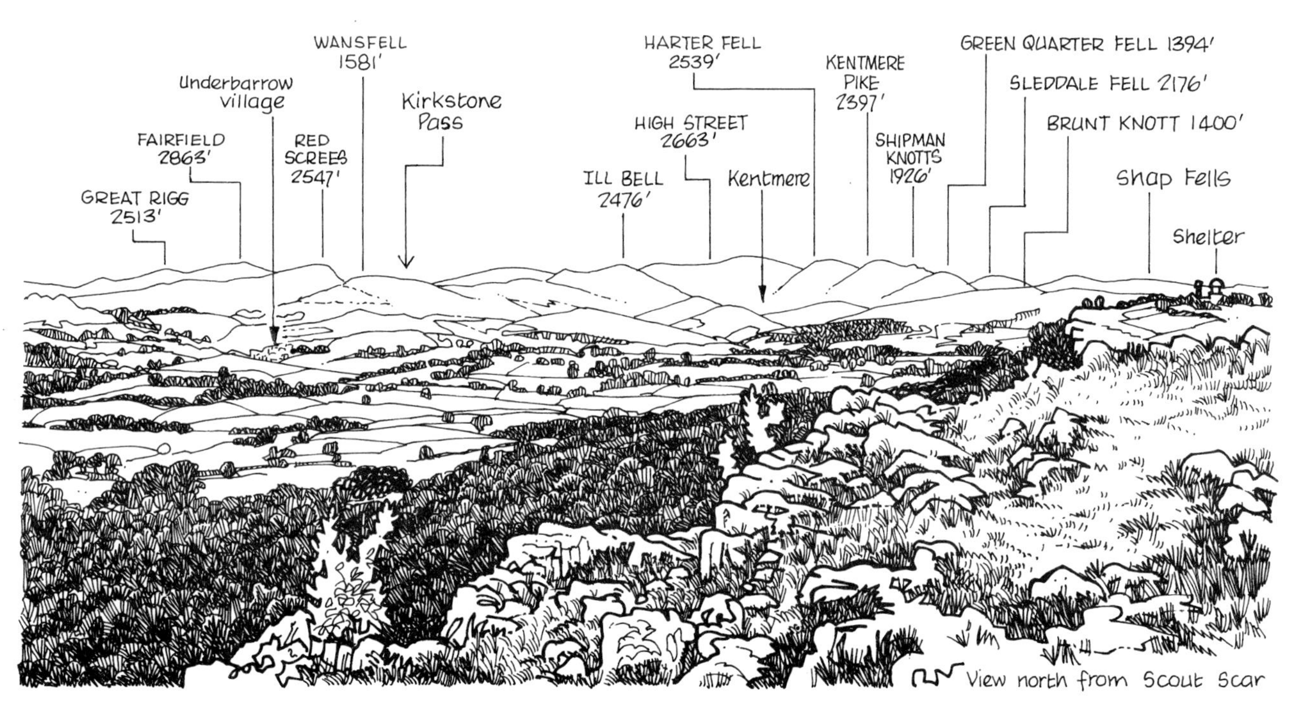

View north from Scout Scar

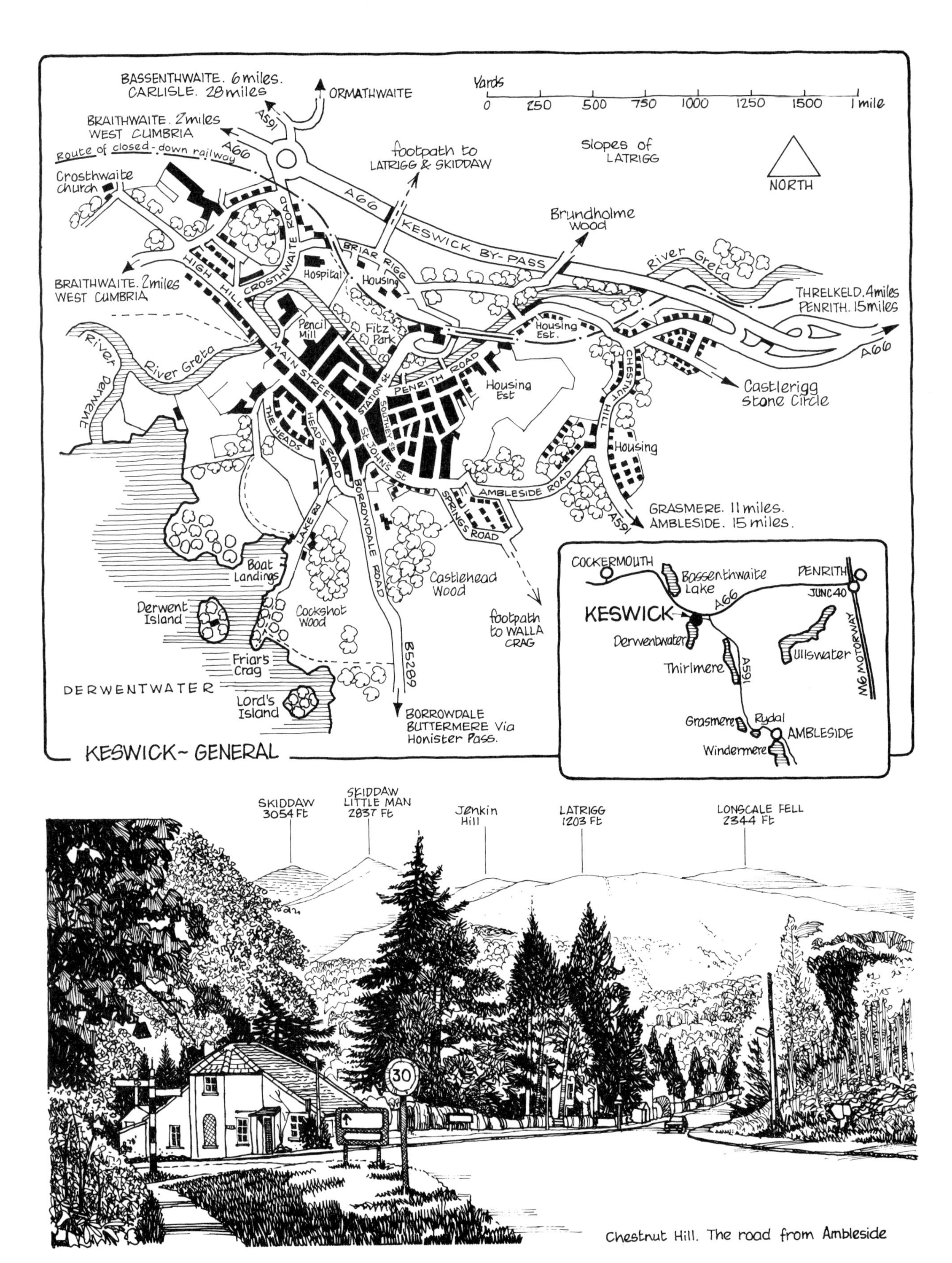

Chestnut Hill. The road from Ambleside

Main Street

Keswick

The bonnet of my car dipped eagerly down Chestnut Hill towards my old home town of Keswick. Derwentwater flashed fleetingly on my left, Bassenthwaite twinkled in the distance and the huge bulk of Skiddaw filled my windscreen. It was good to be back amongst friends.

Here at the northern edge of Lakeland, the scenery is so overpowering the little slate-grey town can seem unjustly mundane in comparison. Becks tinkle, trees blaze with colour, fearsome crags rear dramatically. Wind, rain and mist sweep down Borrowdale in avalanches of atmosphere worthy of grand opera. You have to be made of stone not to be moved by the romance of it all.

I'd driven along the A591 from Ambleside, crossing Dunmail Raise, the scenic and cultural watershed between northern coarseness and South Lakeland gentility, just beyond Grasmere. There had been memorable mountain sights along the way: the steep stony backside of Helvellyn towering over Thirlmere, and a magnificent full-frontal display from mighty Blencathra along St John's in the Vale.

The A66 trunk road takes you from Penrith to Keswick at breakneck speed. Often packed with convoys of heavy lorries, it can make the A591 seem like a peaceful farm track.

Keswick is part of my life. Here I went to school, first fell in love, and tottered hesitantly into the world of work. Only now, thirty years later, do I realise how privileged I was. We've both changed, my old home town and me, but the changes in Keswick are the hardest to take.

The A66 roadbridge, north of Keswick

According to legend, Saint Kentigern was one of the first Lakeland hikers. In AD 550 he preached at Crosthwaite where a church was eventually built in 1181. Worshippers from the valleys began to hold unofficial markets after services, annoying the neighbouring townsfolk of Cockermouth who had a royal charter for their markets.

They petitioned parliament about the illegal competition for over a century, until Edward I finally settled the squabble by awarding a new market charter to a small cheese dairy already established just south of the River Greta. It grew to become the town of Keswick, while the original settlement at Crosthwaite died out, leaving St Kentigern's Church isolated to this day.

Keswick is now locally governed from Cockermouth by Allerdale District Council. Planning decisions it makes for the town are frequently unpopular. However, without the fuss kicked up by its municipal forefathers at Cockermouth, Keswick would now be situated in a more exposed position at Crosthwaite. It just wouldn't be the same there. For that planning decision at least; thanks, Cockermouth.

The town of Keswick developed with the local mining industry. It was a haphazard business until a 1564 decree by Elizabeth I brought skilled miners from Germany to dig for copper ore in Newlands and Borrowdale. A large smelter was built at Brigham where the A66 road bridge now crosses the Greta. There was a century of prosperity until the Civil War, when Cromwell's troops inexplicably destroyed the smelter and with it the Keswick copper industry.

Miners now turned to 'Wad' mines at the head of Borrowdale producing graphite, then a valuable resource with military and medicinal uses. Packhorses carrying graphite to London were guarded by armed soldiers. Locally it was made into pencils, an industry still carried on in the town.

By 1880, the Lake Poets' extravagant descriptions were attracting affluent visitors to the town, but it was the railway opening in 1864 that began the great tourist onslaught. Keswick now has the most bed and breakfast accommodation of any town in Cumbria, absorbing a vast, ever-changing procession of people and, less successfully, their cars.

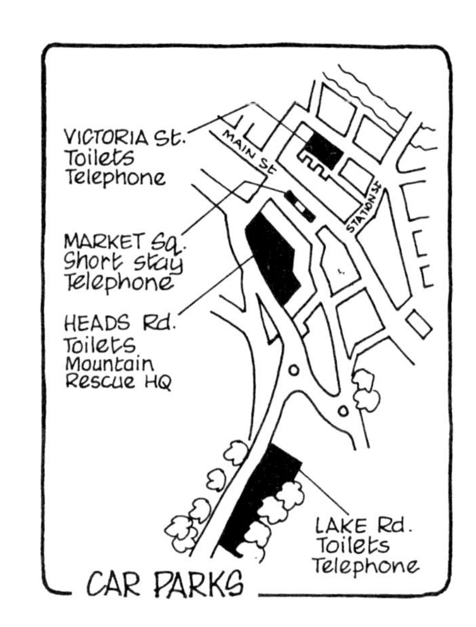

Parking in Keswick is a nightmare. There is not enough space to park local cars so visitors need to get here early. Book some accommodation with car space, even if you're not staying overnight. At least you'll have somewhere to leave your car. Yes, it is that bad. Until recently there was no official parking for coaches at all. Some had to be disgracefully left on the lake shore, ruining the very views their passengers had come to see. Crazy.

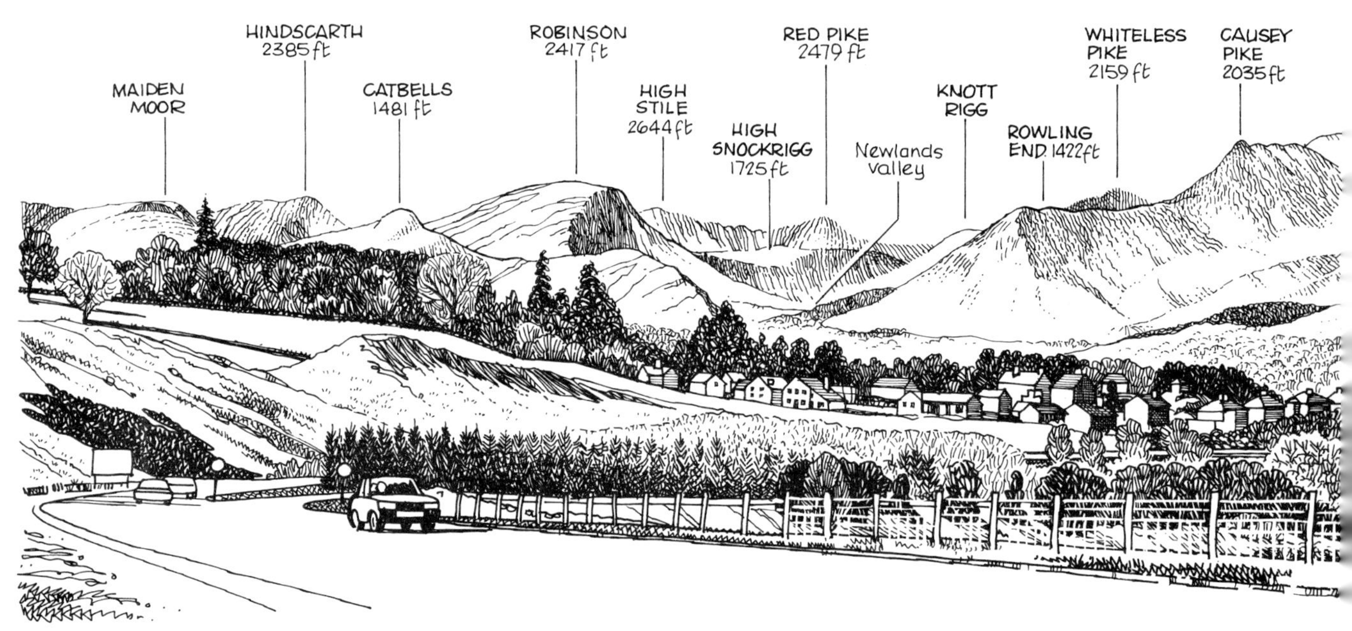

The Keswick fells from near Storms Farm

High Hill

Brigham

I used to see the glorious panorama of Keswick fells from Storms Farm every day on my way to school. Freshly covered in snow on a clear winter morning, the scene was breathtaking. The town would often be obscured by low-lying mist, leaving the apparently untethered fells to float like huge ethereal icebergs in an endless blue sky.

Beware, however; this view is a powerful distraction for motorists all the year round. While driving under its influence, I frequently miss my turn-off for north Keswick.

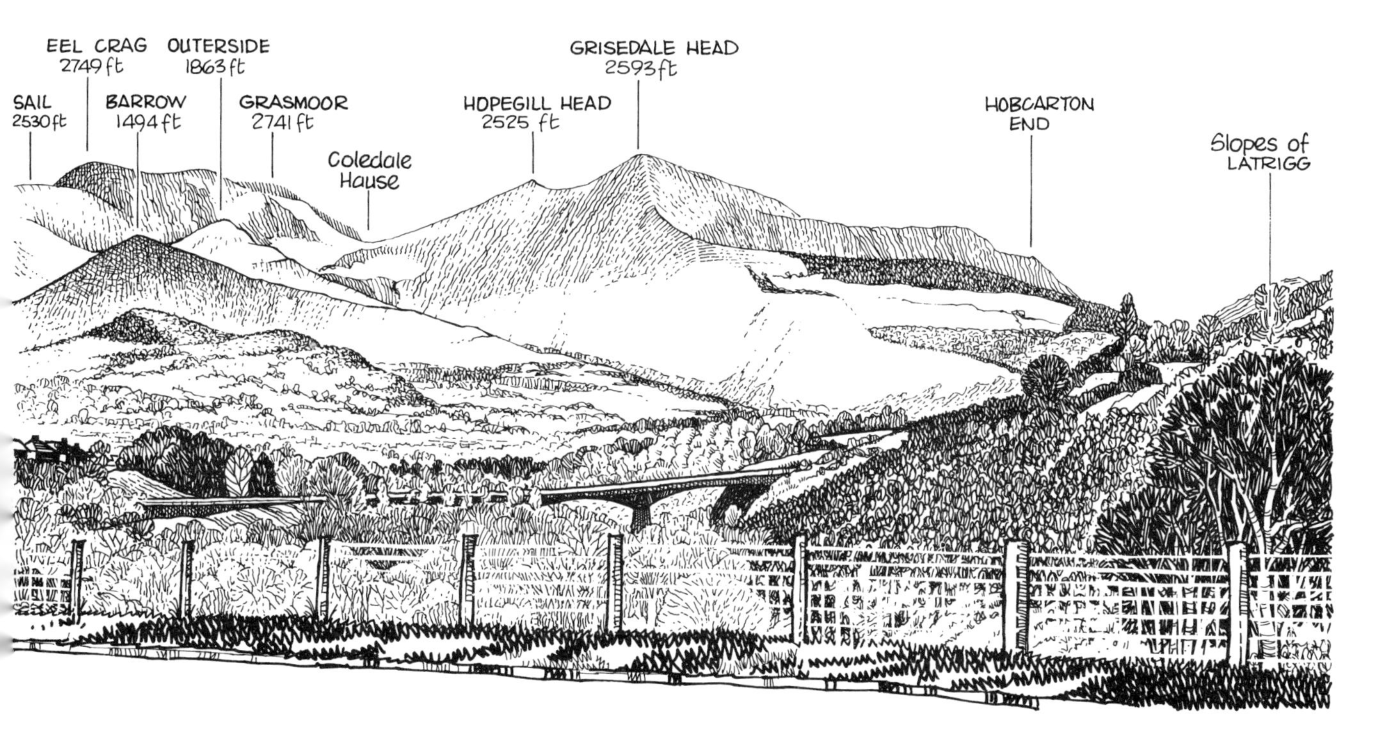

Main Street. Circa 1900

Main Street was busier and brasher than thirty years ago. More noise, more tension. Maybe it was the hot weather. Irate car drivers exchanged opinions about the sanity of another manoeuvring his caravan up Lake Road. Bikers in black leathers offered him raucous encouragement. Grim-faced families strode determinedly past. Walkers scurried for fells. Local folk sagely shook their heads. Suddenly two low-flying jet fighters screamed across the lake. We all looked up, united by fear. A jet had recently crashed only two fields out of town.

TSB Bank building, today

Keswick is not noted for architecture. The Main Street buildings are a chaotic jumble of Victoriana, modernised with variable success by modern shop fronts and repackaged as gift shops full of trinkets or outdoor clothing stores draped with orange anoraks. There was a time when this clutter and lack of sophistication gave central Keswick an agreeable homely character, but it seems to me that is fast disappearing.

I headed for the Moot Hall, still Keswick's best-looking building. Outside, the seats and car parks were filled to overflowing with corpulent young men from the North East. Keswick has always attracted Geordies, many of them accomplished mountaineers and climbers who practised their arts on the Borrowdale crags before refreshing themselves in the local pubs.

These modern lads had eliminated the time-wasting physical activity and gone straight for the boozing. After a heavy morning at the bar they were now topping up with fish and chips. The serious drinking was yet to come. They all wore expansive teeshirts that proudly proclaimed they were on a '12 Hour Sup-Up of Keswick'. Modern tourism knows no bounds.

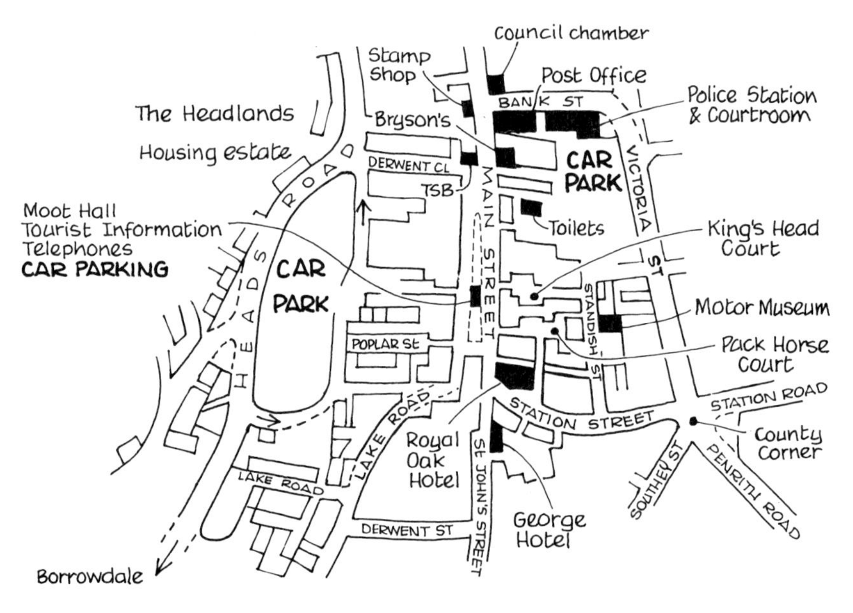

The Main Street buildings seemed little changed, but many had different frontages and uses. A Boots store now occupies the ground floor of the Skiddaw Hotel. An outdoor clothing shop used to be a popular pub. After I drew the Central Hotel it became part of the up-market sweet shop next door. The Geordies were not pleased.

A market is still held in Market Place on Saturdays, causing even bigger traffic snarl-ups than it did years ago. Argument about banning town centre traffic continually rages amongst local traders. Some want the market moved. Please, no.

Poplar Street

Main Street

Both sides of Main Street are perforated by a series of passages, remnants of ancient yards demolished for parking space.

I went into King's Head Court. Stone steps into a furnishing store once led to the cottage of Jonathan Otley, 18th-century geologist, scientist and clock-repairer. In 1823, he wrote the first reliable guide to the Lake District.

All the yards are interesting. One next to the Skiddaw Hotel used to house the local newspaper. Another, Poplar Street, still keeps quaintly dignified.

Pack Horse Inn

Many of us mourn the loss of the Pack Horse Inn, one of the town's oldest institutions and favourite watering hole of generations of walkers and climbers; a place rich with lively banter delivered in the broad Cumbrian dialect, where visitors and locals mixed convivially and life-long friendships were forged.

Sadly, all that unique Pack Horse atmosphere, which I first savoured long before I was legally entitled to, was destroyed in a wanton 1990 modernisation. If Jennings Bitter wasn't so blooming good I'd never sup another drop in protest. I hope they don't modernise their beer.

King's Head Court

Pack Horse Yard ~ 1984

Same viewpoint ~ 1990

In 1990, Keswick's most radical building development for years turned sleepy Pack Horse Yard into a bright, modern shopping area.

Seventeen new shops were created, birch trees, flower beds and ornate lampposts were planted. An arcade was driven through the Royal Oak Hotel from Station Street and wrought iron canopies erected at each end. It all looks great.

But significantly there are no big chain store names, just the usual woollen goods and expensive gift shops. With high rents and only seasonal tourist trade to rely on, there are fears that the prosperous good looks of the renamed Pack Horse Court may be only fleeting.

The famous Moot Hall just squeezes into Market Place on the reputed site of a court-house, built in 1695 using materials from the ruined mansion of the last Earl of Derwentwater on Lord's Island.

The present tall and elegant building dates from 1813, and has been used as a court house, market, prison, museum and town hall. An unusual one-handed clock in the tower is wound every night by a remarkably diligent local man. On the hour a bell tolls, more a miserable clang actually, but well suited for its original 17th-century function as a curfew bell.

For many years the Moot Hall was painted black and white. When all the rendering was removed during renovations in 1975 it was controversially decided to leave the rough stonework exposed. I've just about got used to the 'new' look by now.

Since 1971, the ground floor has been a National Park information bureau, the busiest in Lakeland with 190,000 visitors a year. Slide shows and exhibitions are held on the two upper floors. What appears to be a Punch and Judy show under the stone steps is actually an ingenious booking office for the Century Theatre.

THE MOOT HALL

Police station & Courtroom

Through traffic avoids the town centre by using Victoria Street and Bank Street. Standing appropriately on the corner is the kindly-looking police station and courtroom, kept busy these days by visiting hooligans.

Next door, where the post office now stands, there was once a poorhouse, founded in 1644 by Sir John Bankes, a local man who rose to become Lord Chief Justice and a Privy Councillor.

The dusty council offices, which occupy the opposite corner, were originally built in 1864 as the Cumberland Union Bank, giving the name to 'Bank Street'.

Derwent Close

Demolition of old buildings for access to Heads Road car park has revealed an attractive row of slate cottages in Derwent Close, and a distant view of Catbells.

Bryson's new shop is as good as their excellent bread and cakes, and glorious proof that imaginative design is possible without old buildings having to be demolished.

I had more surprises in Main Street: a scholarly stamp shop, and Skiddaw Gallery with its indoor wells and mining relics.

Council offices, Post Office & Brysons

I remember when the Royal Oak was one of Keswick's most prestigious hotels. Stained glass windows inside commemorate the Lake Poets and other local heroes. Now its elegant ballroom is filled with ubiquitous woollen goods, and a cocktail lounge has become a passageway to Pack Horse Court. Autumn seems to have come to the grand Royal Oak.

Keswick's oldest inn, the George Hotel, survives relatively unaltered round the corner in St John's Street. Dark deeds in plumbago smuggling were reputedly plotted here.

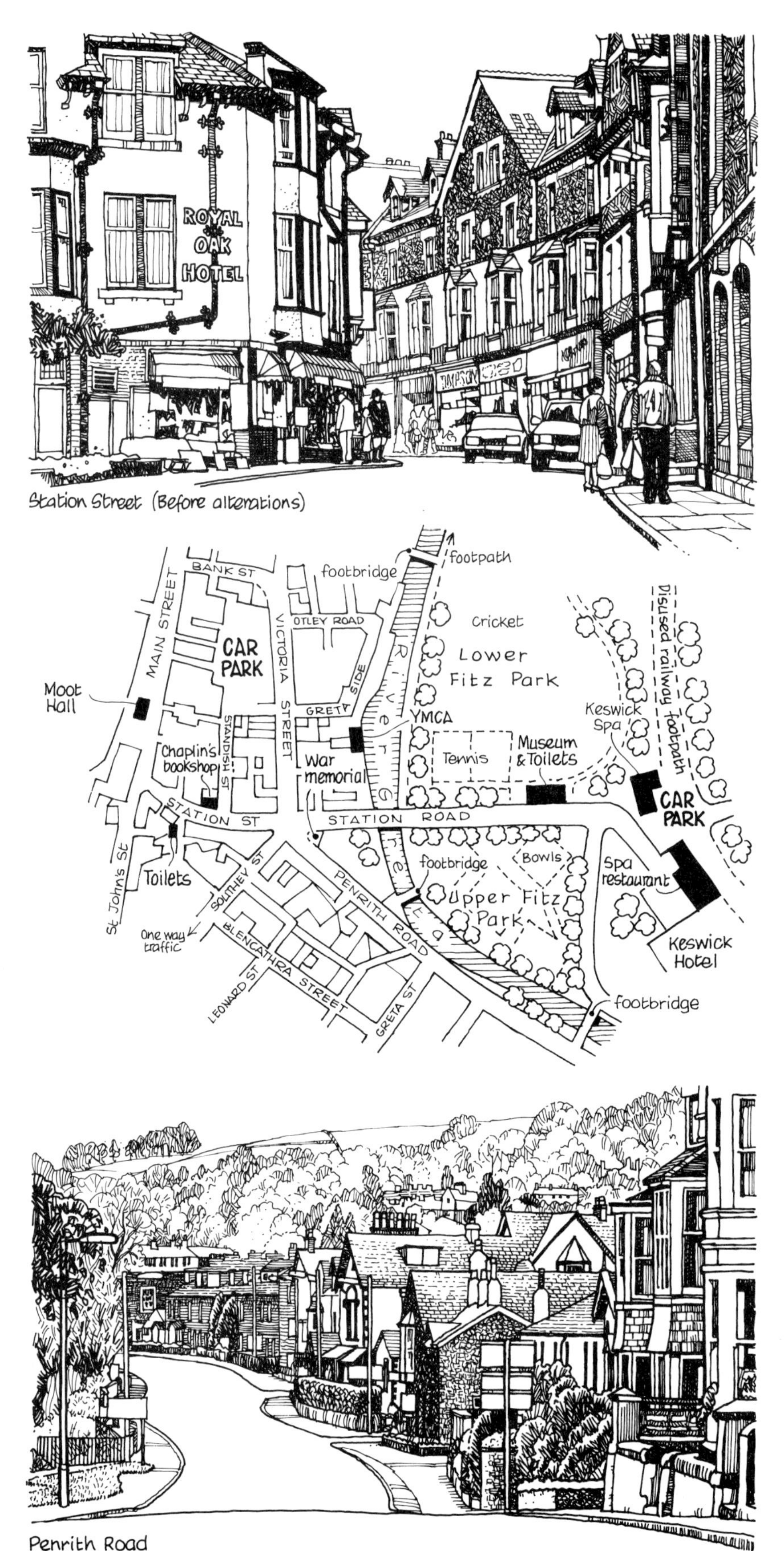

Station Street (Before alterations)

Penrith Road

Chaplin's bookshop

I thumbed through the Lakeland best sellers in Chaplin's bookshop and watched from the wall by a photo-gallery of their authors. Chaplin's distinctive black and white building dates back to the 17th-century when it was a farmhouse standing in open fields.

Along Southey Street I entered Keswick's extensive bed and breakfast belt. The terraces of handsome slate-built houses, three and four storeys high, are laid out in a bewildering maze of narrow streets. More tourists get lost in this area than on Skiddaw.

The north side of Penrith Road is bordered by the Greta, a lovely rock-flecked river that meanders delightfully around the town, but soon swells to a raging torrent after heavy rain. I crossed over a footbridge into Upper Fitz Park, always a delight. It all looked as good as it did thirty years ago.

Museum & Art Gallery

Among the museum's rather sparse collection of curios is a set of musical stones collected from Skiddaw, Turner paintings donated by an American, and documents to do with Wordsworth, Southey, Ruskin and Coleridge, including Southey's original story of *The Three Bears*. Most interesting are the thick volumes of Walpole manuscripts, written in his own flamboyant hand with capital letters picked out in red ink. Don't miss the kiddies favourite: a 500-year-old mummified cat - late of Borrowdale.

Railway passengers from Penrith used to make a spectacular entrance into Keswick through the wooded gorge of the Greta. I was one of the scruffy urchins who greeted them outside the station. We made easy pocket money ferrying luggage to hotels on home-made carts.

In 1972 the line was closed, but the station buildings were re-opened in 1987 as a restaurant for the ill-fated Keswick Spa. I found the skeletal platform off-putting. It was like having a meal in a graveyard.

Old Railway Station

River Greta and Fitz Park

Lake Road leaves Market Place in a short bottleneck that opens out into a small square enclosed by souvenir shops and two of Keswick's best-known pubs: The Dog and Gun, and The Lake Road Vaults. Between the tight buildings there's a glimpse of Causey Pike. One of the great joys of Keswick is the fell views at every street end.

Teeming pedestrians often pack the narrow double bend of Lake Road, making it a hazardous passage for red-faced drivers heading for Borrowdale.

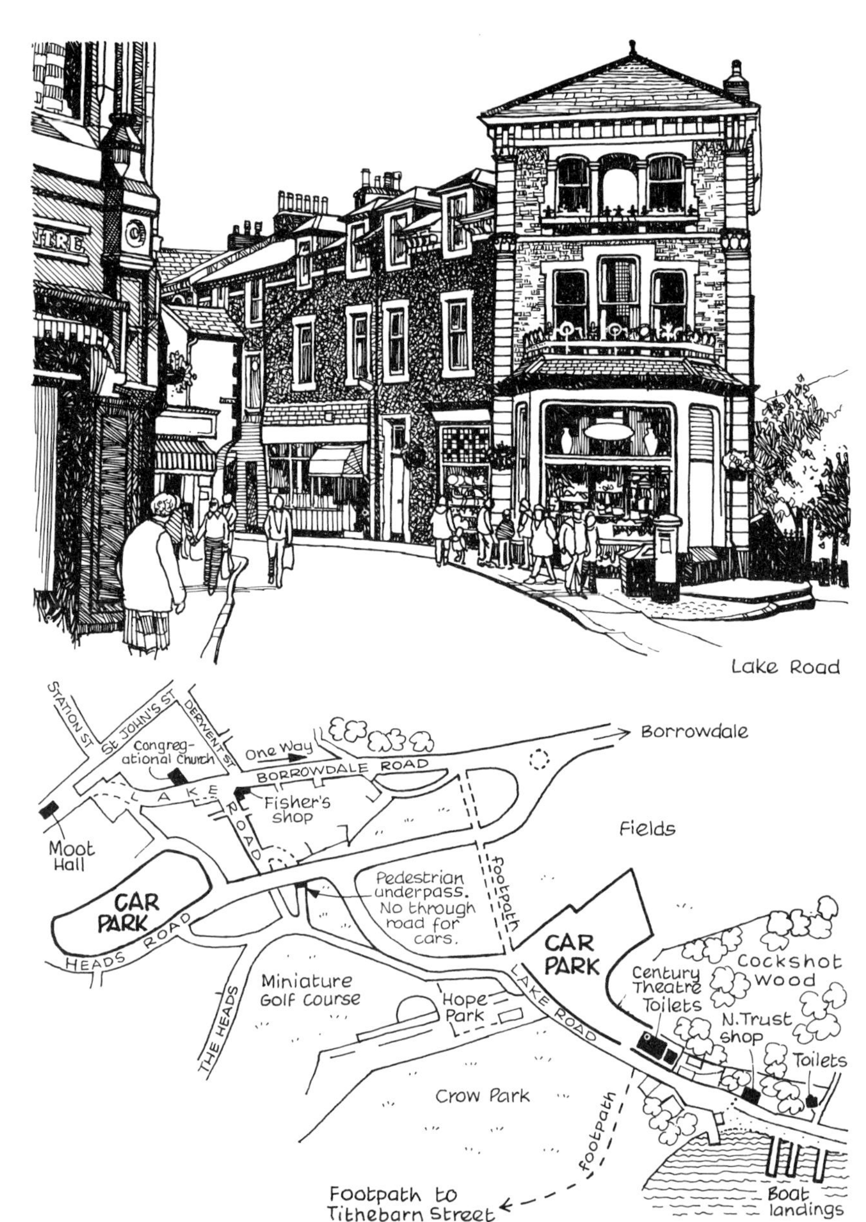

Lake Road

World-famous climbing shop

At a magnificent copper beech tree, Lake Road cuts sharply downhill past the looming edifice of Fisher's climbing shop. The well-known landmark had recently been done up. There is a slicker style in the painting of the ice climber above the entrance, and a twin has appeared on another wall. Inside, the merchandise is even more fabulous and tempting than ever. Enter Fishers only with a fat wallet. Going out on the fells can be an expensive walk.

Congregational Church

Lake Road

A traffic-free part of Lake Road is now dominated by Mayson's splendid up-market gift emporium and coffee shop. Before restoration in 1984, the building was one of Keswick's worst eyesores. It used to be occupied by Maysons, the renowned pioneers of early photography, but when their business closed it fell into ruinous decay. A large relief model of the Lake District was shamefully allowed to crumble away to dust.

The studio of another famous photographic duo, the Abraham brothers, was above Fisher's shop. Their superb monochrome studies of mountains and bygone Lakeland scenes are now classics, eagerly sought after by collectors.

Miniature Golf Course, St John's Church and Clough Head

Adjoining the miniature golf course, where you can practise your swing without too much walking, there's Hope Park. It was donated to the town in 1974 by local dignitary, Sir Percy Hope. My first job was office boy in his architect's practice. I remember him as a large country gent dressed in tweed walking breeches. He always carried a shepherd's crook - even to the office.

Hope Park and Catbells

When you walk down Lake Road, Derwentwater is kept tantalisingly hidden by the low hill of Crow Park, so the first sight of the lake comes as a wonderful surprise at the boat landings.

The Derwentwater promenade was a more sedate version of those I'd seen at Bowness and Ambleside. Pensioners nodded behind newspapers, families fed ducks, teenagers drenched each other in frantically rocking row-boats. All human life was there.

What wasn't there was a decent place for all of us to enjoy a cup of tea. The tea gardens look way past their shelf life. Some discreet development would not go amiss here.

Derwent Island, largest of the lake's four islands, lies only a stone's throw offshore. Once a sanctuary for German miners, it was bought in 1778 by the eccentric Joseph Pocklington. He covered the island with bizarre buildings as a background to his regattas and mock battles on the lake.

The Marshall family took over in 1884 and occupied the 1791 house for over a century. In 1951 they transferred ownership to the National Trust. You need a boat to see the still-occupied house, which remains - with the island - strictly private.

The Boat Landings

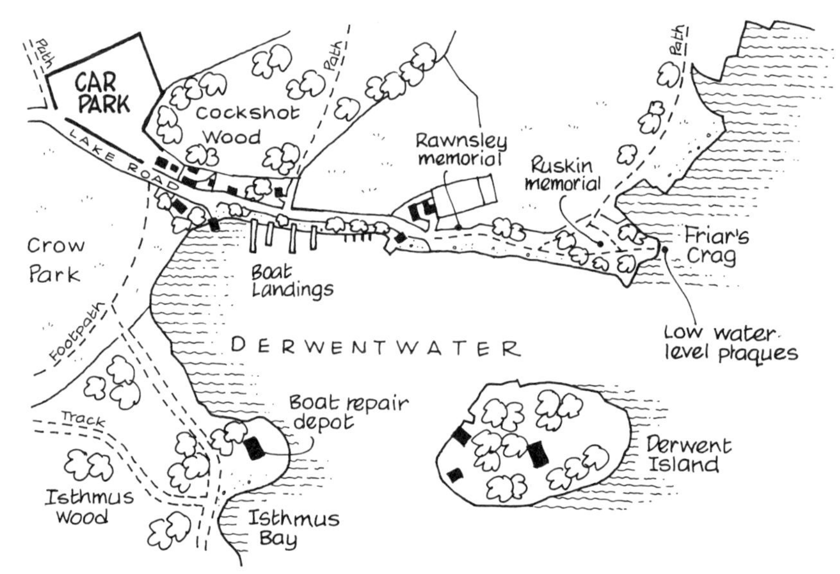

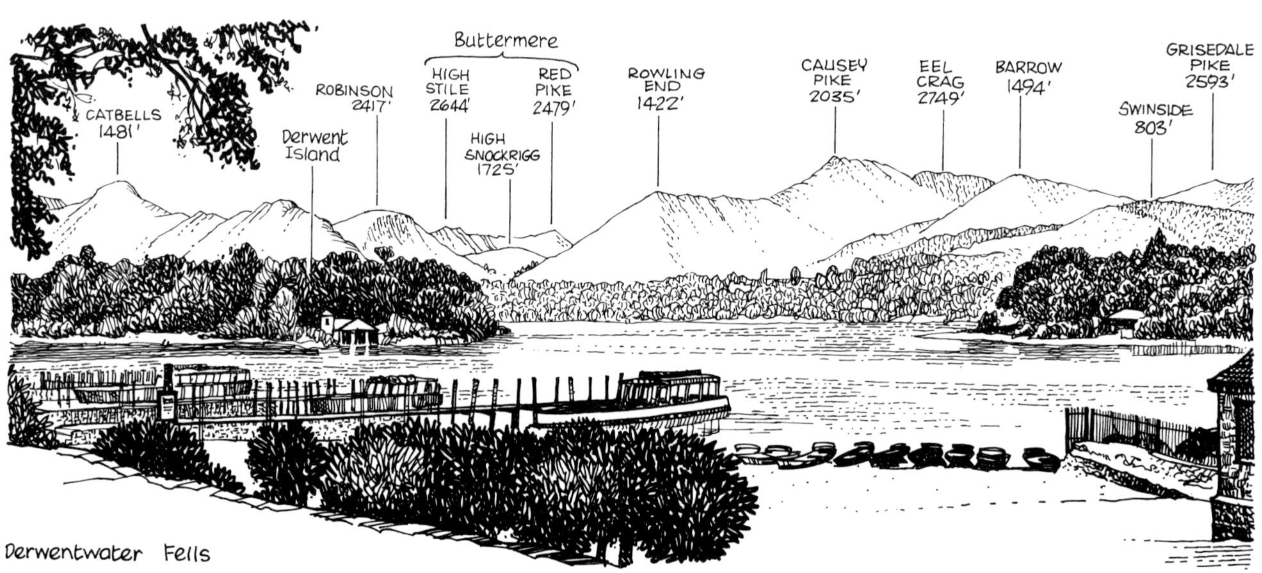

Derwentwater Fells

After a look in the discreet National Trust shop I joined the crowds flocking along the beautiful lakeside path to Friar's Crag. We passed a memorial to Canon Rawnsley, vicar of Crosthwaite and most dynamic of the Trust's three founders. They were all influenced by the writings of John Ruskin, who is honoured by a stone on the crag itself.

Seen from the lakeshore, sunlit Skiddaw resembled a modern sculpture assembly of massive fur-covered cones. Its stark beauty contrasted sharply with the craggy silhouette of Borrowdale, which was created by violent volcanic action. Skiddaw consists of slate, some of the oldest rock in Europe, laid down as marine deposits long before volcanoes became active.

Though easily reached, Skiddaw's summit stands 3,053 feet high, only 150 feet lower than Scafell Pike. The old boy carries great age with dignity. Treat him with respect.

Skiddaw & Crow Park

National Trust Shop

Friar's Crag is one of the most visited spots in Lakeland. Amongst the scraggy Scots pines that sprout untidily from its insignificant top, I stood shoulder to shoulder with crowds of other craning camera clickers, all of us attempting to reduce the panoramic view of Borrowdale up the lake down to photograph size. It cannot be done. But once seen - never forgotten.

I clambered down to the water line where plaques mark the low levels. The current lowest was recorded during the Great Drought of 1983.

Friar's Crag & Walla Crag

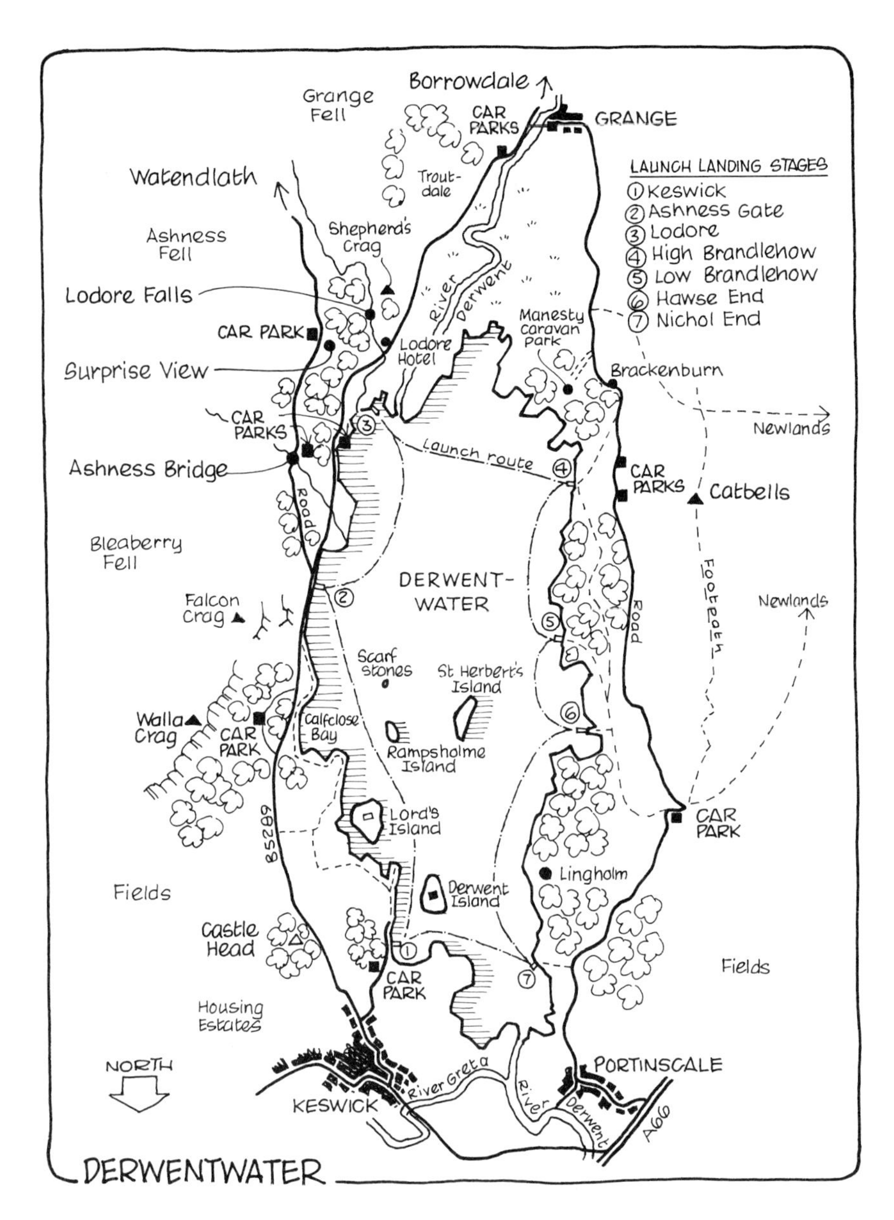

Derwentwater has a compact oval shape, nearly 3 miles long by 1¼ miles wide. The maximum depth is 72 feet, near Ashness Gate - relatively shallow, so it freezes most winters for skating.

The setting abounds with interest and variety: fearsome cliffs on Walla Crag; beautiful woodland around Ashness; wild and wonderful Borrowdale; and the sinuous arm of Catbells embracing the lakeside trees of Brandelhow Park.

Lingholm Island

All four islands have an odd claim to fame. The last Earl of Derwentwater, beheaded in 1716 for joining the Jacobite rebellion, had a manor house on Lord's Island. Iron ore was smelted in a Rampsholme bloomery. St Herbert's is named after its hermit immortalised by Wordsworth. And Derwent Island was home for Joseph Pocklington. He planted many trees, so wasn't all batty.

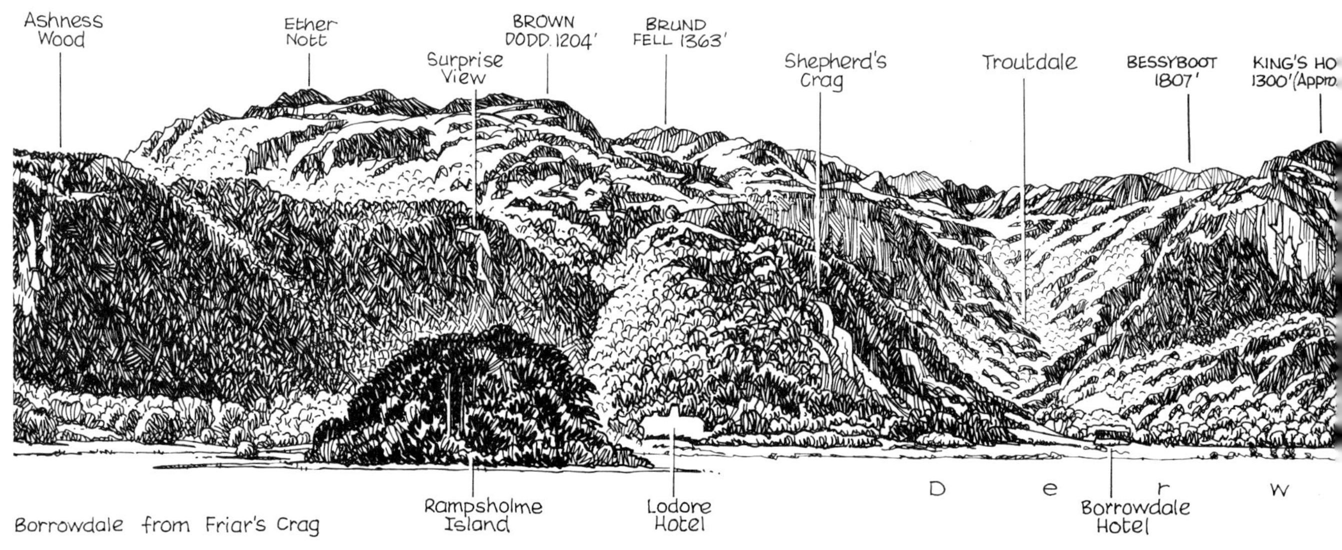

Borrowdale from Friar's Crag

The small islands are equally interesting. Land on tiny Lingholme Island with eight records and pretend you're cast away with Sue Lawley, or watch cormorants drying their wings on Scarf Stones.

Then there's the phantom floating island, a raft of vegetable matter that reputedly rises from the lake bed near Lodore on a cushion of marsh gas. Believe it when you see it.

A Derwentwater Launch

Scarf Stones & Catbells

Derwentwater is a busy highway for boats, but a ban on large motor craft and a speed limit of 10mph keeps traffic peaceful. Rowing boats or self-drive motor boats can be hired at the boat landings.

The most relaxing way to see the lake attractions is aboard one of the popular little launches. They have run a regular service since 1904. Two built of Burma teak over 75 years ago were originally for exclusive use by Lodore hotel patrons.

From March to November the launches call at seven points around the lake where you can board or leave. Clockwise or anti-clockwise circuits are available, each taking about 50 minutes to complete. A launch trip is a fabulous way to begin or end a day's walking.

John Ruskin put the classic view of Borrowdale from Friar's Crag in his top three of Europe, though he did tend to go over the top. According to him, Keswick was 'too beautiful to live in'.

Nevertheless, the view is magnificent in clear conditions. Great End is nine miles away, so you can be peering through a lot of Lakeland mist.

Derwent Island & Skiddaw

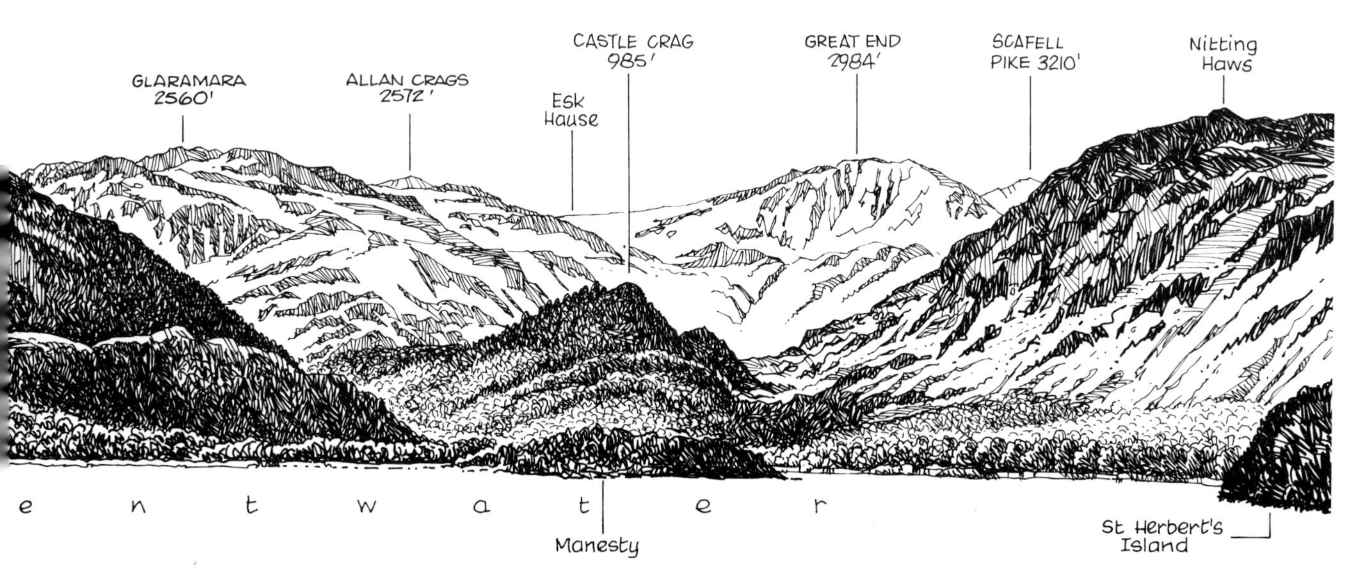

For years the area known locally as 't' bottom end of toon', straggled quietly away to the Lakeland bungalows at High Hill without attracting a lot of visitor attention. Now the tide of tourism flows ever further down Main Street all it touches is transformed. If there was still a tithe barn in Tithebarn Street it would have been turned into some kind of novelty shop.

The street I knew has almost entirely disappeared. Gift shops line both sides these days. A popular pub has been replaced by modern apartments that no ordinary local couple could afford. The draughty old bus station has gone and a sensational new supermarket development built on the site. It used to be a pleasure waiting for your bus to start off when you could admire Causey Pike and rhododendron-covered Swinside from the top front seat of a double-decker, but that lovely view has now been ruined by a stalag-like block of flats.

Only the old Methodist church seemed unchanged. I welcomed it like an old friend. Thirty years ago I never gave the plain slate building a second look.

The local rugger club takes profitable advantage of the town's chronic parking problem by opening its nearby ground as a summer car park. I've always found parking in Keswick a bit of a scrum.

Tithebarn Street & Latrigg

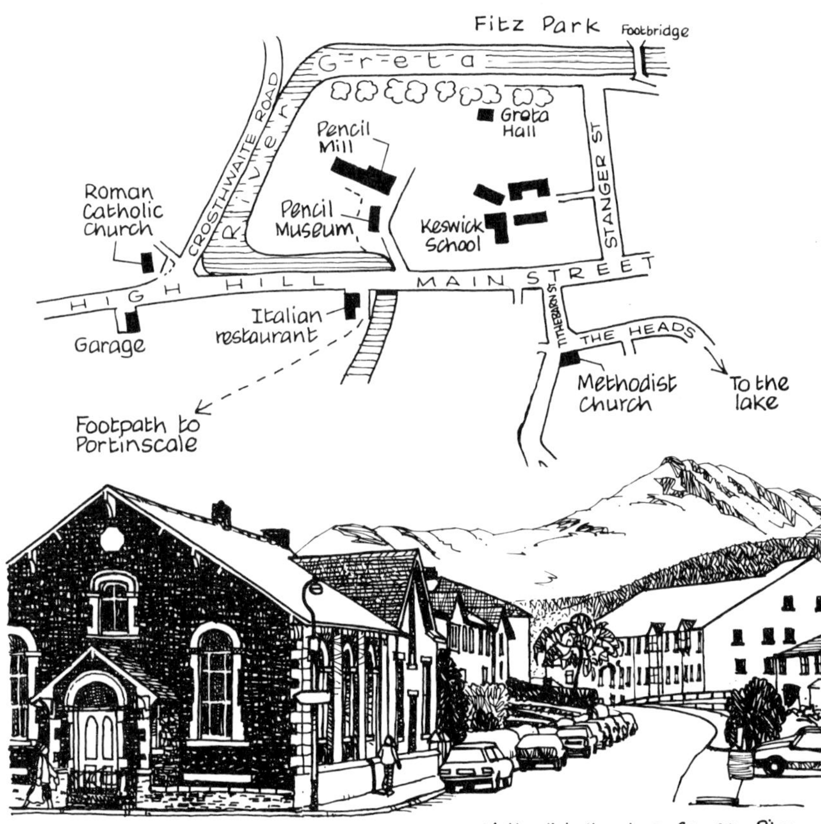

Methodist Church & Causey Pike

Keswick School

I went to Keswick School in the 1950s when it was a toffee-nosed grammar school. Today it's just part of a huge comprehensive.

Now there's talk of the school following the rugger club's example and turning its hallowed lawns into summer car parks to raise money. They didn't need to do that in the 1950s.

Pencils have been made at Keswick since the 1500s. Originally a cottage industry, manufacture expanded in 1830 when the first of several factories opened. Only the Cumberland Pencil Company has survived. Now owned by Rexel, its high-tech factory produces nearly half a million pencils a day.

The history of pencil making is told in the museum, where you can also try your hand at drawing. Alas, not with the world's largest pencil, that's only there for display.

Somehow the museum doesn't match the brilliance of the pencils. I use them all the time - even on the cover of this book.

The Pencil Mill & Museum

The Primavera Restaurant

Opened in 1984, the Primavero Italian restaurant was originally the Keswick School of Industrial Art. The notable training centre for local craftsmen, brainchild in 1894 of Canon Rawnsley and his wife, produced high quality articles in stainless steel, copper and other metals.

A Ruskinesque quotation is prominently displayed across the front of the building: *The loving eye and patient hand shall join together and bless this land.* As I looked back across Greta Bridge to Walla Crag and the fast-changing town it did seem painfully apt. A loving hand and patient eye was just what Keswick needed, but my eye, my hand. I didn't want changes I didn't like. I didn't want any changes at all. I wanted Keswick to be just as it was 30 years ago. But it wasn't really my old familiar home town I was hankering after - it was my youth.

A group of well-preserved cottages nearby lifted my spirits. Ruskin Cottage was the Keswick branch of the great man's Coniston lace industry. Another still has its bay window where tolls were collected. Keswick has similar toll bar cottages at Brigham and Chestnut Hill.

Cottages at High Hill

Keswick's parish church of St Kentigern was founded at Crosthwaite during the 6th century. Parts of the original stone church of 1181 can be seen in the present 1523 building, which was itself extensively restored in 1844.

Though rather austere looking outside, the church is warm and lush inside with many historical relics around the ancient walls. A good place to explore, there's an excellent, if quaintly written, guide on sale.

The churchyard headstones are rich with notable Lakeland names: William Jackson (1797-1809), who built Greta Hall; Jonathan Otley (1766-1856), of King's Head Court, who repaired the one-handed church clock after it had been silent for 50 years; and of course, Canon Rawnsley, best friend to all lovers of Lakeland.

Southey's tomb is a great crowd-puller. Its restoration was paid for by the Brazilian government in 1962, so I was expecting something exotic. It isn't. The tomb is nothing more than a box made of five pieces of slate. Southey himself was much liked in Keswick. He worshipped at St Kentigern's for 40 years.

There are fabulous views from the churchyard, especially of Skiddaw, but my meditation was constantly disturbed by the roar of traffic from the nearby A66.

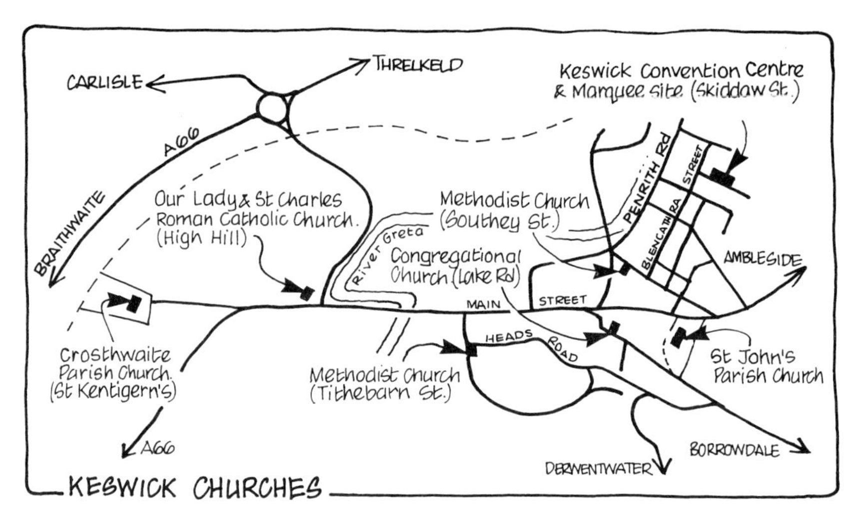

KESWICK CHURCHES

Church entrance

Southey Tomb.

Canon H.D. Rawnsley (1851-1920)

St Kentigern's Church

Hardwicke Drummond Rawnsley was a fearless activist for nature conservation all his life. Best known as co-founder of the National Trust in 1893, he was also a prolific author and keen educationist. Young Beatrix Potter was encouraged to paint and write by his personal attention.

An active churchman, he was vicar of Crosthwaite (1883-1917), Canon of Carlisle (1893), and chaplain to King George V (1912-1920). Millions of people have benefited from his energetic life. Rawnsley's sainthood should be in the post.

The Parish Church of St John's cost £4,103 to build in 1836 using sandstone quarried near Greystoke. It was paid for by a wealthy Yorkshire mill owner, John Marshall, who died before the Early English style building was finished in 1838. Since then two aisles have been added, and the once-controversial tall spire, which has become a familiar landmark. Sir Huge Walpole, the writer, is buried on the terrace overlooking Derwentwater.

Inside, the church is large and spacious, but with a cooler atmosphere than St Kentigern's. While I wandered round two ladies came in, settled in a pew and produced a flask. Armed with a cup of tea each, the couple then proceeded to gossip loudly about all manner of intimate family matters. That warmed things up considerably.

Walpole's headstone

St John's Church

The Keswick Convention, an inter-denominational spiritual crusade, was founded in 1875 by the vicar of St John's, Canon Battersby, and a Quaker friend, Robert Wilson. Two hundred people attended. Now thousands of pilgrims annually pack the town for two weeks in July.

Services are held in a huge marquee erected behind the new convention centre, which unfortunately looks more like a greyhound racing stadium than a religious shrine.

Convention Centre

The Catholic Church of Our Lady and St Charles was opened for worship in 1928 but not finally finished until 1965. It has the distinction of being the only church built of Threlkeld granite - the same kind of stone used in Thirlmere dam. Any religious allegory is entirely coincidental.

Our Lady & St Charles Church

LITERARY CONNECTIONS

Samuel Taylor Coleridge (1772-1834)

Robert Southey (1774-1843)

When Coleridge wasn't writing fantastic verse he'd be off on marathon walks or getting stoned on opium. In 1800 he brought his family to live at Greta Hall. Soon after, the Southeys joined them and Coleridge deserted for the wandering life of a drug-addict poet. He died at Highgate in 1834.

Meanwhile Southey had been busy building his library of 14,000 books and writing the first history of Brazil without ever visiting the country. He also looked after Coleridge's abandoned family. With two women and eleven children to support, no wonder he took on the Brazil job.

Greta Hall is a handsome, three-storey Georgian building overlooking the town and Borrowdale. It has been part of Keswick School since 1921 and strictly closed to visitors, though you can sneak a look by walking along a lane above the Greta.

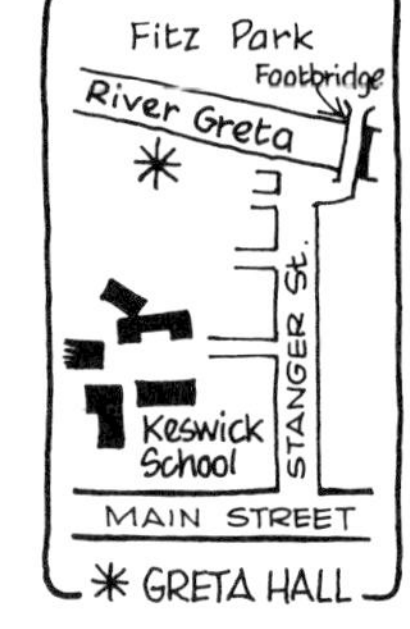

Greta Hall

Brackenburn Lodge

Sir Hugh Walpole (1884-1941)

Born the Bishop of Edinburgh's son in New Zealand, Walpole later divided his time between Borrowdale and London. He wrote 42 novels, most famously the Herries quintet, which has Lakeland settings. Brackenburn, built in 1909, was bought on first sight in 1923. Walpole extended the house several times so he could still see the lake over growing trees. His wide-windowed study is above the garage. Visitors are not admitted.

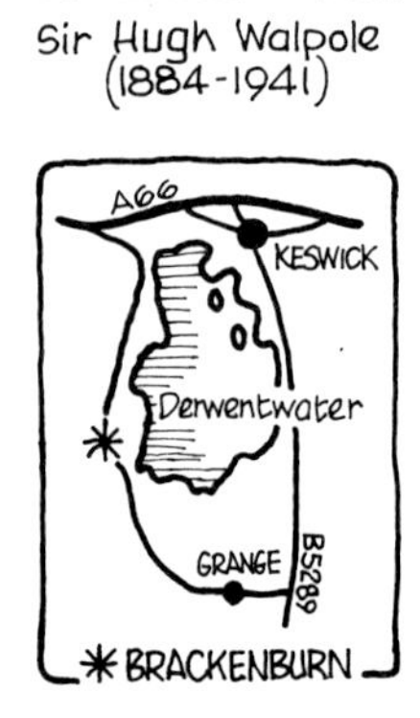

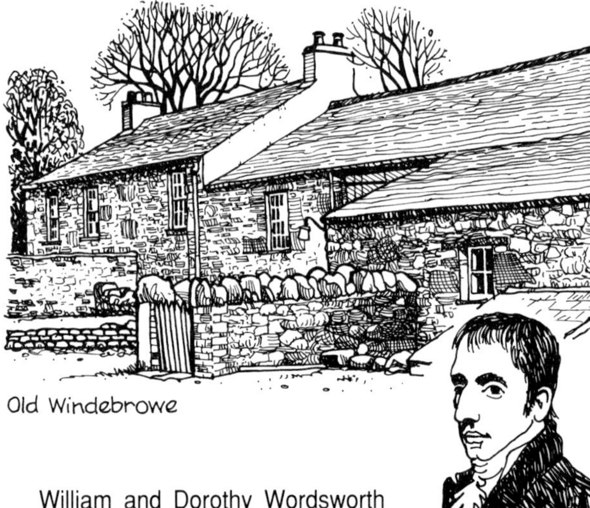
Old Windebrowe

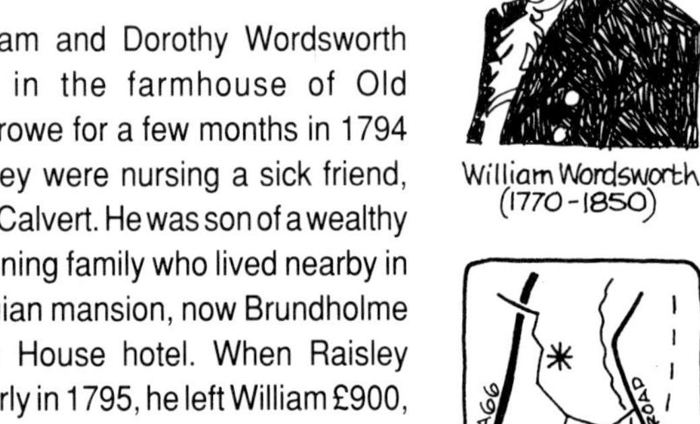
William Wordsworth (1770-1850)

William and Dorothy Wordsworth stayed in the farmhouse of Old Windebrowe for a few months in 1794 while they were nursing a sick friend, Raisley Calvert. He was son of a wealthy land-owning family who lived nearby in a Georgian mansion, now Brundholme Country House hotel. When Raisley died, early in 1795, he left William £900, which enabled him to pursue his career as a serious poet.

Old Windebrowe now belongs to the Calvert Trust which provides adventure holidays for the disabled. All trace of the Wordsworths' unhappy stay has long since disappeared.

A66
BRUNDHOLME Rd
River Greta
PENRITH ROAD
Old railway
STATION ST
✳ OLD WINDEBROWE

ENTERTAINMENT

The ornate Alhambra Cinema, opened in 1913, is Keswick's only red-brick building. With no Lakeland slate to be seen on the building, it would have difficulty these days getting planning permission.

When I was one of Keswick's young cinema-goers we were welcomed by Mr Jack Simpson, resplendent in evening dress. Now owned by the local Graves family, today's Alhambra has a more relaxed, friendly style. A steady supply of current blockbuster films is shown during the summer months.

Alhambra Cinema - St John's Street

Keswick Spa - Station Road

Trumpeted as an 'indoor resort', the Keswick Spa opened its expensive doors in 1987. There was a 'fun pool' with 'real waves', a 'tropical paradise' temperature, and enough junk food to satisfy the unhealthiest of diets.

The venture struggled to survive and in 1989, with rumoured debts of £10 million, it was closed. Allerdale Council has now re-opened the pool but the ghastly building remains, an awful blot on the landscape and a terrible warning for potential developers.

What looks like a collection of abandoned Portakabins in Lakeside Car Park is actually a highly regarded theatre. Formerly a touring group, the company made Keswick its home in 1976 and has been looking for a permanent site ever since. As I write, the enormous sum of money for a new theatre building has not been raised.

However, I found the mood optimistic. Gradual rebuilding will now convert the Portakabins to brick and mortar permanence. Live theatre will continue at Keswick. Hooray!

Century Theatre - Lake Road

TOWN WALK

From Moot Hall take in the variety of shops down the LH side of Main Street to Tithebarn Street. Go round the block, returning past Walter Wilson's supermarket. Cross Main Street into Bank Street. At the top end go through the pretty-gardened housing estate to Fitz Park footbridge.

Visit the museum and pass the ill-fated Spa, then go into Upper Fitz Park. Leave by the footbridge and cross the busy Penrith Road - easier here than at the war memorial.

After more shops in Station Street and St John's Street, rest in the church. Then enjoy great views down Lake Road to boat landings and, if you wish, go on to Friar's Crag.

Retrace your steps back to Hope Park then take the underpass into Lake Road. More assorted shops, then a bar meal in the Dog and Gun will round off a good morning's exploration.

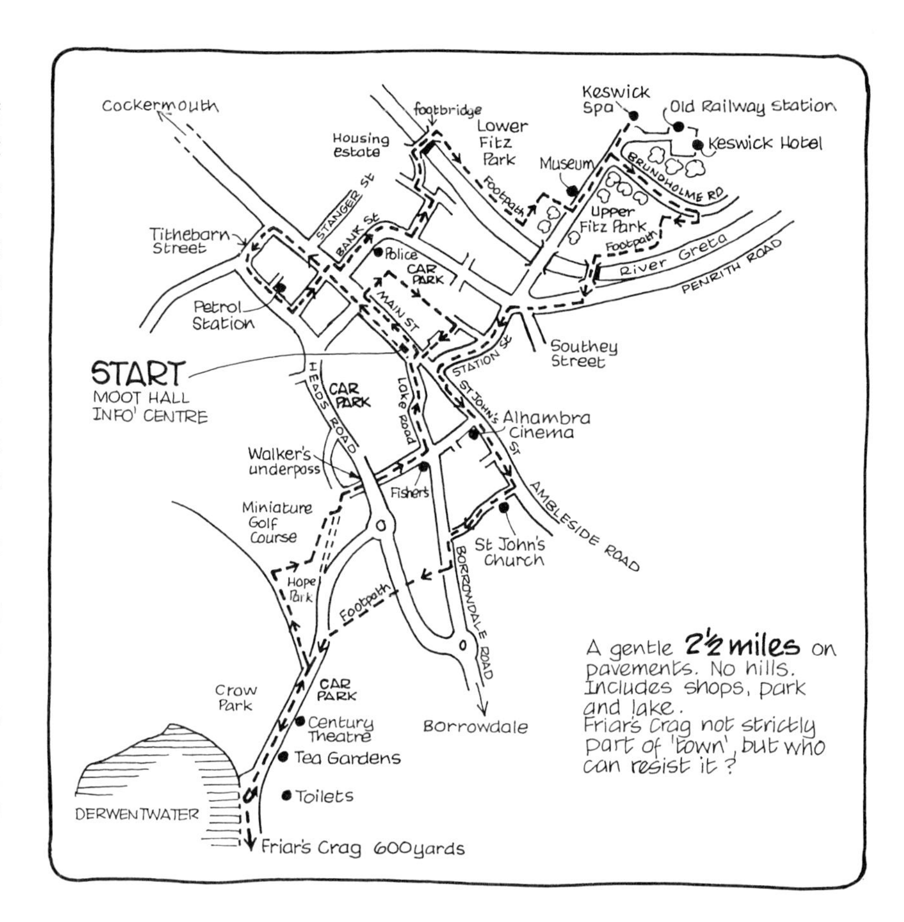

Carlisle
Old Windebrowe
Go between the 2 Calvert Trust buildings and follow the lane down through woods
Brundholme Wood
Crosthwaite Church
Lane
School
A66
Garage
Hospital
Briar Rigg
Roadbridge
Brundholme Rd
Old railway footpath
High Hill
Footpath
River Derwent
River Greta
Spa
Fitz Park
Penrith
Old Railway
Penrith Road
START
Tithebarn Street
Main Street
Chestnut Hill
Heads Road
St John's St
Old Toll House
Caravan Site
Footpath
Manor Brow
Crow Park
Housing Estate
Toilets
Springs Road
Ambleside
Footpath
Boat landings
Castlehead (viewpoint)
Borrowdale Road
Friar's Crag
Footpath
DERWENTWATER
A grand tour of 6¾ miles on roads and good footpaths. Some hills. Take refreshments. Views brilliant. Best town outskirts walk in the Lake District.

OUTSKIRTS WALK

Go down Main Street to Greta Bridge. Turn left before Primavero Restaurant for the footpath across open fields to the suspension bridge at Portinscale. Return along the lane to Crosthwaite Church. Go up the lane past the school to the A66 roundabout. Turn right down the road. At the garage go left along the lane to the railway bridge. Go along the footpath on the embankment to the Spa. Take Brundholme Road to Old Windebrowe. Go down through the wood to the river. Across the bridge turn right for main road. Walk up Chestnut Hill to old toll house. Down Manor Brow take Spring's Road on the left, then the footpath right to the rocky viewpoint of Castlehead. Views are stupendous - get the flask out. Descend to Borrowdale road, go left then take first right onto a well-marked lakeside path. Pass boat landings. Cross Crow Park to Tithebarn Street.

ROUND DERWENTWATER WALK

Begin at the Tithebarn Street corner of Main Street. Over Greta Bridge, go left past Primavero Restaurant for the footpath across open fields to the suspension bridge. Cross into Portinscale village, then follow the road left into a beech wood. At a signpost marked 'Nickol End' go left along a track, then right onto a well-marked woodland route through Brandelhow Park to Manesty Park.

Beyond the caravan site, cross the flat flood plain to Lodore; classic view of 'Jaws of Borrowdale'. Visit the waterfalls behind the Lodore hotel if in spate. You will have seen and heard them if they are.

Return to the road. Use the woodland path on the right-hand side of the road to avoid traffic. At the lakeside car park take the path along the shore to Calfclose bay. Follow the path round onto a wooded outcrop, then on past Stable Hills farm. A well-marked route through the wood takes you to Friar's Crag. Join the crowds on top for superlative views across the lake. Carry on to boat landings. The path through Crow Park returns you and your camera full of memories back to Tithebarn Street.

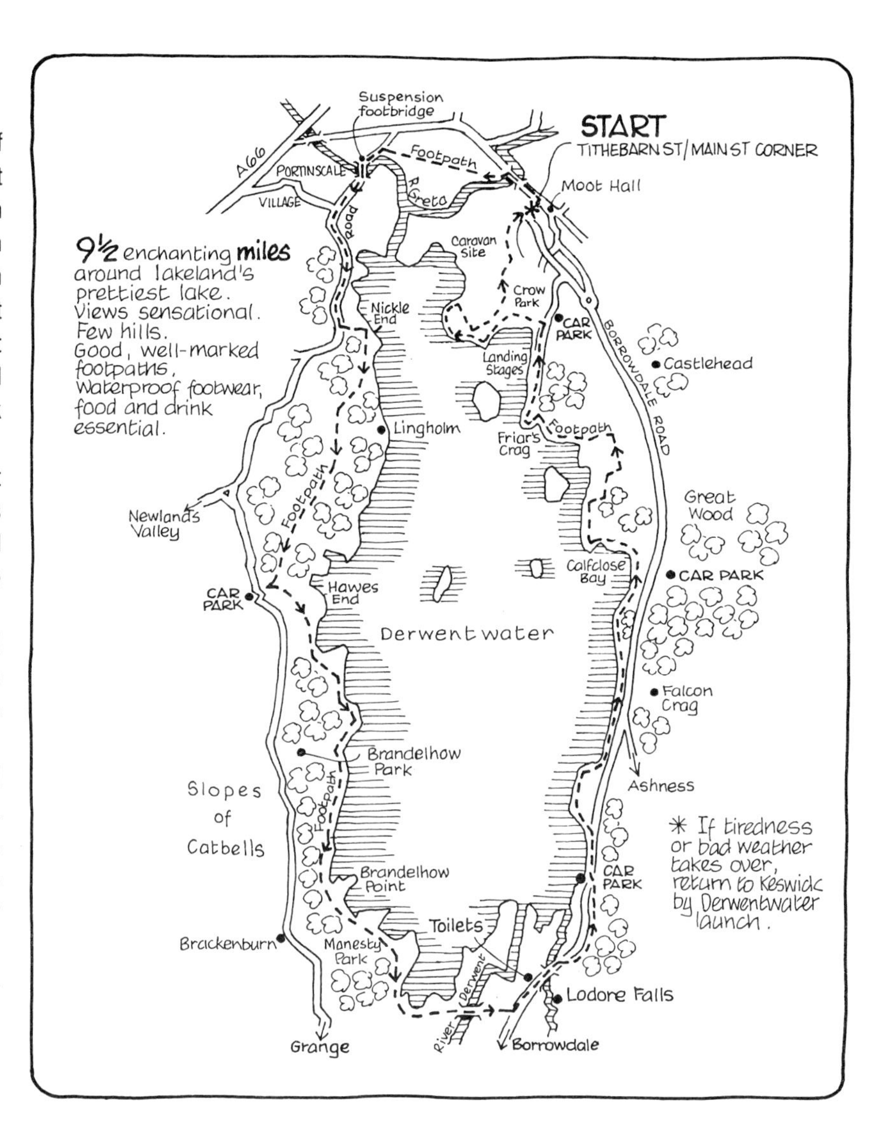

OLD RAILWAY WALK

Follow the track from Keswick station into a wooded gorge of the Greta. The river meanders attractively under steel bowstring bridges. The trees clear for a while then you enter another woodland gorge approaching Threlkeld. When you see the concrete A66 road bridge over the river, go through the wood under the A66 to the old bridge where the two rivers meet.

Walk towards Threlkeld and cross the A66, taking no chances. Continue along the village road to a lane signposted 'Wescoe' which takes you back to Keswick through Brundholme Wood - terrific views. Walk through the wood off Brundholme Road if you prefer. For anyone like me who remembers the trains this can be a sad walk.

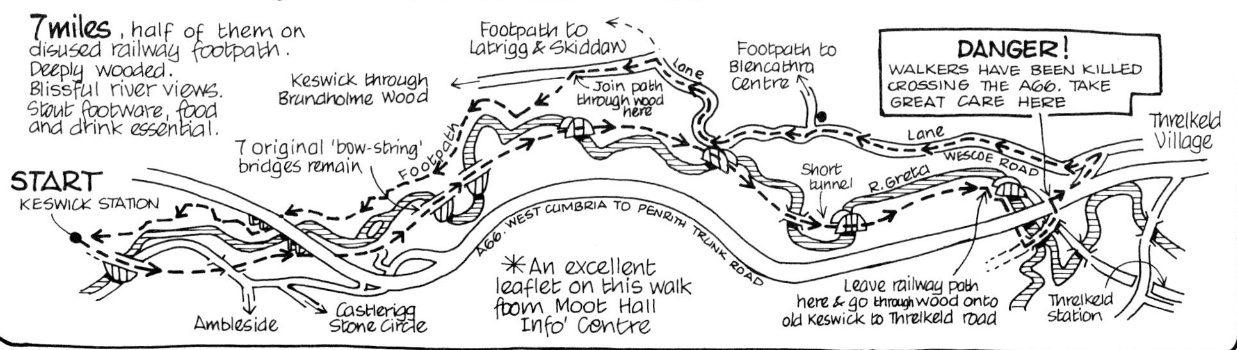

THE KESWICK FELLS

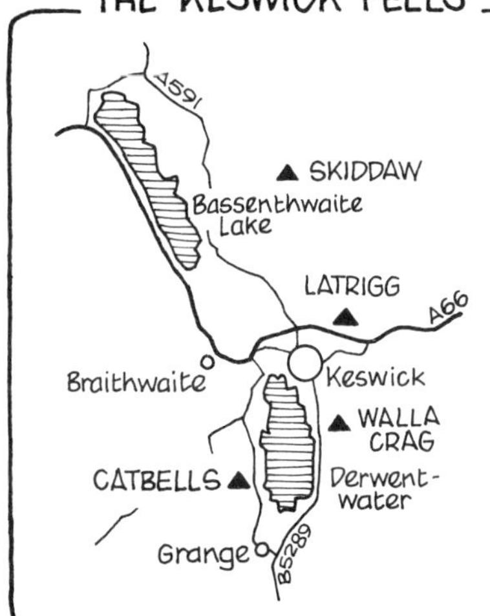

The Keswick experience is incomplete without setting foot on one of the surrounding fells. Whatever your age or fitness, you are well catered for. Superb viewpoints abound. Strong footwear is essential, dress sensibly, and take something to eat and drink.

Watch where you put your feet. According to local mountain rescue statistics, the most common fell accident is a twisted female ankle about four o'clock on a Sunday afternoon.

Walla Crag from the South West

WALLA CRAG - 1234 ft

Though looking unattainable from Borrowdale Road, the top of Walla Crag is easily reached via Spring's Road and Rakefoot. Descend by the same path. Going up Cat Gill is steeper. Return to Great Wood car park by Rakefoot.

A satisfying circular route of about 4½ miles is to precede the Cat Gill route by Friar's Crag lakeside path from Keswick. Leave the top by the Brockle Beck path, visit Castlehead, then take Borrowdale Road back to town.

The dangers of the Walla Crag cliffs will be obvious. Take care.

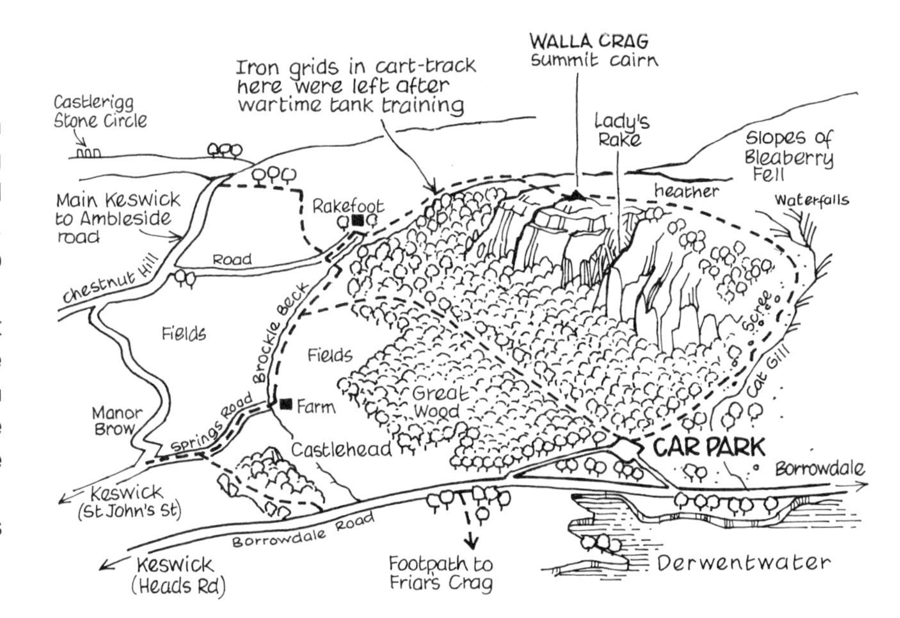

THE VIEW

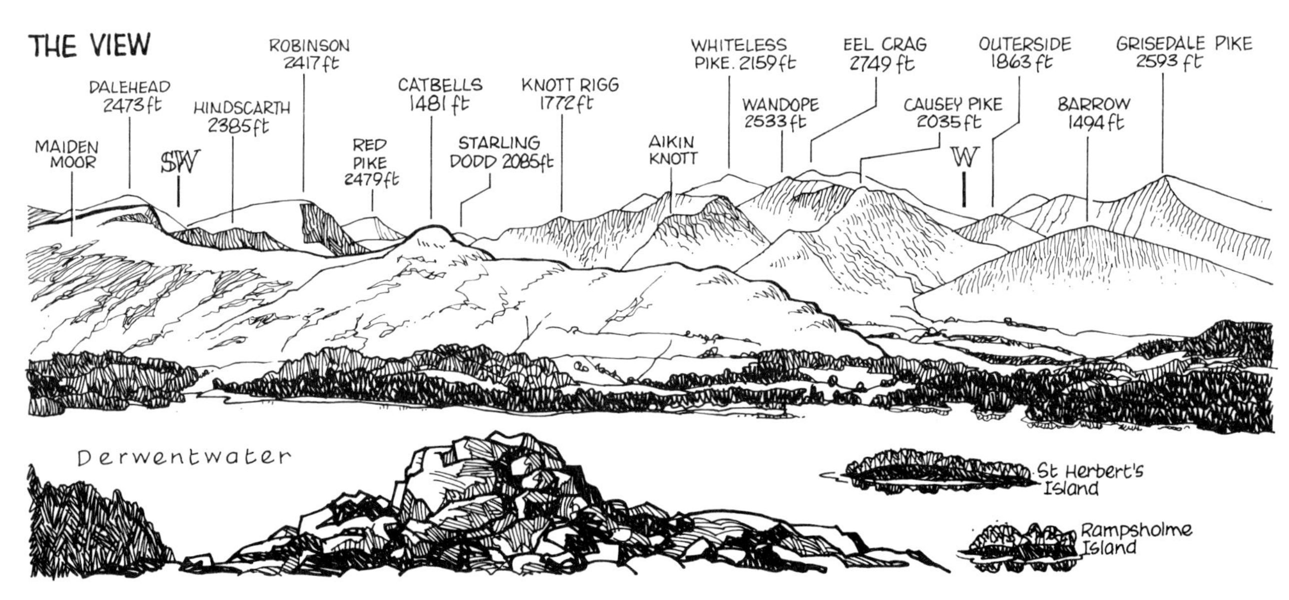

CATBELLS ~ 1481 ft

Everyone loves Catbells. It's great for family walks and picnics. The easy-peasy ascent is from the road at Manesty. At a pair of slate gateposts take the obvious path onto the fell. Pass behind Brackenburn, then up the wooden stairway to Hause Gate. Cross a grassy slope for the easy climb onto the rocky summit.

Best route is from the north end car park. After a steep, sweaty start there's fabulous views from the wide ridge, then a zig-zag climb takes you to the summit.

You can also reach Hause Gate from Little Town in Newlands, along a well-worn miner's track. Boring.

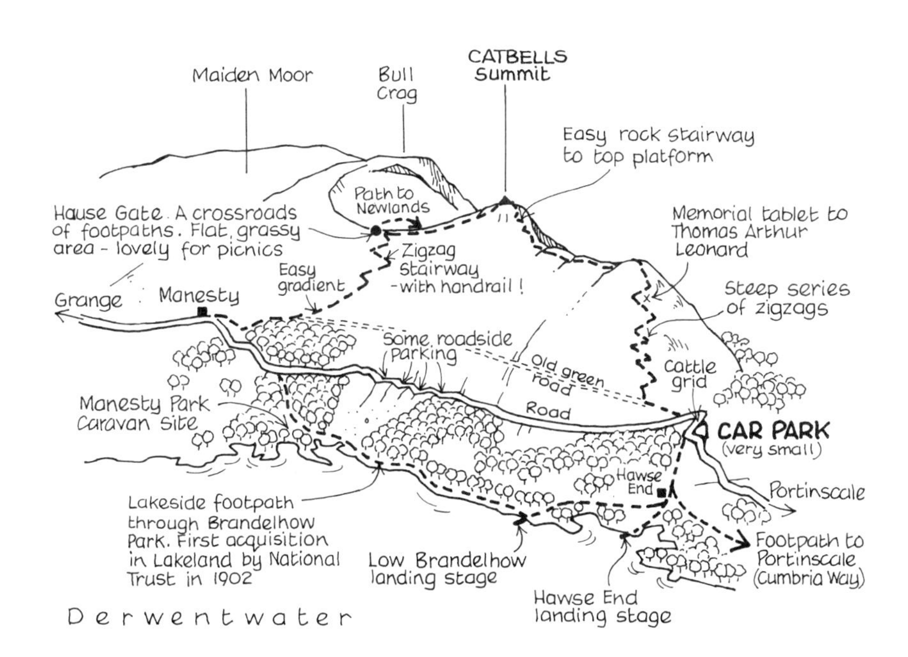

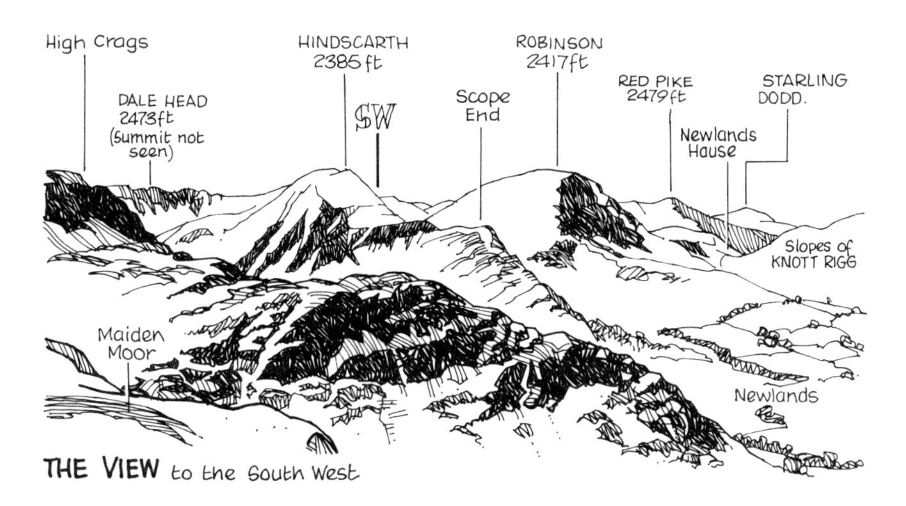

THE VIEW to the South West

Catbells's top get crowded, but the scenery is sensational. When Ruskin maintained that the most aesthetic views are from lowly fells, he must have been thinking of Catbells. Borrowdale, Newlands and Derwentwater all look exquisite. If you climb only one hill at Keswick, let it be Catbells.

For a memorable half-day, combine a launch trip from Keswick to Hawse End with a walk along Catbells's ridge. Descend to Manesty and return to the launch through Brandelhow Park.

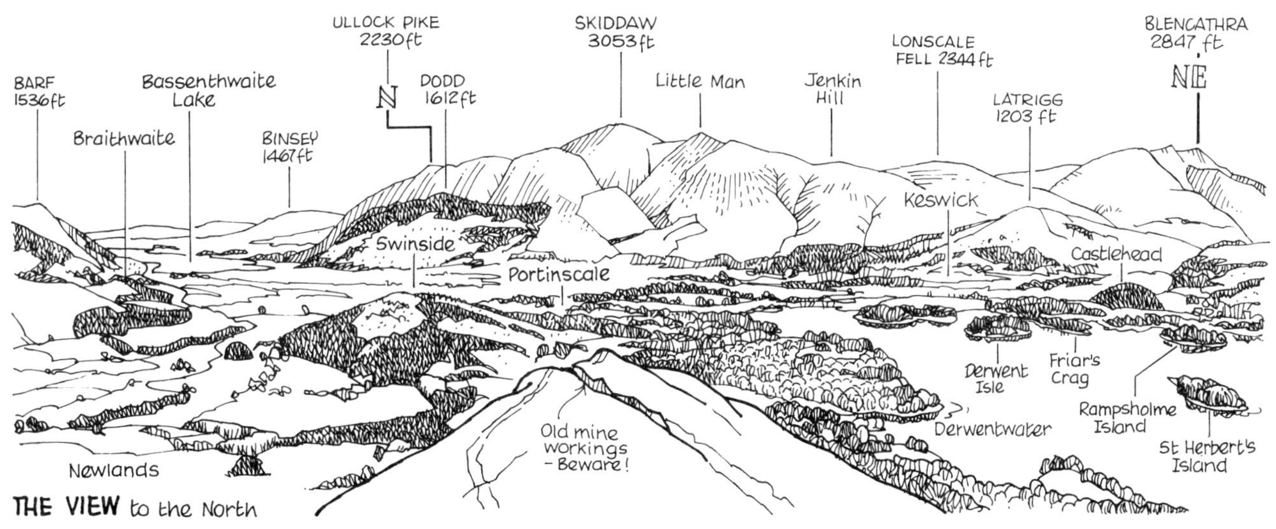

THE VIEW to the North

LATRIGG ~ 1203 ft

A low outcrop of sombre Skiddaw, Latrigg has its own individual, lively character. You can drive up Gale Road nearly to the grassy summit, but if you respect car tyres, you'll walk. It's easy; just follow the lane opposite Briar Rigg housing estate. For a round trip descend the beckside path to Old Windebrowe.

Fell racers at Keswick Sports used to run up and down Latrigg in about 20 minutes. That's rushing it a bit. You need time to take in the incredible panoramic view. Wait for a clear day for Latrigg. You will not be disappointed.

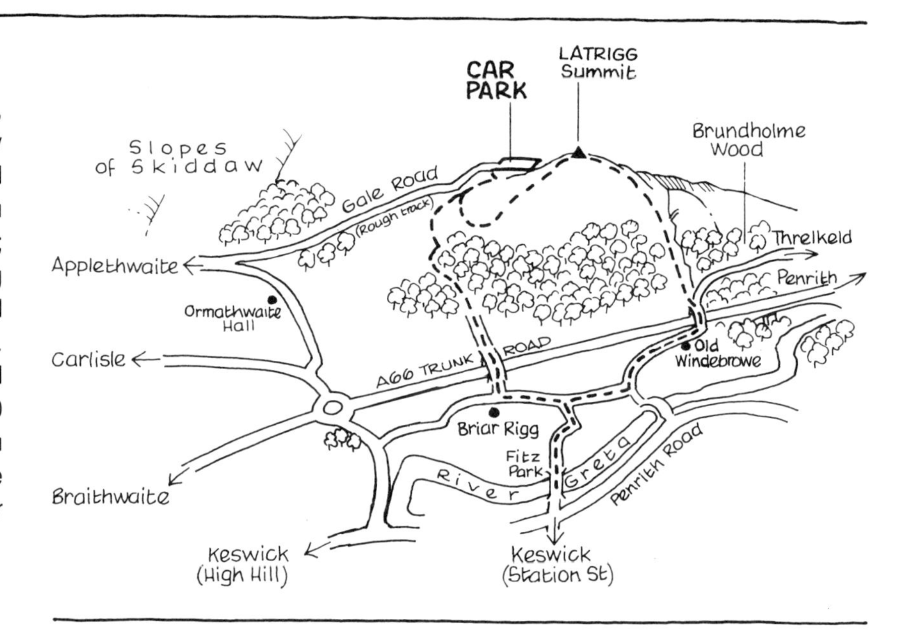

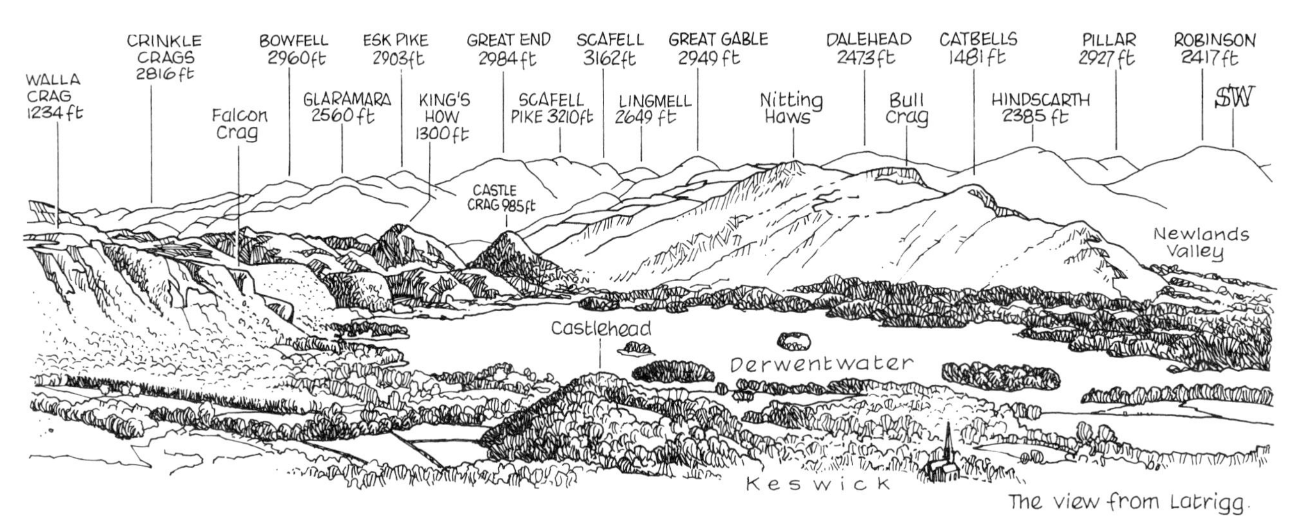

The view from Latrigg.

SKIDDAW ~ 3053 ft

The popular way up Skiddaw begins at Latrigg car park followed by a long, tedious pull up Jenkin Hill. Across the top it's like strolling a country lane until you reach a ruined gateway, then suddenly realise you're on a high mountain. Skiddaw summit ridge can be extremely cold and bleak, even in summer.

The view is extensive but too distant to be interesting. Skiddaw is boringly safe, often climbed just because it's there, but, make no mistake, this is a real mountain.

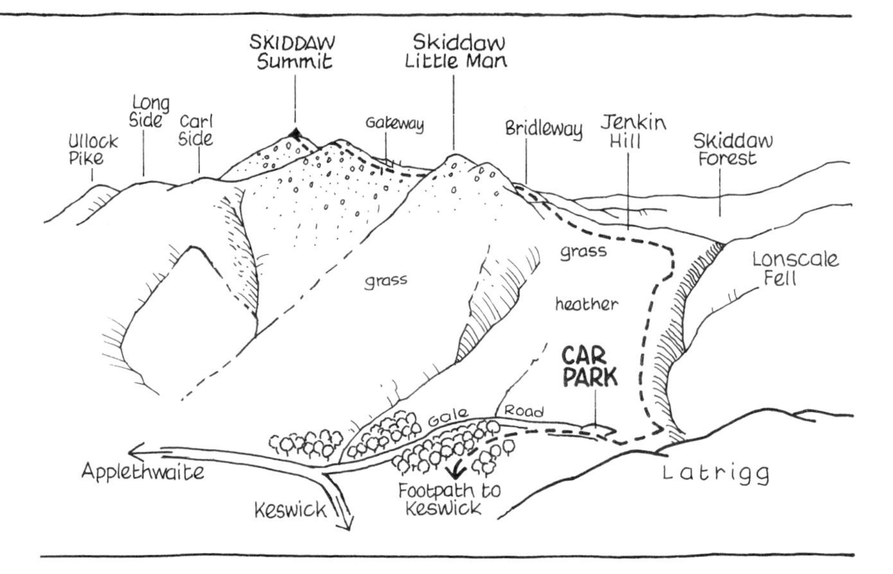

CASTLERIGG STONE CIRCLE

The mysterious Castlerigg Stone Circle stands surrounded by some of Lakeland's finest fells on a grassy plateau 650 feet above the Keswick streets, a setting of spell-binding magnificence.

With such competition I always find the stones themselves slightly underwhelming. To academics, however, they are endlessly fascinating.

Latrigg & Skiddaw

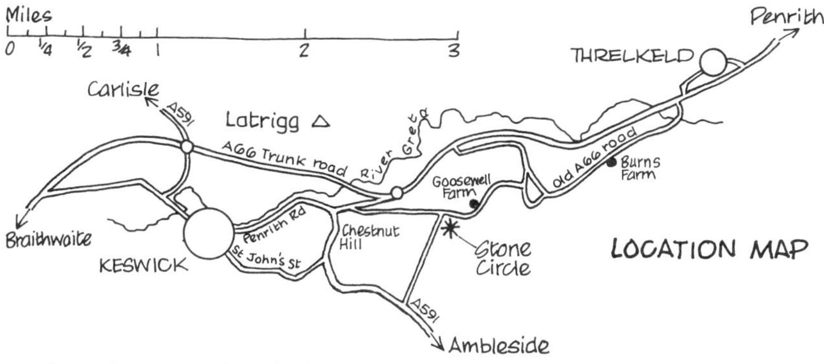

Castlerigg consists of 38 stones - Stukely counted 50 in 1725. The tallest is 7½ feet, average height is 3 feet. They are set in a rough circle of 30 yards diameter. Another 10 stones are arranged in a rectangular enclosure inside the south-east side. This is unique to Castlerigg. No other stone circle has an enclosure. Excavations within it during 1881 revealed - surprise, surprise! - soil and stones.

Three stone axes have been found within the circle, but no trace of organic matter.

The mystery goes on.

As early as 1725, Lincolnshire antiquarian William Stukely established that this is not a 'Druids' circle, though the name still persists locally.

The precise purpose of stone circles remains a mystery, despite many elaborate and fanciful theories. Even dating is difficult. Castlerigg is thought to be about 5,000 years old. The stones themselves are glacial erratics dating from 14,000 years ago.

One thing is certain - it's old.

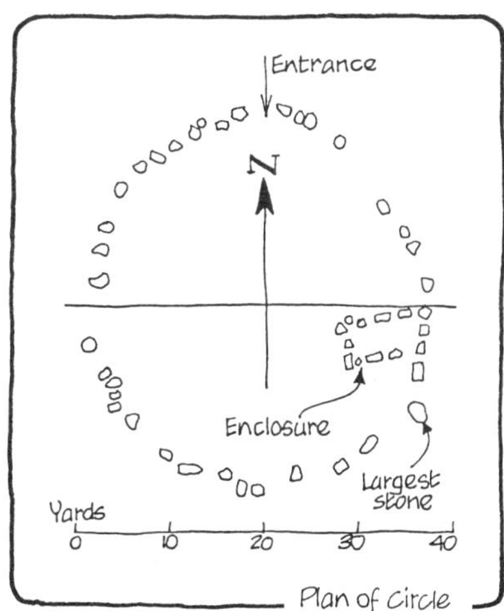

Plan of Circle

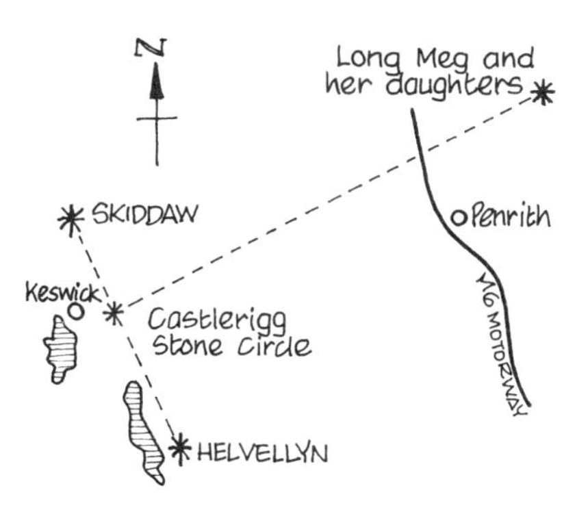

Blencathra

There are some strange oddities about the Castlerigg setting. A line drawn on a modern map between the two highest visible summits - Skiddaw and Helvellyn - passes through the stone circle's centre. Another line drawn eastwards at right angles to the first, goes through another stone circle, Long Meg, 20 miles away.

I find this creepy. Castlerigg can do that. You get caught up in the mystery.

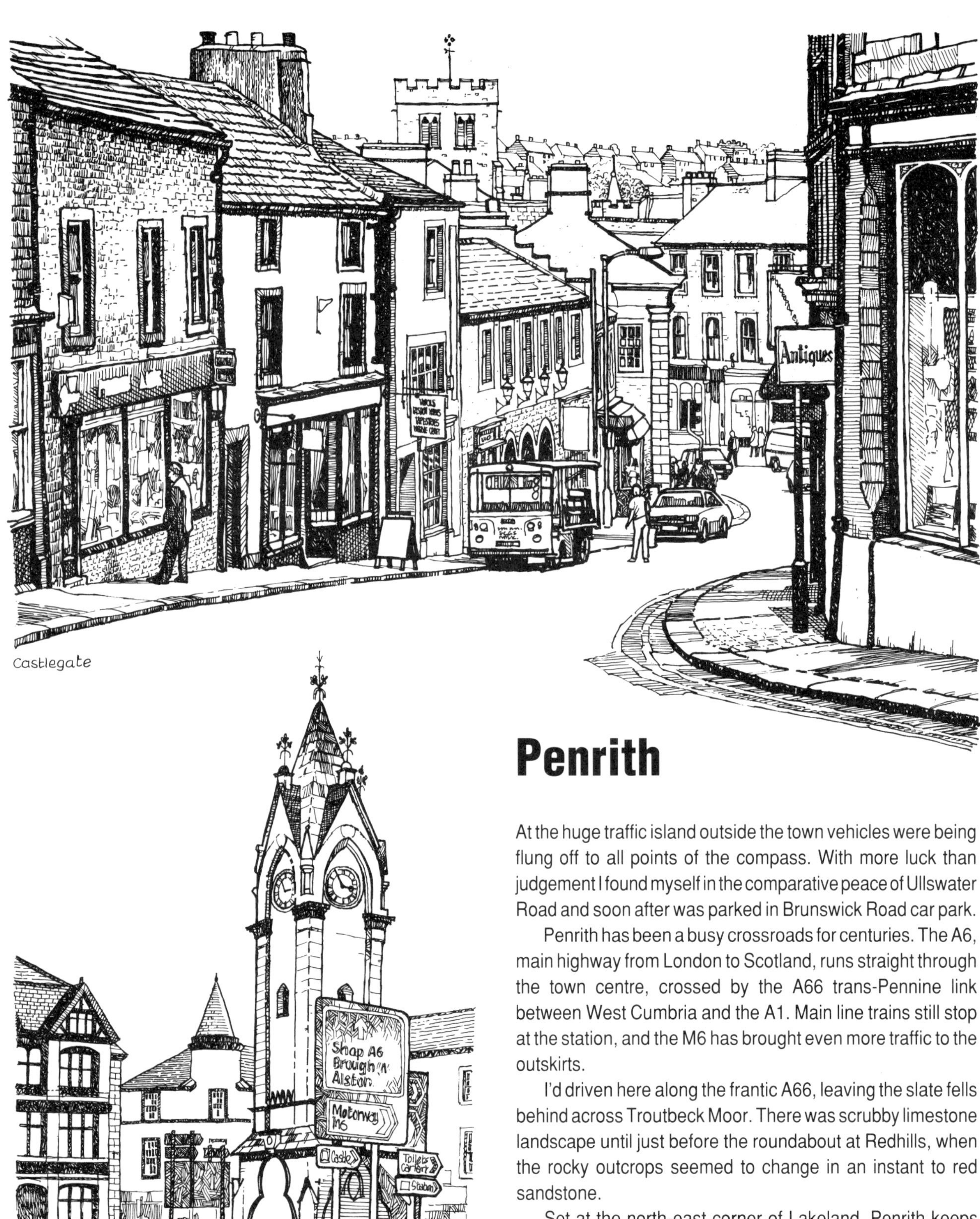

Castlegate

Old & new - Musgrave Monument & Angel Lane

Penrith

At the huge traffic island outside the town vehicles were being flung off to all points of the compass. With more luck than judgement I found myself in the comparative peace of Ullswater Road and soon after was parked in Brunswick Road car park.

Penrith has been a busy crossroads for centuries. The A6, main highway from London to Scotland, runs straight through the town centre, crossed by the A66 trans-Pennine link between West Cumbria and the A1. Main line trains still stop at the station, and the M6 has brought even more traffic to the outskirts.

I'd driven here along the frantic A66, leaving the slate fells behind across Troutbeck Moor. There was scrubby limestone landscape until just before the roundabout at Redhills, when the rocky outcrops seemed to change in an instant to red sandstone.

Set at the north-east corner of Lakeland, Penrith keeps well out of the tourist mainstream. The friendly old town is no worse for that. I was born here and spent much of my childhood in the surrounding area. In Brunswick Road I treated myself to some home-made toffee from the same shop where my Granny used to buy me it forty years ago.

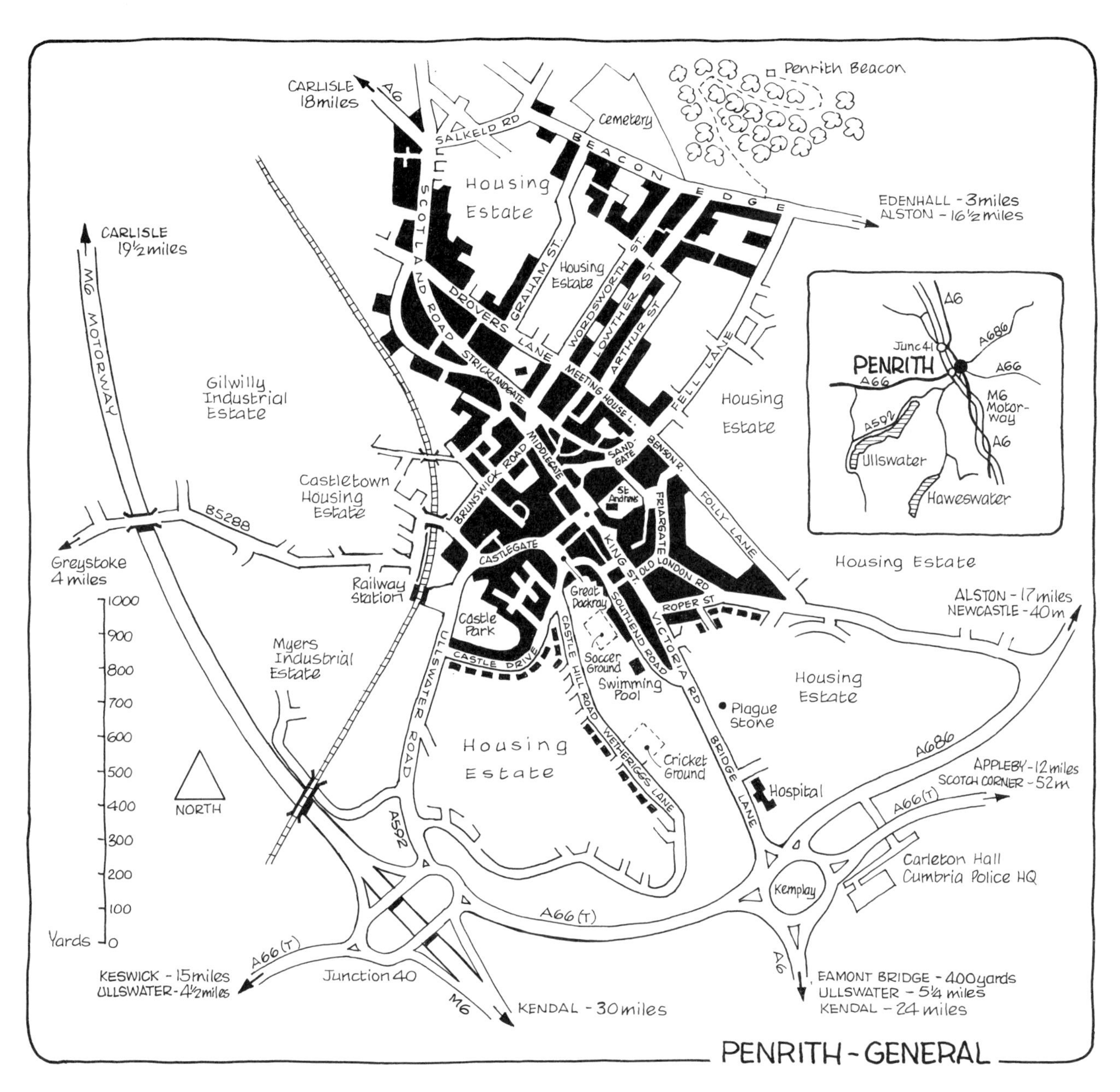

PENRITH - GENERAL

Penrith lies in a shallow open-ended valley that stretches northwards from the River Eamont towards Carlisle. Castle ruins on the west side of town look across to the Beacon, a familiar landmark set on a tree-covered hill.

Despite being hemmed in by the network of ugly roads and large ever-spreading housing and industrial estates, the old town centre is a delight to explore. For senses dulled by pretty-pretty scenery, Penrith is the perfect antidote.

Victoria Road

Penrith has a long and often violent history. Once part of Scotland, the town was seized for England by Edward I in 1295. Fifteen years of border skirmishing followed. Penrith was burnt to the ground three times. The marauders were finally brought to heel by a garrison of troops stationed in specially re-built Penrith Castle. Today's town layout, a confusion of small squares and yards connected by narrow streets, passages and alleys, developed as a defence against border raids.

Sucking contentedly on treacle toffee, I began my exploration at the north end of town, where the architecture is as rich as the warm red sandstone. Stricklandgate is named after William Strickland, the 14th century Bishop of Carlisle who re-built Penrith Castle. There are six churches here, of all denominations from Roman Catholic to the Salvation Army. The United Reform church in Duke Street used to be attended by Mary Wilson, wife of the former Prime Minister. Her family have long associations with Penrith.

The beautiful Adam-style town hall was originally two houses built in 1791. William Wordsworth's cousin lived in one of them. They were converted to municipal use in 1905 with an original staircase and fireplace retained.

Junction of Stricklandgate & Duke Street. United Reform Church nearby

Corney Square & Town Hall

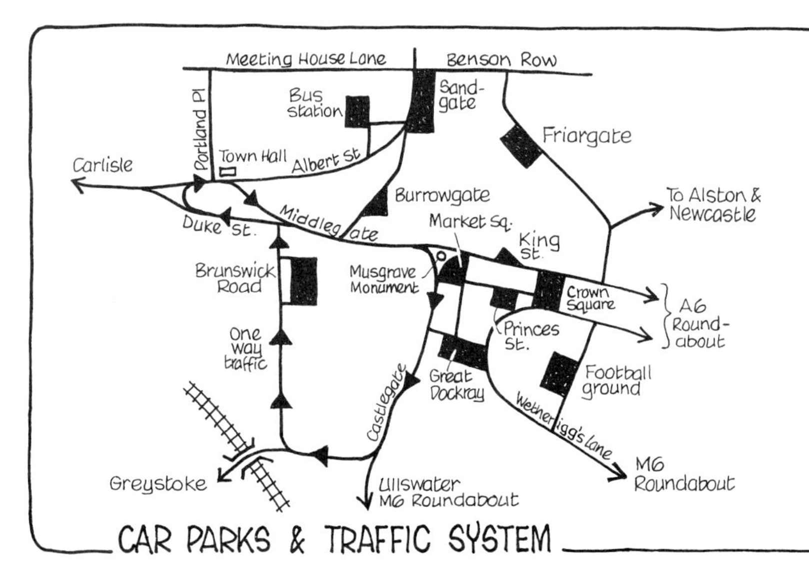

CAR PARKS & TRAFFIC SYSTEM

Penrith is no pleasure for motorists. I can't get used to the one-way roads. Going round a mile-long gyratory system two or three times to find somewhere to park is no way to enjoy a town. The squares seem to be perpetually filled with cars of local workers. Well it *is* their town. These days I settle for parking behind Brunswick Road school and walking. It's handy for shops and most of the Penrith goodies.

Junction of Albert Street & Queen Street

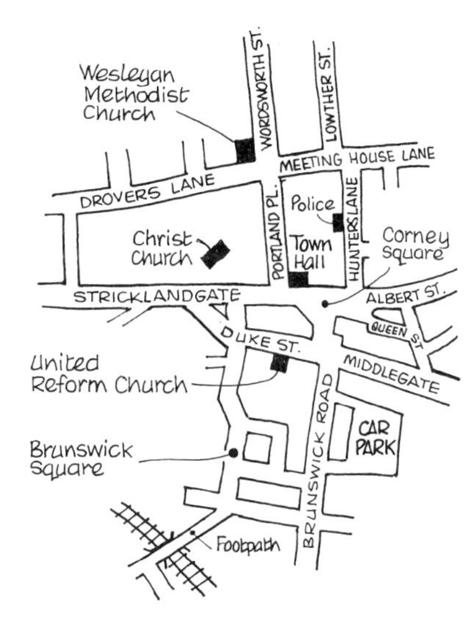

Brunswick Square & Christ Church

A quaint house-end separates Queen Street and Albert Street like the bow of a ship. It has a chimney intriguingly-placed directly above four windows. Where does it go inside the house? Queen Street used to be called Fallowfield Bridge when it was the main entrance from the north. There's still a slight hump in the road where the town's only beck flows underneath.

I was born at 30 Brunswick Square, an ordinary house that served as a private nursing home in those impoverished pre-NHS days. It cost 12 guineas for a fortnight's confinement. Quite a sum in 1942. Quite a confinement too, compared with today's lightning turnrounds.

Wesleyan Methodist Church

Christ Church

Now lined by rather characterless shops, Middlegate used to be inhabited by weavers, tanners, and tailors. The entrance to William's Yard, near Woolworth's has a lintel marked with a pair of shears and the date 1697.

Musgrave Hall was once the town house of the Musgraves of Edenhall, who were great Penrith benefactors. Their family coat-of-arms is on the building. In the 1920s it belonged to Countess Ossalinsky. Her family sold Thirlmere lake to Manchester Corporation as a water supply. Stand outside the hall and hiss if you wish. Careful though, it is now a British Legion club and could be packed with highly-trained fighting men.

The door lintel of Robinson's School displays the date of 1670, though the building may be older than that. Its founder, Penrith-born William Robinson, died in 1660 after making his fortune in London. He left £55 a year to the town, £20 of it to go specifically for 'education and upbringing of girls'. They were housed on the school's upper floor and were taught the three Rs, plus spinning and weaving. Boys were kept out until 1770.

Robinson's School

The poorest scholars wore badges lettered PS that allowed them to beg in the streets. They all had a miserable time, enduring eleven-hour working days and frequent beatings. A new 'rod of chastisement' was provided every week. Schooling of a less brutal nature carried on here until 1970.

The old schoolroom has recently been extended and now houses Eden Council's tourist information centre and museum. It was opened in 1989. I wasn't impressed by the mock-Elizabethan style extension. Penrith has few modern eyesores. This is one too many.

Thacka Beck runs behind the information centre courtyard. The four-miles long watercourse flows under much of the old town. It was cut by hand in 1382 from the River Pettril, north of the town, to the River Eamont in the south, as a clean water supply. Penrith has no natural stream or river.

Devonshire Street

Middlegate constantly throbs with vehicles stopping and starting for traffic lights at the 12 feet wide 'Narrows', said to be the narrowest road passage between London and Glasgow. It's a miracle how the tall buildings still stand after the years of shaking they've had.

Close by there's a toy and cycle shop, a warren of narrow passages and little rooms, all packed with an incredible selection of boxed toys and games. Finding your way out is a game in itself.

Middlegate

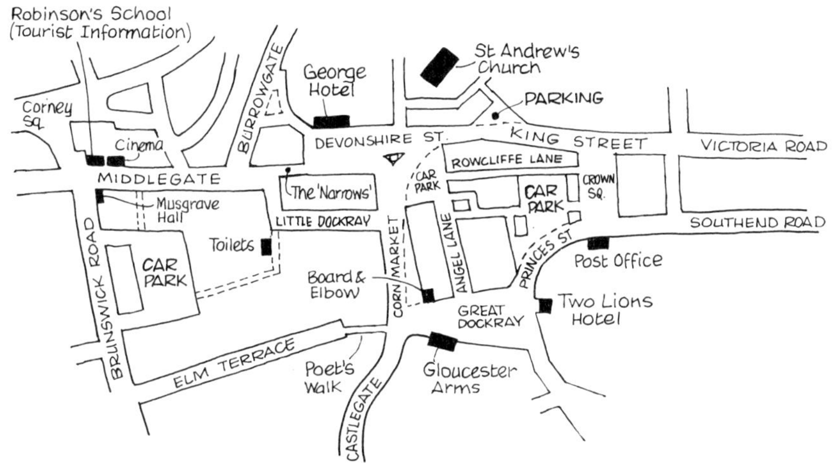

Shaking, I emerged from the Narrows into Devonshire Street, which has bustled with activity since Henry III granted Penrith a market charter in 1223.

At the north end, where there was once a Moot Hall consisting of five shops and a courtroom with prison underneath, Arnison's store now stands. A wall plaque says Wordsworth's grandparents, William and Ann Cookson, 'lived here'. That isn't strictly correct; they lived in an earlier building on this site.

The distinctive Musgrave Monument stands at the other end of the broad street. Architectural critic Pevsner, dismissed it as 'utterly insignificant'. Not to local people, who affectionately refer to the landmark as 't' Clock'.

It was erected by public subscription in 1861 as a memorial to Phillip Musgrave, eldest son of the town's benefactor family, who died tragically, aged 26, in Spain.

During the 18th century the Market Cross stood here. It was a simple shelter used as a butter and egg market, where itinerant traders sold spices and hardware from stone slabs and 'Hirelings' gathered looking for farm work.

A group of shops nearby, known as the Roundabout, was demolished around 1900 to be replaced by the Midland Bank. All three Devonshire Street banks compete for attention with wildly differing architectural styles. Barclays goes way over the top with sandstone Gothic. National Provincial is cool in white marble. Most handsome is the classical-style Midland.

Railings outside the bank are oddly bent and twisted, the result of generations of local men leaning on them, 'hevn't t' crack' (gossiping). On market days the railings are regularly lined by farmers. Wags used to say it was so they could be close to their money. With the state of modern farming I doubt whether there's still any truth in that.

The street is named after the Dukes of Devonshire, who owned the George Hotel, a solemn sandstone building where Charles Stuart stayed in 1745 on his way south to claim the English throne. An archway next to the George leads to the Market Arcade, built in 1860 for stalls and extended in 1866 for public and political meetings. I found it a bit dilapidated and under threat of demolition, though I've heard since it has been rescued and a wrought iron walkway erected outside. I don't think I want to see that.

The Narrows

George Hotel

King Street looks much as it did 100 years ago, though old photographs of the time show most of the buildings on the eastern side were either hotels or garages.

Lloyd's Bank now occupies the site of the cottage where an unfortunate carrier of the plague lodged in 1597. A third of Penrith's population followed him to a mass grave on Beacon Side.

Mitre House in King Street, has a datestone of 1669 and a large British Legion wall plaque states Trooper William Pearson (1828-1903) lived here and survived the 1854 Charge of the Light Brigade at Balaclava. The building is now occupied by Mounsey's solicitors. Alas, too late for Trooper Pearson. After that infamous cavalry charge he could have used a good solicitor.

King Street

Two Lions Hotel

The Cornmarket

West of the Clock is the Cornmarket, where rye, oats, barley and wheat used to be sold outside the inns. In 1983, an unpleasant public toilet was replaced by the splendid Market Cross. This is no more than a Westmorland slated roof supported on wooden pillars, similar to one that once stood where the Clock now is. But it's effective and beautiful, and enthusiastically used by market traders, the town band, and love-struck teenagers.

Nearby, the Board and Elbow Inn guards the corner into Great Dockray like an impenetrable fortress. Wonderfully atmospheric inside with good pub grub.

In the 18th century, Great Dockray was the town's beast market and entertainment centre. There's still a market here on Tuesdays. No beasts, but the entertainment's good.

Gerald Lowther's town house is now the Two Lions Hotel, dated 1585, probably older, with mysterious passages and stairs, and a beautiful plaster ceiling in the bar.

The Market Cross, Board & Elbow and Great Dockray

Penrith's horrid traffic system sweeps through the Cornmarket and roars determinedly up steep Castlegate, passing a trio of elegant arches, the entrance to a pedestrian way of pretty little craft shops. Poet's Walk is probably too quiet, too out of the way for mega-business, but nevertheless an attractive contrast to the great hulking buildings on Castlegate.

Poet's Walk

Castlegate

Angel Lane connects Great Dockray and the Market Square. The narrow street once had dressmakers, confectioners, boot dealers, and iron-mongers, but by the beginning of the 1980s it had become a rather dark and depressing part of town. Then a large draper's shop was demolished and a new pedestrian area of shops built. Angel Square is now one of Penrith's busiest and most attractive areas.

The Angel Square development is only about a dozen shops, but that keeps it human-scaled and friendly. Victorian-style buildings are painted in a variety of pastel colours and the overall effect is not unlike strolling about a stage set. It's almost Dickensian at one end where there's a fruit shop barrow and an attractive old archway. I wouldn't have been surprised if a gang of raga-muffins had come dancing round the corner, belting out choruses from 'Oliver'.

Angel Square

Angel Square

Angel Square has an excellent bookshop, 'largest in Cumbria', says their advertising. There's certainly plenty of books, which is the main thing, and all the latest titles. They overflow the shelves onto piles on tables and even on the floor. Perfect for a good old browse.

There's a more clinical approach to bookselling at a W.H. Smith's store across the way, but their presence, with other chain stores names, seems to assure the development's future. Good.

Rowcliffe Lane, which runs parallel to the shopping area, was once the main street into town where wagons and later stage coaches used to rumble. Incredible, considering it's only eight feet wide in places. The main post office was situated here, also tailors, coopers, saddlers, rope-makers and whitesmiths. Today the lane is mainly back entrances and storerooms for the King Street shops, but there are still one or two signs of its busy industrial past.

Penrith's modern post office stands in Crown Square at the lane end. The King Street side of the square used to be the Crown Hotel, but when it was bought by a large supermarket chain, the fine old facade was removed. There's now a three-storey-high blank wall right across one side of Crown Square. It looks appalling.

Angel Square from Princes Street

Rowcliffe Lane

The traffic was getting on my nerves and the toffee had run out, so I relaxed in the soothing ambiance of the aromatic blossom trees and tranquil Georgian architecture of St Andrew's Church Close.

The sandstone church looks quite grand, very square, like a huge slab of rich brown fruitcake. It was built between 1720 and 1722, incorporating the west tower from an earlier building. There are three galleries inside supported on Tuscan columns. Two brass chandeliers were given to the townsfolk by the Duke of Portland for their support in the 1745 Jacobite rebellion.

St Andrew's Church

Main entrance

The Giant's Grave consists of two 11th century stone crosses connected by four hogback tombstones. It was once alleged to be the resting place of Owen Caesaries, King of Cumbria in AD 900. Whether it is, or indeed if the person buried here was almost twelve feet tall as the length of the grave suggests, continues to be a mystery. As a child, I never had any doubts that there was a giant down there. I've still not seen any evidence that there isn't.

Giant's Grave

An ugly rectangular monument, topped by sharp pinnacles and tightly enclosed in the churchyard by iron railings, commemorates the Superintendent of the 1844 construction of the Carlisle to Lancaster railway. The designer can't have been a train spotter.

The Giant's Thumb at the main gateway is the remains of a Saxon cross. It has been dated AD 920, which suggests that there has been a church here for a long time, perhaps even 1,500 years, ever since St Ninian brought Christianity to the area.

Giant's Thumb

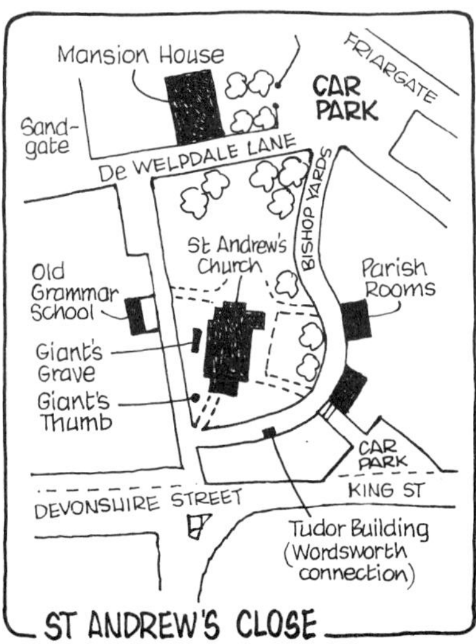

ST ANDREW'S CLOSE

The lane at the east end of the church close is named after John de Whelpdale, one of the original governors of Penrith's free grammar school, which was founded by Royal Charter in 1564. Today's plain and simple building replaced the old schoolroom on the same site in 1857. The events are recorded in Latin on stone scrolls above the door. In 1915, the school was moved to a new, neo-Georgian building in Ullswater Road.

Old Grammar School

North-west corner of the Close

Bishop's Yards curves round the south side of the close, with a modern Job Centre at its bottom end and the ancient Tudor building at the top (See page 145). A Georgian town house is now a solicitor's practice. The imposing Church Rooms stand on the site of a cock-fighting pit where raucous crowds reputedly drowed out the vicar's sermons in the church.

De Welpdale Lane

Bishop Yards

Burrowgate and Sandgate are the town's oldest streets, going back to the 13th century. Burrowgate had a horse market and rows of open butcher's shops, known as the 'Shambles'.

Forty years ago this was one of the town's busiest shopping areas. All one side of the street was taken up by the little shops of the local Co-operative Society: a grocers, butchers, bakers, even a chemist. Folks stood about outside chatting in friendly groups. As a small boy, I stood about with my Granny, who was a formidable chatterer.

Burrowgate

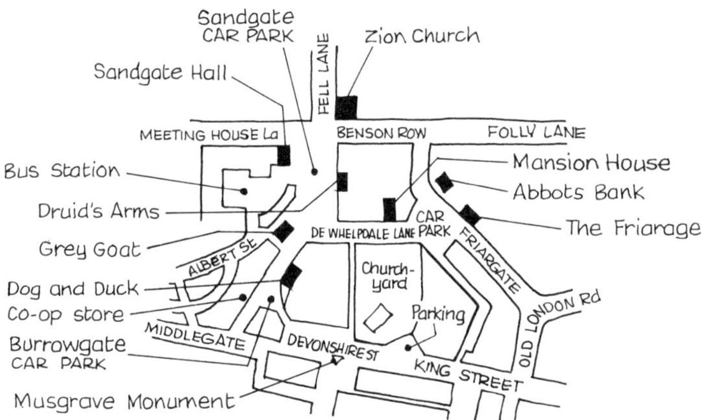

Now the Co-op is isolated from the street, nobody stands outside chatting. However, I found a much happier scene across the street, where brightly coloured fruit and vegetables were displayed across the broad pavement.

The Dog and Duck Inn next door is painted black and white like many of Penrith's pubs. In 1829 the town had 57 public houses for a population of 5,383. And you still couldn't get a seat.

Inside the Co-op, there was a series of mysterious hissing pipes rising up from each of the counters. An assistant put Granny's money into a small canister, which, with a satisfied gasp of compressed air, was sucked into a network of pipes spreading across the ceiling.

After a short wait, when the weather was discussed, various illnesses diagnosed and surprise shown over how much I'd grown, the canister clattered back across the ceiling and dropped out of the pipe into a wire basket. There inside was Granny's change. Amazing.

All's different today. The Co-op is one huge store with its ground floor windows blanked out and doors only at each end, 100 yards apart.

Burrowgate

Burrowgate opens out into Sandgate, peaceful these days but it once rang horribly with the sound of bear baiting. Penrith was well-known for its ferocious bull terriers. Baying crowds were kept well lubricated at inns around the square. Three that have survived are now eminently respectable and serve generous portions of no-nonsense pub grub.

The acres of parked cars gave the square a dreadful lifeless atmosphere. I can remember Sandgate when it was the town's bus terminus and full of movement. Excited queues of people climbed aboard red double-deckers to exotic-sounding places such as Lazonby or Shap. There were great white stratocruiser coaches roaring powerfully away to foreign parts: Newcastle or Manchester.

Sandgate

Grey Goat

As a small boy I used to wait for the bus to Pooley Bridge outside a YMCA club at the bottom end of Sandgate. In summer, the games room windowsills were usually draped with teenage boys chatting up girls in bus queues. With their undone ties, drooping cigarettes, and billiard cues held at rakish angles, these lads were sophisticated role models to my impressionable eight-year old mind. Unfortunately, before I was old enough to enjoy the club's dubious pleasures it was demolished. However, that has revealed an interesting part of old Penrith behind the Market Hall.

A row of three houses at the square's top left corner was once Sandgate Hall, the town house of the Fletcher family, who owned Hutton-in-the-Forest. In 1745, the Duke of Richmond stayed here while engaged in despatching Bonnie Prince Charlie back to Scotland. They almost met face to face at Penrith. Only a month earlier, the Young Pretender had made The George Hotel his first headquarters in England.

Sandgate Hall

Druid's Arms

Zion Church

Friargate isn't pretty. A bleak car park overlooked by gaping backyards, it is named after a contemplative Friary that was established here in 1291 by Augustinian Friars from Newcastle. When Henry the Eighth shattered their peace by demanding an Oath of Supremacy from all religious orders, they joined the 1536 rebellion against him. Three years later the king took terrible revenge on other local conspirators, so the friars hurriedly left town, never to return.

Abbot's Bank

No trace of the Friary remains. The Friarage, a house with leaded windows, was built on the same site in 1717 and is still in excellent order. A restaurant, Abbot Bank, now stands where the Abbot's house was. When the foundations were being dug in 1820, parts of the Friary and the remains of buried friars were uncovered.

The Friarage

Cottage dated 1716 in Benson Row

The handsome Mansion House was built in 1750 for the De Whelpdale family. Screened by huge beech trees, the Georgian-style building has been headquarters of Eden District Council since 1919. I found it being heavily picketed by members of NALGO, who were dedicatedly following the example set by the friars all those years ago and rebelling against a modern authoritarian imposition - the Poll Tax.

Mansion House

THE WORDSWORTH CONNECTION

William Wordsworth must have been profoundly affected by two tragic deaths at Penrith. Had they not happened he may never have written a worthwhile word.

The first death was that of his mother, Ann. After catching a chill on a visit to London, she was returning home early to Cockermouth when her condition worsened at Penrith. She was taken to her father's house in Devonshire Street but died later. An entry in Penrith's 1778 parish register reads tersely: 'March 11th - Mrs Wordsworth, wife of John Wordsworth, Esq, of Cockermouth, aged 30. Buried.' The site of her grave is unknown. William was almost eight years old. A year later he was banished to school at Hawkshead, separated from his brothers and his beloved sister, Dorothy.

Tragedy again hit the four Wordsworth children five years later at Cockermouth. Their father caught a chill while riding through Lorton Dale and subsequently died aged 42. Dorothy came to live in Penrith with an uncle, and William continued in Mrs Tyson's care at Hawkshead.

But their unhappy relationship with Penrith was not yet over. Fifteen years later, in 1794, they were nursing a consumptive friend, Raisley Calvert, at Keswick. After deciding that his recovery would be helped by a warmer climate, the Wordsworths set off with him for Lisbon. Unfortunately they only got as far as the Robin Hood Inn in Penrith, where young Raisley died. A demise strikingly similar to that of their mother.

Tudor Building

Robin Hood Inn

Apart from a couple of blue plaques Penrith does little to foster its Wordsworthian connections. When William was five years old and staying with his grandparents, he attended Anne Birkett's dame school in St Andrew's Place. It was here he first met local tobacconist's daughter, Mary Hutchinson, who became his wife 27 years later. Part of the picturesque school building is preserved behind the Tudor Cafe, but there is no reference to Wordsworth anywhere in the sandstone remains. Now if it had been in Grasmere...

The poet's last recorded visit to Penrith was with his daughter, Dora. She wrote in her diary about attending a ball with her father, who was then aged 42. Funny, I can never picture William dancing.

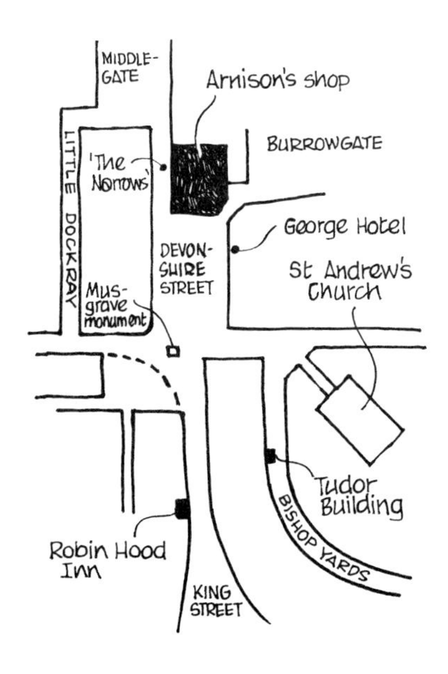

East of Eden ~ Angel Lane

Chemist ~ Middlegate

Penrith has some wonderful old shop fronts, potent reminders of less stressful times and blissful antidotes to the rush and roar of traffic.

An inscription above the ancient double-door entrance of the Angel Lane branch of the Appleby-based 'East of Eden' cosmetics and toiletries company, tells that the building was acquired in 1722 by a merchant, Robert Miers and his wife, then rebuilt in 1763 by 'WM', who was possibly their son.

The rather drab shops in Middlegate are enlivened by a substantial black and white painted building housing a chemist's. Unfortunately, its attractive Dickensian looks are spoiled by the modern illuminated advertising signs in the window. Close examination of a cast iron rain water down spout reveals the date 1786.

Cornmarket

The most attractive shop fronts are in the Cornmarket. Those of Thomas Edmondson Ltd and the adjoining pipe shop are of lightly stained natural wood, and look superb. Walking sticks and packs of agricultural products arranged outside add to their friendly charm. This delicious duo were a delight to draw.

Next door to them is Birtles toys and sports goods. Mercifully, they've avoided the modern dayglo-coloured sporting look and gone for a handpainted muted scheme on their Victorian frontage. Ronnie Barker from TV's 'Open All Hours' would look well at home here.

Little Dockray

Cornmarket

Little Dockray connects the Cornmarket with Middlegate missing out the 'Narrows'. There were once eight inns along the 80-yard-long lane. None of them survives today. A saddler's shop has stood at the top end for ages, with a distinctive white carved horse's head above the door. To the dismay of children and shoppers alike, this popular landmark recently had to be taken down when it became unsafe. My drawing has returned the horse to its rightful place. I hope the real thing is restored soon.

My greatest surprise in Little Dockray was Mounsey's Fish and Chip shop, elegantly turned out in grey and white livery with lettering of gold. How could I resist chips in splendour like this?

Well, the meal didn't quite match the decor - champagne a teensy bit warm - but the Mounsey style is impressive.

I now live in a town infested by modern chain stores, so tend to look at Penrith's old shops through mists of nostalgia. Though forty years ago, when this was my home town, I can never remember thinking them even remotely attractive.

Little Dockray

PENRITH CASTLE

The jagged castle ruins overlook the west side of town. Attractively set in manicured lawns like rotted teeth in a smile, you can't miss them.

The oldest parts date from 1399 when the Bishop of Carlisle, William Strickland, was given licence to extend a pele tower. In 1471 it was added to by Richard Neville, who later became King Richard the Third. He actually lived in the large, draughty place. Living rooms were on the first floor and the ground floor was used for storage and services.

By 1547 the castle had fallen into ruin and the sandstone was being plundered as building material. Some was used to build Castlegate and a prison outside the town.

Early photographs show the ruins much as today, but enclosing an abundance of trees, a long lean-to shed and a substantial house. They were the business premises of Joseph Tremble and Sons, Castle Nurseries.

Castle ruins 1990

Castle ruins 1910

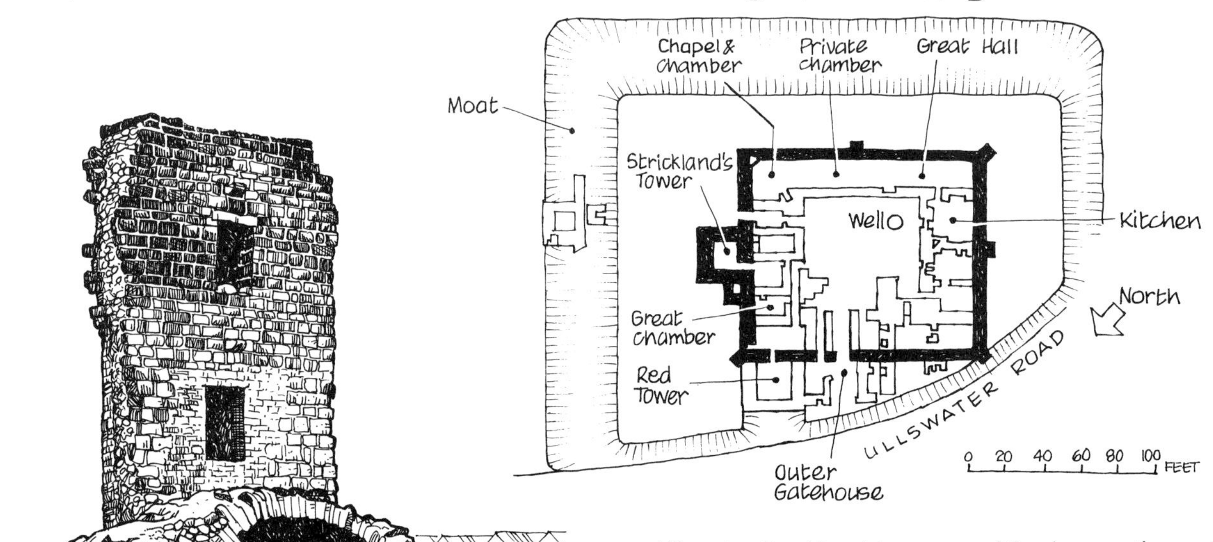

Red Tower

Ullswater Road has taken some of the deep castle moat, but most of it remains, neatly grassed and much enjoyed by small children who love to roll down its steep sides. Flymo mowers must have been godsends for the park gardeners.

Penrith UDC bought the ruins from the London and North West Railway Co in 1910 and manage to keep them in good order, despite the worst efforts of graffiti scrawlers and teenage rock climbers unconcerned by the crumbling nature of sandstone.

There's enough of the ruins left to give a good idea of the scale of the original structure. The high, battered walls, built by Richard the Third, would be a fabulous setting for Shakespeare's humpbacked villain version of the diminutive king to roam about in. What an amazing place it must have been 500 years ago! Under Strickland's Tower huge cannon balls have sunk into the chamber floor.

The remaining slab of the Red Tower consists of a sandwich of sandstone blocks with the centre filled by stone cobbles. A similar building method is used in dry stone walls all over the Lake District.

Beyond the ruins there's a park with tennis courts and a bowling green set amongst attractive gardens. I sat for a while by the pavilion where pupils from nearby schools had gathered for a midday smoke. The girls were most addicted, puffing out great clouds of billowing smoke, while their sturdy Cumbrian thighs, inadequately covered by micro-skirts, turned delicate shades of blue in the chilly breeze.

Eastern corner

The main entrance to the park is through a war memorial gateway from where a broad rose-covered drive leads straight up the hill to an impressive bandstand, built in 1923. In front of this stands the Boer War memorial, first unveiled outside the town hall.

To assist traffic flow through Corney Square the statue was moved to this less congested site in 1964. Unfortunately, the memorial now attracts the attention of vandals and on a number of occasions the beautiful 'Black Angel' has been toppled from her plinth by senseless attacks.

Park gateway

The 'Black Angel'

One of my visits to Penrith was on the train. I left home in the Midlands at 6.30am, travelled in comfort on a British Rail Intercity express with coffee brought to my seat, and arrived in Penrith three hours later, early enough for a full day's exploration, rounded off by a blissful nod all the way home. I couldn't do that on the M6 - and all for about £25 return.

With that kind of convenience and economy, it's a pity more visitors don't use the railway. The ones that do seem to be hairy climbing types, who are speedily minibussed from the station to remote adventure schools and turned loose on mean Lakeland crags. I strolled round the town instead.

Penrith has an attractive sandstone and slate-built station with long curving platforms. For many years there was a break in the line between Lancaster and Carlisle while engineers figured out how best to cross Shap fells. With the considerable help of 10,000 navvies, the bleak obstacle was eventually crossed and the main line completed in 1846.

Railway Station

There was considerable friction between the English, Scottish and Irish workers employed on the railway construction. Following a quarrel between an English ganger and an Irish navvy at Yanwath, south of Penrith, 700 angry Irishmen armed with blackthorn sticks marched from their camp at Plumpton, north of the town, to retaliate. When they began to rampage through Penrith, some hard talking from local magistrates persuaded them to turn back.

But despite the Irish climb-down, the English camp wanted a fight. Next day a huge mob marched north into Penrith and attacked anyone who spoke with an Irish accent. Some tinkers were left for dead. Shops and banks were closed for a week and local folk hid in fear. Finally, Sir George Musgrave, aided by cavalry soldiers and a Roman Catholic priest, managed to restore order. Penrith's notorious Navvy Riot was over.

Gloucester Arms

Of all the famous visitors to Penrith, Richard Neville (1452-85), Duke of Gloucester, reached the highest position. At the age of 31 he was crowned King Richard the Third, only to die two years later at the Battle of Bosworth Field.

In 1471 he stayed at what is now the Gloucester Arms, while Penrith Castle was being made habitable for him. Tradition has it that there is a secret passage from the inn to the castle. Much modified since, the Elizabethan house was originally owned by the Docura family who gave their name to Great Dockray where it stands.

During the 16th century, the poor of Penrith lived in appalling conditions, crowded together in tiny yards with no sanitary facilities at all. The plague was a frequent visitor. In the 1598 epidemic 2,260 local people died. Social position was no barrier; both the wealthy Musgrave and De Whelpdale families had victims.

While the plague raged in the town farmers would not enter, so temporary markets were set up on the outskirts. Townsfolk paid for supplies by tossing coins into hollowed-out stones containing disinfecting fluid. One such receptacle is preserved in the grounds of Greengarth old folk's home in Bridge Lane. Birds now use it for a bath.

The road maker, John McAdam (1756-1836), lived for a while in Cockell House at the north end of town. Born at Ayr, McAdam went on to make his fortune in New York, then returned to Scotland to devise new ways of road making. So successful were they in Bristol, the government gave him the job of improving all British roads in 1827. He invented granite chippings, lethal for modern windscreens and paintwork. Thanks, Mac.

Cockell House is a plain building with some eccentric windows. It was the headquarters of a computer company for a while but has now reverted to a dwelling.

After a bit of searching down a side street near the railway I found Page Hall, an ordinary house that takes in B & B visitors. For ten years it was home of the young Samuel Plimsoll (1824-98), who later became a social reformer, Member of Parliament and deviser of the 1875 Merchant Shipping Act. This required every owner to paint a circular disc with a horizontal line through it on all his ships, indicating the maximum depth to which the vessel could be loaded, known ever since as the Plimsoll line.

Plague Stone

Cockell House

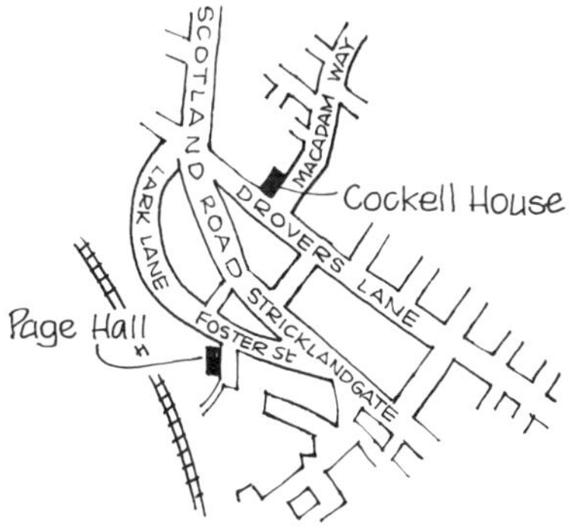

The family name is also carried on by the cheap black plimsolls worn by generations of schoolchildren for gym lessons. Recently teenage girls such as my daughter have adopted the flimsy footwear as a serious fashion statement.

Over the years, Penrith has played a part in many significant events of British history. Discovering the town's historic sites was an unexpected pleasure.

Page Hall

PENRITH STEAM MUSEUM

Yes, that's just what I thought too - yawn, yawn, another boring collection of carefully preserved relics only interesting for steam minutiae freaks. Well, the Penrith Steam Museum, hidden away at the top of Castlegate, isn't at all like that.

There are some magnificent steam engines to drool over, but I liked the things not kept in pristine condition best; wonderful old engineering workshops packed with mind-boggling arrays of gently rusting tools, implements and machines; and a tiny worker's cottage, straight out of a Melvyn Bragg novel.

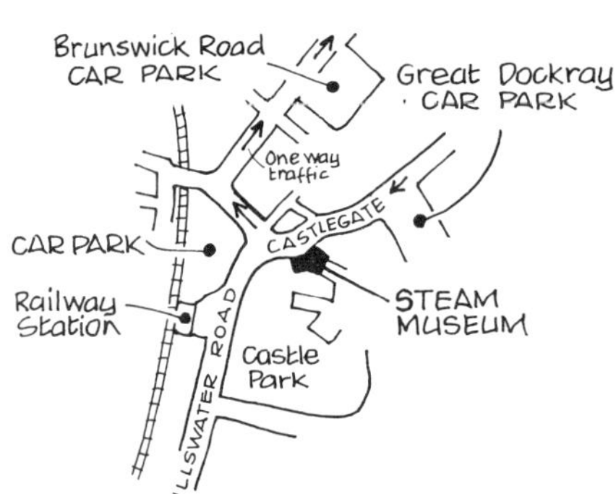

Entrance

The centrepiece collection is ten gleaming traction engines. Even cold and silent each has its own personality and you can imagine what they might have been like at work.

The diminutive Ruston and Horsby portable probably rushed about all over the place squealing excitedly "Please, let me help!"

'Little Jim' is a sturdy Leeds-built tractor. What a workhorse he must have been. "Aye, thus nowt a can't tackle, lad."

'Anne' is a more stately tractor; always wore a hat, good home, helped out on farms at threshing time, upper-class voice, 'Oh, do leave it to me, dear!' A suffragette too, I shouldn't wonder.

The 'Admiral Beatty' is a big lad. Heavily tattooed, he's been about a bit. Started his career as a road locomotive in 1916, then travelled round the fairgrounds with William Thurston and Son. Retired in 1946, but he can still dominate the hall. "Look, pal, this is my patch, right?"

Public relations for Jennings Cockermouth Brewery is admirably handled by the restored 1927 Foden wagon. Immaculately turned out in blue and gold livery, he's the perfect cheery barman. "Now, what'll it be, gentlemen?"

The lumbering 1926 road roller went round with the roadmen. He's the amiable giant who never quite grew up. "Hello, Auntie Nelly, it's me again!"

Ruston & Hornsby portable (1932)

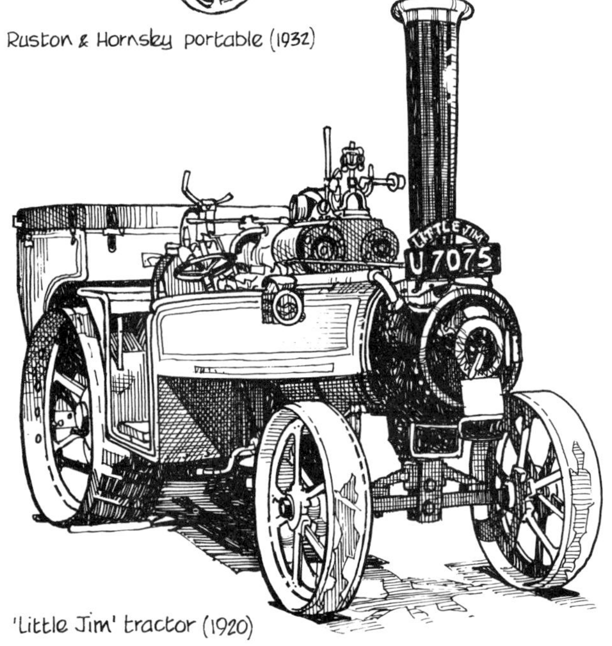

'Little Jim' tractor (1920)

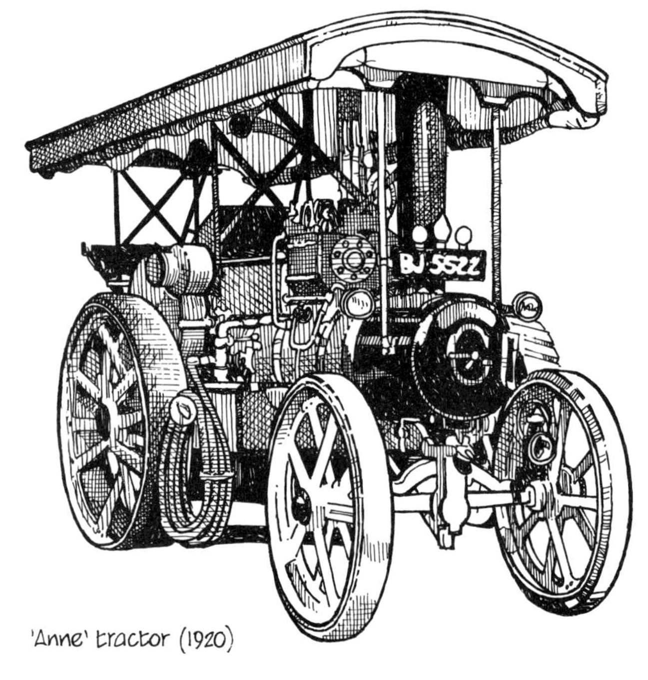

'Anne' tractor (1920)

Blacksmith's shop & yard

Rickety wooden steps lead to the old works office, which has a large opening in the floor for management to keep an eye on workers below. In the yard outside there's the pattern shop, stores and a Robey steam engine usually in steam.

The three-roomed worker's cottage is amazing. As my teenage son remarked: "No bathroom, no central heating and no telly." He couldn't survive in it for five minutes. It's all correctly furnished with a pair of boots by the black-leaded fireplace, a small table set for tea, and lace dresses hanging from cupboard doors upstairs. You feel the inhabitants have just popped out for a minute. Magical.

The whole museum is. I just wish it had a printed guide or at least more labels on the exhibits. A tiny quibble. This place is unique. Don't miss it.

Rivalling this formidable bunch for attention in the main hall is a huge 1899 Pollit and Wigzell stationary engine, the 'Judith Hannah', which once powered a Yorkshire mill. It is regularly working, accompanied by a steam organ playing lively fairground music.

The steam museum was opened in 1980 as part of the preserved Castle Foundry agricultural engineering works, founded in 1851 by blacksmith Jonathan Stalker.

Through the old foundry machine shop, packed with finishing and fettling curios, I came to the blacksmith's shop, where the walls, benches and floor are covered with iron-mongery bizarre enough for a medieval torture chamber. Goodness knows what they were all for. Some of them are still used. Wrought ironwork is still turned out here.

Foden wagon (1927)

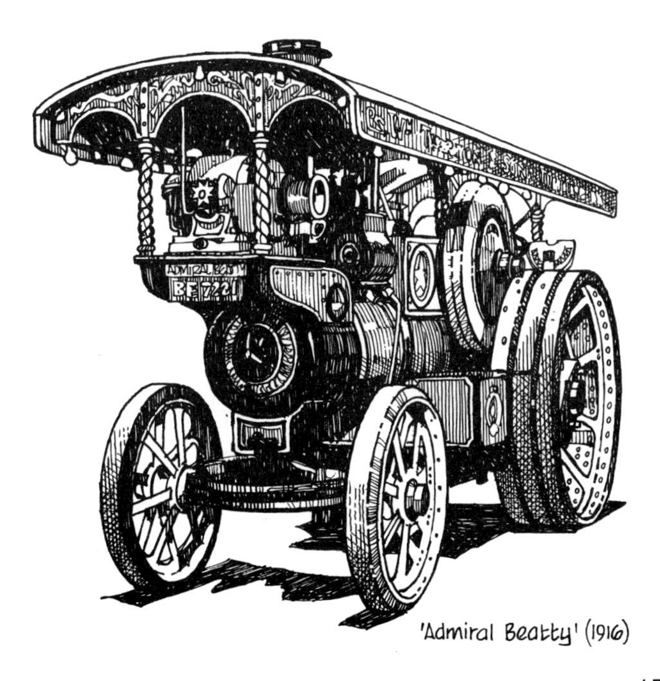

'Admiral Beatty' (1916)

Fowler's Road Roller (1920)

THE BEACON

The streets rising steeply from Meeting House Lane are lined by attractive sandstone houses, but are a long drag to walk up to the Beacon. Take a bus from Sandgate or drive and park along the Beacon Edge. Don't panic, that's a wide road - not a precipice.

As part of the extensive Lowther Estate, Beacon Hill Plantation is noticeably well managed, and the sandy pathway, meandering between the trees, is securely fenced. Years ago it had a broad drive entrance and was a popular walk for the gentry. A visitors' book signed by royalty was kept at the lodge. That's now been turned into an eccentric-looking private house so we have to enter the plantation less regally, along a narrow pathway down the road. It's a gentle walk to the 937-foot-high top , part of a series of sand dunes that straggles away eastwards towards the Pennines.

The red sandstone tower is as tall as a modern semi, and despite the high railings, pitted with names and dates scratched by generations of determined visitors. Close examination revealed that in the thirties they were named Ethel and George. These days they're Tracey and Wayne.

A beacon was recorded here in 1468. The present one, dating from 1719, was restored in 1780 as a monument to the town's involvement with the 1745 Jacobite rebellion.

The Lodge

With the town spread out below me and a distant view of the Ullswater fells and Blencathra as a reminder of how close Lakeland was, I contemplated what it is that makes Penrith so special. 'Friendly' was the description I kept returning to. Friendly buildings, friendly people. Ask someone in Penrith for directions and you could get their life story. An old chap offered to take me round the sights in his van. Women showed their knees for my camera. Cheeky kids pulled faces.

Lakeland still beckoned, but first I returned to the town for another cup of tea and more local 'crack'. Penrith is no better for being my birthplace, but I like to think I'm better for being born here.

TOWN WALK

Surrounded by busy road, Penrith is not a place people flock to for peaceful countryside walks. However, with its historic architecture and surprisingly tranquil corners the town itself has much to offer the inquisitive walker.

Begin by stocking up on information at the Robinson School Centre, then take in the trio of prominent churches - United Reform, Christ, and Wordsworth Street Methodist.

Down Portland Place visit the sparkling town hall and Albert Street, one of the oldest parts of town and unaltered for ages. Continue to Sandgate and go up to Benson Row at the top. Look out for the pele tower on the corner. Friargate is very historic, as is St Andrew's Church Close - THE place to linger, eat your sandwiches and soak up the tranquil atmosphere. Walk round the close to see the Tudor building.

Continue across the bottom of Sandgate into Burrowgate. Through a narrow cobbled passageway beside Arnison's store you're into Devonshire Street where there are shops, banks and the indoor market. Don't miss the inaccurate Wordsworth plaque on Arnison's wall. Go past the Robin Hood Inn into King Street. At Crown Square, turn right up Princes Street into the new Angel Square shopping precinct. If you haven't already eaten, the Bluebell Bookshop Restaurant is well worth trying. Or you may prefer one of the three ancient pubs in Great Dockray. There's a market here on Tuesdays. The delights of the Cornmarket follow, then Little Dockray takes you back to the busy shops of Middlegate.

Don't rush the walk - it takes time to appreciate Penrith's sometimes elusive charm. Three hours is a minimum - you might meet one of the town's friendly chatterboxes.

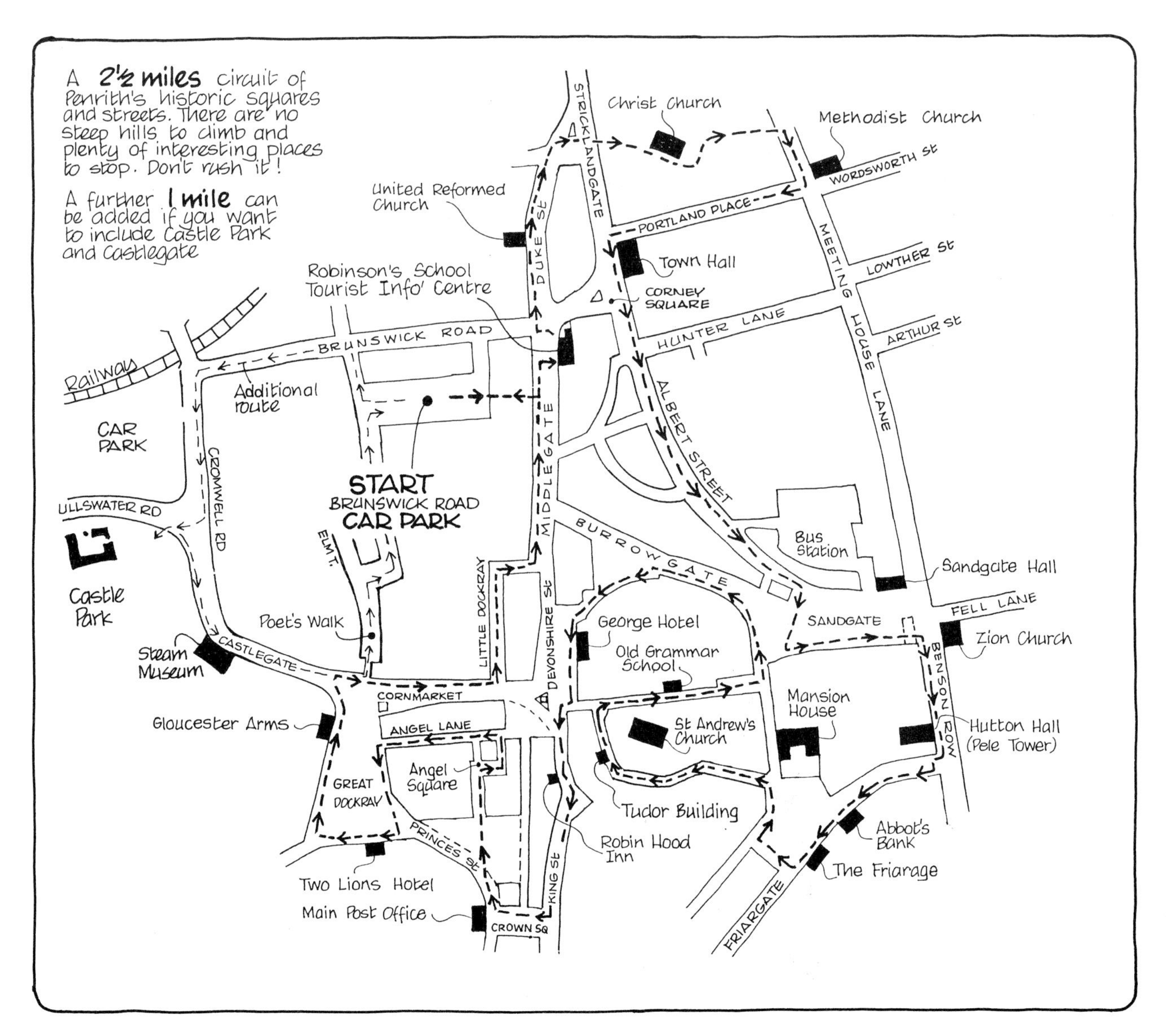

Windermere

Shops in Cresent Road

The town bottleneck was clear when I drove through Windermere from the A591 to Broad Street Car Park at nine o'clock in the morning. By dinner-time it would be packed with cars, all going somewhere else - slowly.

Windermere is one of Lakeland's best-known place names, but its precise location can be confusing. Originally spelt 'Wynandremere', from the Norse-Viking personal name of Vinand, it referred only to the lake. These days 'Windermere' can mean lake or town, even the surrounding countryside too.

The town of Windermere drapes itself untidily across the lower slopes of Orrest Head, part of a conurbation spreading down to the Bowness lake shore. Here 18th-century Lakeland rolled up its sleeves and built a railway station and a town to serve the fledgling tourist industry. Though the narrow streets are now seen only as an irritant by motorists heading for exciting water sports on the lake, less frantic visitors find the town centre has an appealing old-fashioned charm that is refreshingly untouristy.

I did try the train to Windermere, but the branch line from Oxenholme is a disgrace. The trains are ramshackle, the unmanned stations filthy vandalised wrecks. What an appalling introduction to England's premier tourist area.

As I walked up Crescent Road, Windermere seemed like a peaceful country town. A butcher in a striped apron was sweeping his pavement. Next door, racks of picture postcards were being put out. The tourists were coming!

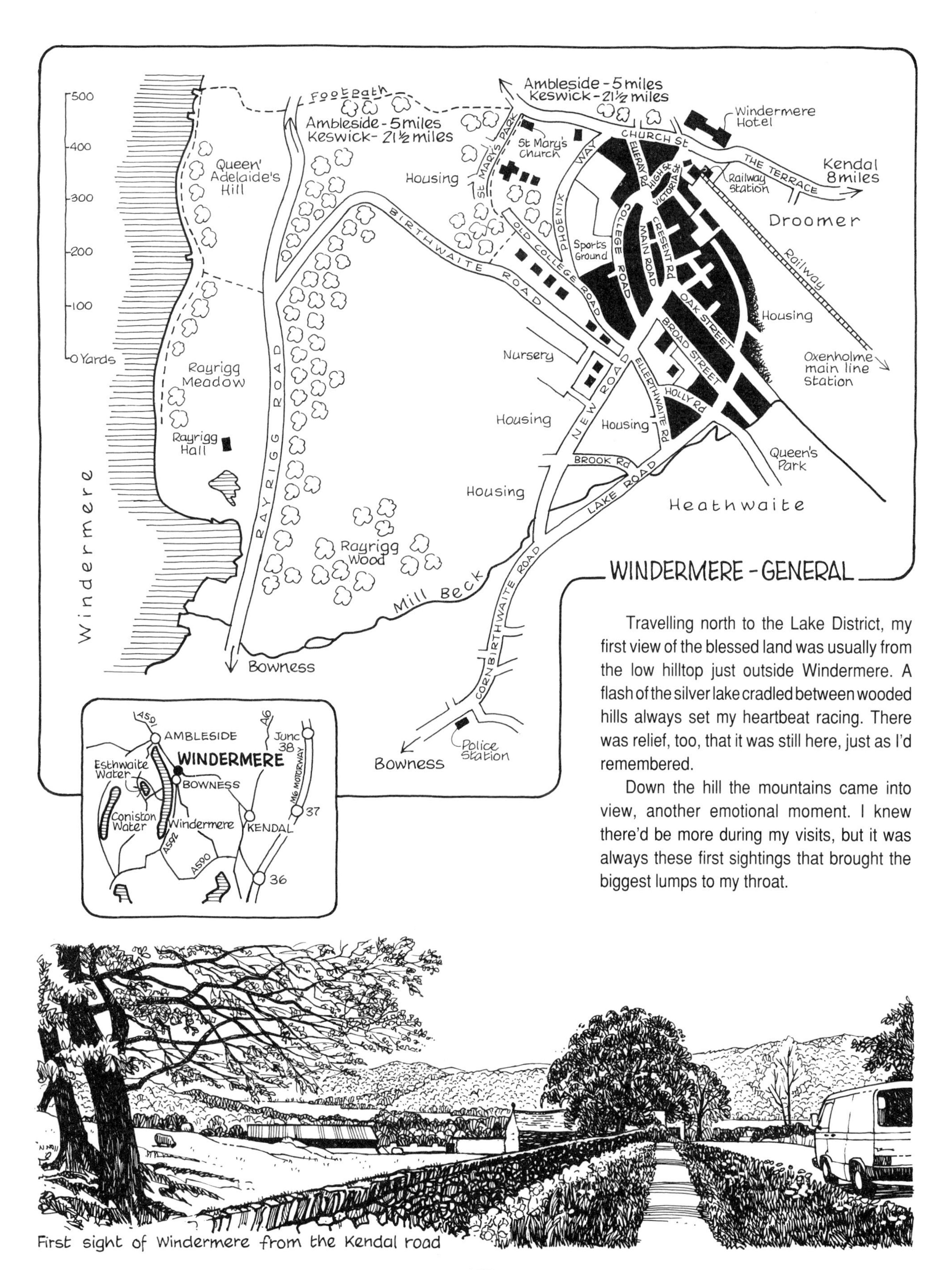

WINDERMERE - GENERAL

Travelling north to the Lake District, my first view of the blessed land was usually from the low hilltop just outside Windermere. A flash of the silver lake cradled between wooded hills always set my heartbeat racing. There was relief, too, that it was still here, just as I'd remembered.

Down the hill the mountains came into view, another emotional moment. I knew there'd be more during my visits, but it was always these first sightings that brought the biggest lumps to my throat.

First sight of Windermere from the Kendal road

Lakeland fells from Windermere Terrace

Windermere's story is reflected in the buildings gathered round the small square just off the main A591 road. Ancient cottages huddle below the railway station and an outdoor equipment store glows with modern colours. There's a new tourist information centre and a substantial bank. A sternly Victorian hotel dominates them all from a hilltop perch.

A large sign across the road indicates the lane to Orrest Head (see page 164). A stroll to this popular viewpoint is an essential part of a visit to Windermere.

I found the local Job Centre hidden away in the bowels of the prosperous-looking National Westminster Bank. There was plenty of menial hotel work available, but nothing remotely interesting or decently paid.

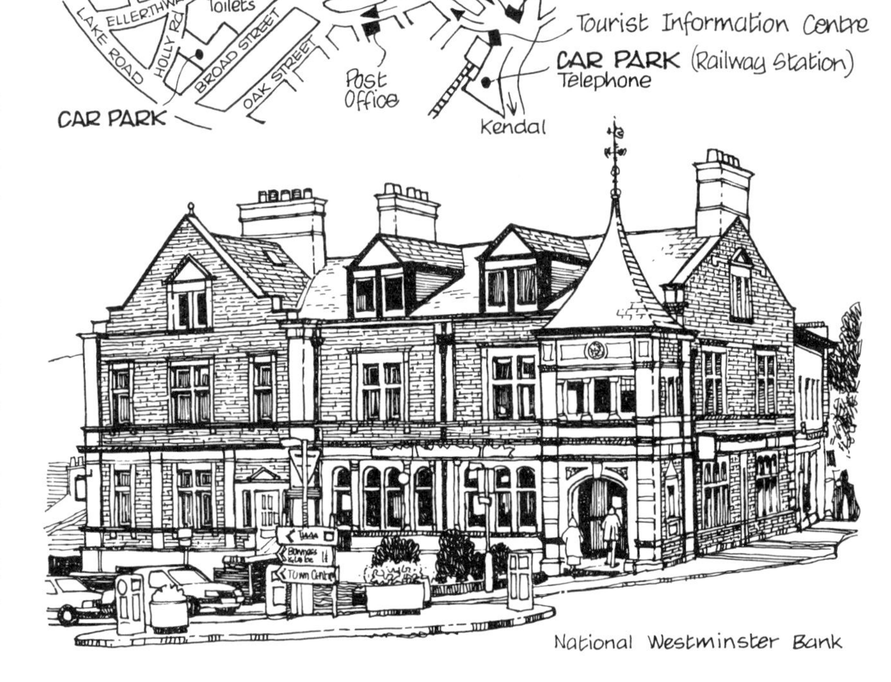

National Westminster Bank

Tourist Information Centre

The new tourist information centre is a welcome and necessary addition to Windermere visitor facilities. I'm a big fan of these places where you can see the best kind of public relations in day-to-day action. I've never seen impatience or heard a cross word from any centre staff. Unfortunately, I can't say that for all of us tourists.

Most English towns began with a market charter. Windermere began with a railway station. It opened in 1848 at the hamlet of Birthwaite, which rapidly developed into a holiday town and eventually adopted the station name of Windermere.

Plans to extend the line to Grasmere were abandoned following furious opposition led by Ruskin, Rawnsley and Wordsworth. What a tourist attraction that line could have been today.

Railway Station ~ 1910

Railway Station ~ 1990

A new £90,000 station was opened in 1985, paid for by a joint BR and local action group effort. Built of wood in the Furness Railway fashion and hung with baskets of flowers, the station is a credit to them. What a pity the rest of the line is so depressing!

An ornate drinking fountain that once stood in the old station forecourt has been retired to more peaceful surroundings at the Brewery Arts Centre, Kendal (see page 77).

The station was built by the local company of Pattinson's. At the same time they put up Rigg's splendid Windermere Hotel, which has a beautiful Indian-style veranda overlooking the town.

In its first year the railway carried 120,000 passengers, but by the 1960s a decline had set in. Some winter trains carried only ten people. In 1976, one track was taken up, leaving just a single line to Oxenholme.

The large station was abandoned in 1983. A year later it re-opened as Booth's supermarket, creditably retaining the striking colonnaded porte-cochère that once led to the station booking office. There are interesting stained glass windows inside the supermarket. One came from Booth's cafe at Preston and depicts their old store in Highgate, Kendal.

Windermere Hotel

Oak Street

The chaotic progress of summer traffic through Windermere town centre is not helped by the lay-out of the sombre slate buildings. Acme House is a substantial barrier, thrusting like a wedge between Crescent Road and Main Road. It was once the Embassy Cinema. Coincidentally, 'Acme' was the fictitious trade name used in numerous Hollywood films and cartoons to avoid litigation. The round Gothic window in the wide end wall is Windermere's best architectural feature.

Two prominent buildings look oddly out of place amongst the brown slate. The Queens Hotel is starkly black and white with tables set at the fume-laden roadside so contented drinkers can jeer at overheated drivers crawling past. Barclays Bank next door, which is faintly Elizabethan-looking and covered in red ivy, appears to have strayed from a Cotswold town. Completing the unplanned scene, a Methodist church across the road is set at a crazy angle to the main road.

Junction of Cresent Road and Main Road

Confusion about Lakeland place-names was tackled by the Cumbrian writer and poet, Norman Nicholson, in his excellent book, *The Lakes.* He argues that the inclusion of 'mere' or 'water' in the name is enough to identify it as a lake. Only when the name also refers to a town or village is it necessary to add the word 'lake' to differentiate one from the other, for example at Elterwater, Coniston or here at Windermere. Bassenthwaite is a special case, it being the only lake which officially has 'Lake' in its name.

Traditional Cumbrian nomenclature is to put the plain topographical term second - 'fell', 'beck' and so on. How ridiculous to say Fellsca Pike, Becktrout or Daleborrow. So in the case of names of lakes which need to be differentiated from town or village, we should say Elterwater Lake, or Coniston Lake, not Lake Elterwater, Lake Coniston, and never Lake Windermere - a very common error.

Modern designers have done their bit too. A new block of flats in Elleray Road has a strange black turret. Possibly influenced by the proximity of Acme House, it reminded me of one of those space rockets in old black and white films, usually belching smoke and about to blast off for the moon with a mad scientist aboard - a drastic way to escape Windermere traffic jams.

In reality, a desperate measure to reduce summer traffic volume through the town centre was experimented with in 1990, when all road signs to Bowness were covered over for three months. Lakeside businesses were not pleased.

Oak Street is a quiet haven just off the busy bottleneck, where a large beer and spirits warehouse used to serve all the local hotels.

Queen's Hotel

Cresent Road

Crescent Road looks more like a main street than adjoining Main Street does - another Windermere eccentricity.

Architecturally, the street is gloomy Victorian Gothic, but the shops are terrific, like they were 30 years ago - the butcher, baker, grocer, chemists, news-agent and sweet shop variety.

There is a sprinkling of modern additions - a supermarket, even a patis-serie - but nothing flash. All of them are visitor friendly. Not so the constant stream of traffic outside their doors. Yes, we're back to that again. You can't escape it here.

While waiting on the kerbside, I asked an old chap stood next to me if it was ever possible to cross busy Cres-cent Road.

"Aye...maybe int' night," he replied. Then dolefully indicated a tiny Jack Russell terrier sat at his feet, "I wouldn't bother, but he plays war to come out."

Smoke from passing vehicles bil-lowed round the dog like dry ice at a rock concert.

"Likes his walk, does he?"

"Walk?" snorted the old chap, real-ising that he was dealing with an idiot visitor, "Hates walking!" The dog looked up, glassy-eyed, and grinned. "Likes exhaust fumes, though. Addicted to 'em."

College Road runs parallel to Main Road. There's little traffic here and plenty to interest the nosey passer-by. Applegarth Hotel, as solidly built as a Lakeland fell, has a wonderful array of turrets, porches and extensions.

Applegarth Hotel

The first chapel of St Mary's, accommodating 200, was built in 1848 as chapel to nearby Old College by its headmaster, the Rev. John Aspinall-Addison. He was responsible for a number of Gothic buildings in the area. One, a house for his masters, is now the Vicarage. The college, where the actor James Mason was once a student, has become the Phoenix Community Centre.

After the chapel was bought by the town in 1855, Windermere became part of Carlisle Diocese. The first incumbent was installed in 1857. Since then all nine of the successive vicars of St Mary's have added to or altered the church building in a remarkable line of unbroken dedication.

The present vicar, Rev. W.E.Barker, has possibly faced the biggest challenge of all.

St Mary's Church Rectory

In August 1988 the church was extensively damaged by fire in an arson attack by a disturbed teenager who had been sleeping rough in the organ loft. The cost of rebuilding ran to £400,000. Most of it was recovered from insurance but £40,000 still had to be raised.

I had a look round the church in 1989 when it was a depressing sight. The interior was burnt and blackened, and charred beams were sticking through the roof. However, after what the Rev. Barker describes as 'two years of headache', the church has risen phoenix-like from the ashes and been triumphantly re-opened. The handsome Victorian church is now, in the words of the vicar, 'more beautiful than before, while still keeping its original character'. A remarkable achievement.

St Mary's Church

ORREST HEAD

'Here the promised land is seen in all its glory.' In his 1974 book, *The Outlying Fells of Lakeland,* Wainwright sums up perfectly the appeal of Orrest Head. Indeed, it was the view from this rocky outcrop, first seen by him while on holiday from Blackburn, that set young Alfred on route to the fells and the production of his seven extraordinary guidebooks.

Start of path beside main road

The signboard in Windermere gives a time of 20 minutes to Orrest Head top. More like half an hour, I'd say. It's an easy walk, but why rush it?

The first section is up a narrow road that meanders between huge banks of rhododendron bushes. Despite their exotic blooms, I always find them dark and forbidding. An imaginative film maker could make a frightening film about these evil plants marching across the landscape and destroying all in their path.

Where the road becomes a path, the summit is first seen. The beech trees look wonderful here after all those killer rhodies. Don't look behind you until you're right on the top, then the wide panoramic view will come as a delicious surprise.

The 'Wagon-wheel' gate

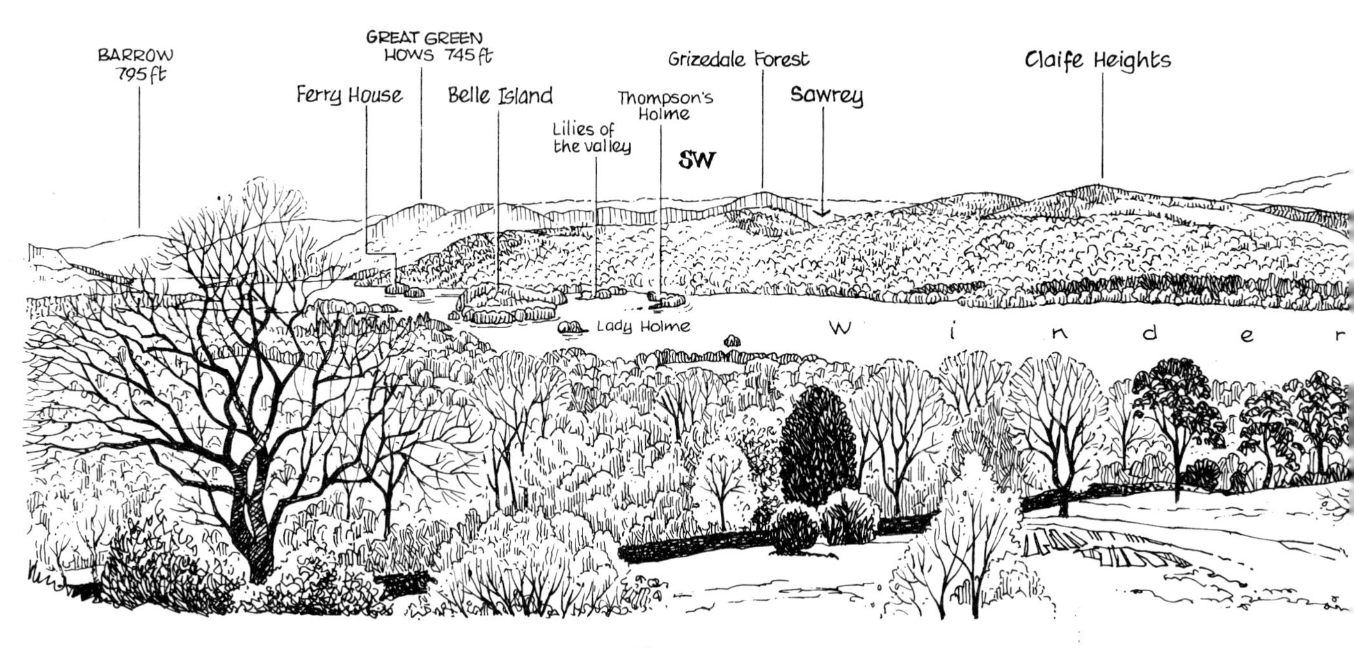

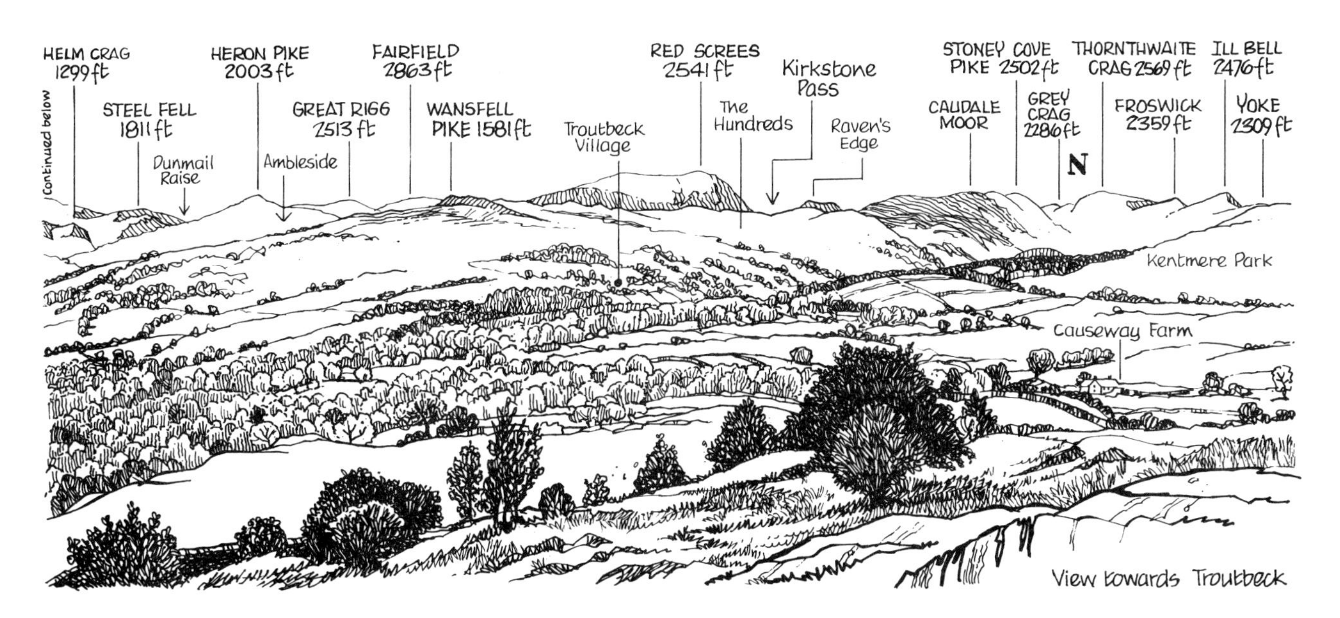

From Orrest Head the effect on the landscape of the two main groups of Lakeland rocks is clearly seen. To the south-west, across Claife Heights, there are gentle rolling hills, laid down as sea bed sediment in Silurian times, 400 million years ago. In contrast, the jagged crags of central Lakeland were formed by violent volcanic action 50 million years earlier.

I last visited the Head during a June heatwave and was amazed to find it both deserted and litter-free.

To complete a pleasant circular walk of about 2½ miles, leave Orrest Head by a grassy footpath descending steeply towards Causeway Farm. Then, at a stone stile, turn left and follow the lane for about half a mile to where it joins the main road. Go through a large iron gate on your left onto a stony path, signposted 'To Orrest Head'. This takes you past some fine houses set in lovely woodland, back to the railway station.

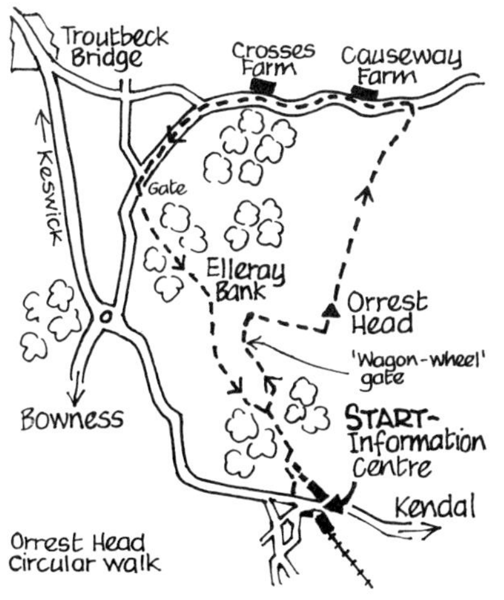

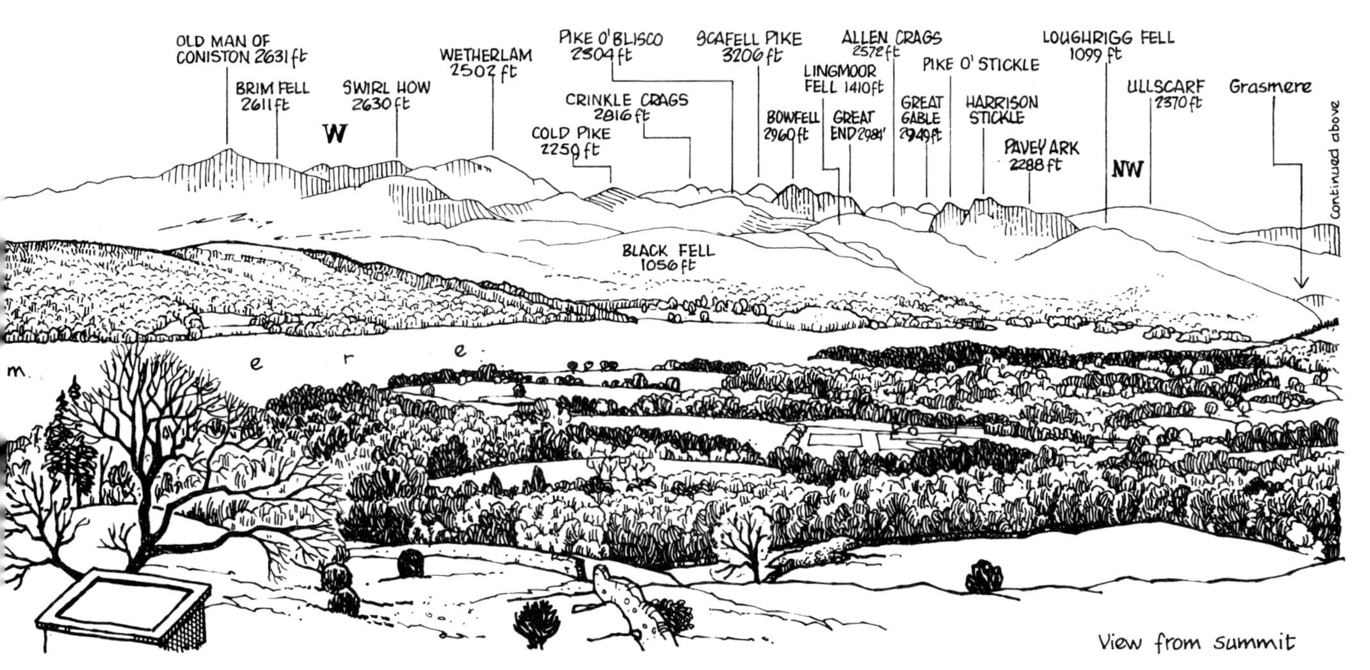

New Road

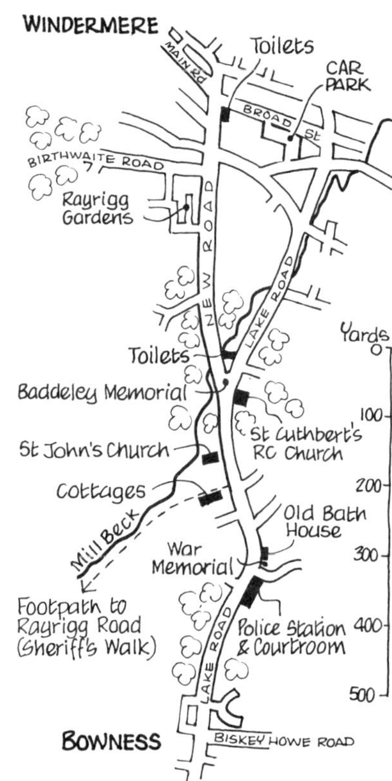

One of the best ways to compare the differing characters of Windermere and Bowness is to walk from one town to the other.

After leaving restricted Crescent Road you come into the broad highway of New Road. Over on the left, a magnificent 200-foot-high Californian redwood tree marks the public library in Ellerthwaite Gardens. On the right there's some horrid garden centre glass houses; a climatic necessity here, I suppose. Across the road, you can hire 18-speed mountain bikes in a wide range of lurid colours. No thanks, I'll walk.

At the junction of New Road and Lake Road, the elegant hexagon-shape of St Herbert's RC church contrasts wildly with the memorial to Mountford John-Byrde Baddeley, which is as exuberant as his splendid name. He wrote one of the best Lakeland guidebooks. Grateful readers contributed to a public fund to erect the squat clock tower in 1907. It looks decidedly toytown these days, as if designed by Larry the Lamb and built by Noddy using Lego bricks. I think the tower is very appropriate. All Lakeland guidebook writers should be remembered with a smile.

St Herbert's RC Church

Baddeley Memorial

St John's 1887 church is a gloomy place. Broken windows and locked doors don't help, but a lively kindergarten school in a west end annexe does bring some welcome life to the dilapidated building.

St John's Parish Church

Ye Olde Bath House

Ye Olde Bath House provided remedial baths before Bowness Hydro opened. A terraced memorial garden nearby commemorates a long list of local men who died in two world wars. Two separate stones each record single deaths in 1951 and 1985. Their isolation makes these two lonely names the most poignant of all.

Goodly Dale Cottages

I strayed off the main road at Goodley Dale to have a look at some pretty cottages. A lady determinedly swept up her garden 'mess' before letting me take a photograph.

Another 400 yards brought me with a shock into the pulsating commercial jungle of Crag Brow. I was tempted to turn around and walk straight back to peaceful Windermere.

While I was exploring Windermere the strap on my haversack broke. I easily found a shop selling needles and thread but when the lady behind the counter heard what they were for she insisted on sewing the strap back on herself. For free!

Would I have been so lucky in Bowness? I rather doubt it.

TOWN WALK

Begin at Broad Street car park. If this is full you can be sure every other car park in Windermere is. Walk through gardens past the library onto broad Lake Road. Cross carefully, then bear left at the garage up Main Road. Continue along Elleray Road. Turn left down Church Street. Have a look through St Mary's Church. Take the footpath beside St Mary's Park. Go between some houses, then turn right for Birthwaite Road. Turn left back to Lake Road. This time walk up College Road where there are some attractive large houses. Cross Main Road and go up High Street to the square at the top. Visit the tourist information centre. Return down Victoria Street and Crescent Road, then back along Broad Street to the car park.

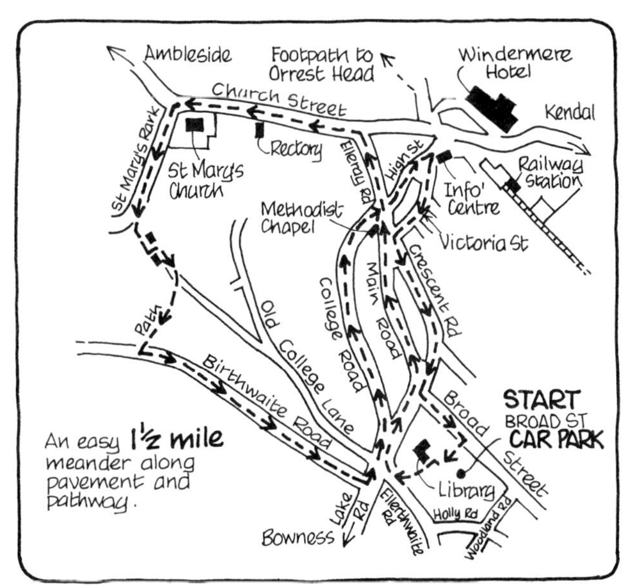

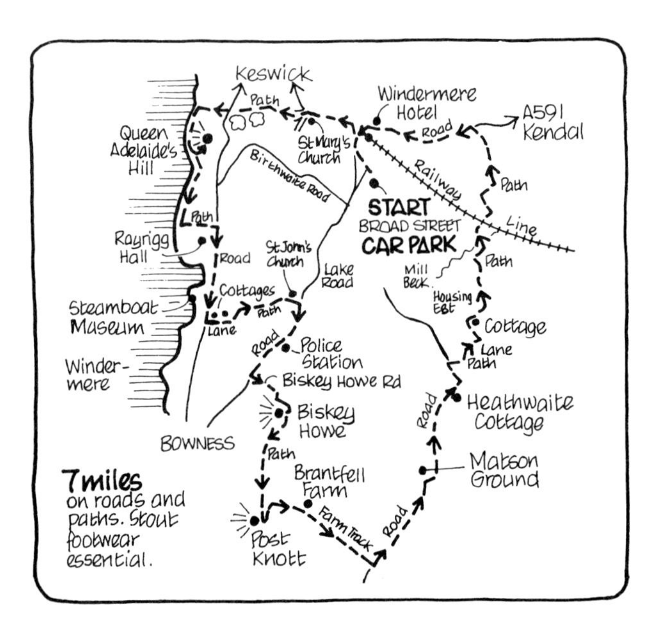

COUNTRYSIDE WALK

From Broad Street head up Main Street, then down Church Street. Just beyond St Mary's Park take a lane between stone walls on the left across Rayrigg Road to the lake at Low Millerground. Follow the lake shore to Queen Adelaide's Hill. Visit the summit for a view. Return to the lake shore footpath. Follow it to the main road. Walk towards Bowness, then beyond the steamboat museum go left up a rough lane past stone cottages.

The footpath leads to Lake Road. Go right, towards Bowness. Just before the cinema, turn left up Biskey Howe Road to the viewpoint. Continue up the footpath to Post Knott. Go down the other side of the hill, then turn left along the road. Two hundred yards past Heathway Lodge take a lane on the right between stone walls. At a Y-junction bear right, then left by the cottage across the beck. Over a stile into the field follow the path across the railway to the main road. Go left back to Windermere.

View from Queen Adelaide's Hill

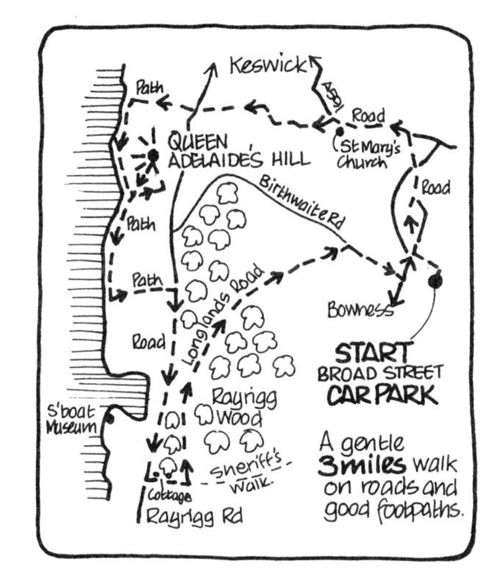

QUEEN ADELAIDE'S HILL

From Broad Street car park walk up Crescent Road and Elleray Road to Church Street. Turn left downhill. Just past the church take the lane on the left between stone walls. Proceed to Rayrigg Road. Cross over to the footpath down to the lake at Low Millerground. Follow the path along the lakeside to Queen Adelaide's Hill. Walk along the hard footpath up to the picnic area, then climb to the top of the hill for superb views. Watch where you put your feet.

Return to the lakeside path and follow it sharp left back to Rayrigg Road. Walk towards Bowness. Just past the steamboat museum turn left up a rough lane passing stone cottages. At the top of the hill turn left along a broad track through Rayrigg Wood to Birthwaite Road. Go right to Lake Road. Cross back to Broad Street and the car park, or try one of the excellent little cafes in Main Road.

'Morecambe Yoof' spray-painted in three-foot-high red letters across the toilet block should have warned me what to expect.

I walked down the tarmacadam path from the regimented picnic area to where a wooden pier juts out into the lake. The popular tourist spot was not deserted. A group of sour-faced youths leant against broken and scarred trees, smoking determined cigarettes and swigging strong lager from a considerable stock hanging from their belts. They eyed piles of expensive scuba-diving kit on the pier, left by the divers frolicking noisily in the water.

On the lake shore, amongst the blackened rocks, rusting cans and cold charcoal of barbecue parties, two women changed their babies' disposable nappies. Disposal of the soiled articles was in a nearby bush. My look of angry disapproval was answered by defiant stares. Sensing amusement, the Doc Martens stepped eagerly from behind the trees. I retreated back along the path and dissipated my aggression on the steep climb up Queen Adelaide's Hill.

The top was almost covered by thistles. What remained was covered by droppings from grazing sheep and cows. Wainwright's advice to 'watch where you put your feet' was never more apt.

In blissful contrast, the view up the lake was wonderful, easily the best I've seen from Windermere lakeside. But it was tainted for me and I did not linger long. A view like that requires contemplation. Here there were only distractions.

I headed back down the hillside with a heavy heart. If this is what good management of beauty spots brings, forget it. The best of Lakeland should be kept difficult to reach. 'Facilities' shouldn't be provided to attract lazy louts, of any age. What is worth seeing is always worth making an effort to see.

Below me, in the car park glistening with broken glass, a policeman was checking my car to see if I'd paid the parking fee. I had. A pound for twenty miserable minutes. I won't be rushing back here

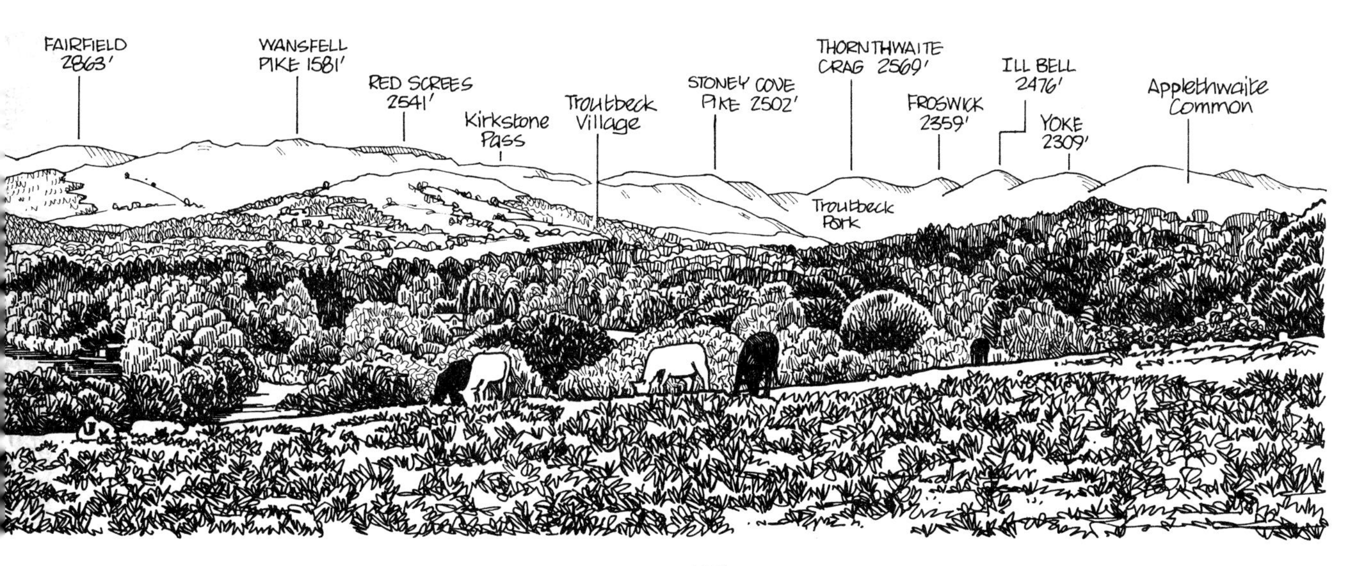

Brockhole

The Lake District National Park Centre at Brockhole is smaller than I'd imagined. After reading about everything that goes on here, I was expecting something palatial. And in a way it is, a fun palace about the Lake District for all the family. This is the most visited building in Lakeland, with 140,000 visitors a year. It gets terribly crowded.

In addition to all the permanent displays and audio-visual shows, there is something different going on here every day except Sundays, from March to September. The range of events is amazing. They're all listed in the *What's on at Brockhole* leaflets available from all the tourist information centres.

Brockhole was built in the late 1890s by William Gaddum, a wealthy Manchester textile merchant. After his death in 1945 the house became a convalescent home. In 1966 it was bought by the Lake District Planning Board and opened to the public as Britain's first visitor centre in 1969.

The extensive 30-acre grounds of gardens, picnic spots and adventure areas run down to the lakeside where launches from Bowness call. Since my visit the restaurant and shop have been redesigned. I had a coffee watched by child-sized models of Beatrix Potter animals. Very creepy.

In a permanent exhibition telling the National Park story, a square plastic column reaching from floor to ceiling contains a substantial collection of litter. Displayed like this, it looks perversely colourful and attractive. The shock effect of litter would be more vividly demonstrated by scattering the stuff over the immaculate lawns outside.

Publicity leaflets say Brockhole is relaxing. It had the opposite effect on me. I was so stimulated by all the exhibitions, lectures and demonstrations about Lakeland life and landscape all I wanted to do was rush out and experience it first hand.

But it was all over for me. My exploration was done, all the pics were taken. It was time to leave. I was disappointed to see so little about the seven Lakeland towns at Brockhole. Over the last two years I'd become very attached to them. We'd shared many happy hours together.

As I drove south along the A591 the weather rapidly deteriorated. Up the hill out of Windermere I caught a last glimpse of the Langdale Pikes in my rear view mirror. By the time I got to Kendal it was raining.

Castle Terrace - Penrith

BIBLIOGRAPHY

Penrith

Portrait of Penrith and the East Fellside by Michael Ffinch. Robert Hale.

Penrith in Times Past by Lawrence Marlow. A Countryside Publication, 1987. One of the familiar collections of local photographs. This one is particularly good.

Places of Interest. Compiled by children of Beaconside C of E Junior School as a project and sold in local shops. A splendid 64-page booklet packed with information.

Cockermouth

Cockermouth in Pictures, written, drawn and published by the town's very own 'Wainwright', J.Bernard Bradbury. A series of eight (to date) booklets on all aspects of Cockermouth.

A History of Cockermouth by J.Bernard Bradbury. Phillimore. All you'll ever want to know about the town - and more. Mr Bradbury certainly knows his home town.

Kendal

Kendal Town Trail by Arthur R.Nicholls. Westmorland Gazette, 1986. A must for serious explorers. Interesting, chatty and comprehensive.

Kendal in the 19th Century by A.Wainwright. Westmorland Gazette, 1977. Drawings from rare photographs by the old master. Brilliant.

Portrait of Kendal and the Kent Valley by Michael Ffinch. Robert Hale.

Keswick

Keswick Town Trail. Lake District Special Planning Board. Excellent booklet sold at tourist information centres.

Windermere and Bowness

Windermere Lake and Town in Times Past. A Countryside Publication of old photographs 1987.

Portrait of Windermere by C.D.Taylor. Robert Hale.

General

Lakeland Towns and Villages by Colin Selbourn. Forster Davies, 1988. Handy-sized, invaluable guide. Plenty of opinions to disagree with!

The Companion Guide to the Lake District by Frank Welsh. Collins, 1989. An excellent read.

An Illustrated Companion Into Lakeland by Walt Unsworth. Oxford Illustrated Press, 1988 and Cicerone Press, 1991. Good read. Excellent on anecdote and history.

The Good Guide to the Lakes by Hunter Davies. Forster Davies. Handy-sized. Lively, packed with information and opinion.

The Lake District by Millward and Robinson. Eyre Methuen, 1970. Superb. Detailed history of landscape and towns.

The Lakes by Norman Nicholson. Robert Hale, 1977. Packed with interest and opinion. A delight .

Vernacular Architecture of the Lake Counties by R.W.Brunskill. Faber and Faber, 1974. The classic work.

TYPESETTING BY CARNMOR PRINT & DESIGN, LONDON ROAD, PRESTON.
PRINTED BY MARTIN'S OF BERWICK LTD